A Micro Handbook for
Small Libraries and Media Centers

A MICRO HANDBOOK
for
SMALL LIBRARIES
and
MEDIA CENTERS

BETTY COSTA   MARIE COSTA

Illustrations by W. Y. Regan

LIBRARIES UNLIMITED, INC.
Littleton, Colorado
1983

LIBRARIES UNLIMITED, INC.
P.O. Box 263
Littleton, Colorado 80160-0263

Library of Congress Cataloging in Publication Data

Costa, Betty, 1931-
    A micro handbook for small libraries and media
centers.

        Bibliography: p. 205
        Includes index.
        1. Libraries--Automation--Handbooks, manuals, etc.
2. Instructional materials centers--Automation--Hand-
books, manuals, etc. 3. Microcomputers--Handbooks,
manuals, etc. 4. Library science--Data processing--
Handbooks, manuals, etc. I. Costa, Marie, 1951-
II. Title.
Z678.9.C64   1983   025'.0028'5404   83-11294
ISBN 0-87287-354-4

Libraries Unlimited books are bound with Type II nonwoven material that meets
and exceeds National Association of State Textbook Administrators' Type II
nonwoven material specifications Class A through E.

For Larry Costa

Table of Contents

List of Illustrations

Preface

You are about to enter a largely uncharted, mysterious, and challenging territory, one which, furthermore, is constantly changing, so that literally no one knows what might appear around the next bend. It is a territory full of exciting possibilities and opportunities for learning, for growth, and for a new kind of freedom from the routine and tedious chores that, until now, have consumed so much of our time and energy. It is a land of dramatic achievements, and small but significant accomplishments. It can also be a land of tremendous disappointment for someone who ventures into it unprepared and unwary.

This book is intended as a guide for the novice traveler in that section of the vast microcomputer territory which relates specifically to small libraries and media centers. Although the landscape is changing too rapidly to provide an actual map, we have tried to provide the necessary equipment, as well as certain rules of navigation, for a successful and productive journey.

We suggest you read the book all the way through before you begin, then keep it as a handbook to use for future reference. Chapter 1 is a brief survey of the history of computers and their role in society, particularly in libraries. Chapter 2 is an introduction to software, the programs that make computers run. Chapter 3 covers some basics of hardware. Chapter 4 discusses in detail a variety of specific types of software and applications for microcomputers in libraries. Chapter 5 is a discussion of the library/media center's new role as a computer resource center. Chapter 6 tells you how to choose and implement your new computer system, and chapter 7 is an account of one media specialist's experiences with computerization. The five appendices include a glossary, an extensive resource section, advice on caring for your computer, suggestions for funding possibilities, and sample evaluation charts.

Writing this book has been a highly rewarding experience for both of us. We can't begin to list all of the people who responded to our letters and phone calls regarding their activities with microcomputers and libraries. Many of their names are listed in the resource section. We are grateful to all of them for taking time to write to or talk with us, and to the software vendors who willingly answered questions about their products. We would especially like to thank the following people: Dr. Janet Naumer of the University of Denver Graduate School of Librarianship and Information Management; Dr. Fred Jurgemeyer of the Colorado State Department of Education; Walter Prelle of Saugus High School, Saugus, California; the staff of San Bernardino Public Library, San Bernardino, California; the library media specialists and the staff of the District Media

Center, School District No. 12, Adams County, Colorado, for their support and encouragement; the staff at Mountain View Elementary School, Broomfield, Colorado, especially Principal George Moyer, for his constant support, secretaries Cogie and Garnette and library aide Ruth Sorenson for putting up with all the letters and phone calls regarding Computer Cat™ and this book; our families, who patiently listened to "When the book is done ..."; our editor, Heather Cameron, for believing we could do it, and for her patience; and most of all, our technical consultant, who read patiently through endless drafts with a remarkable attention to detail, the person who got us into this whole computer business in the first place—our respective husband and father, Larry Costa, to whom this book is gratefully, respectfully, and lovingly dedicated.

Good luck, and please remember: Have Fun!

1 Libraries in a Computer-Dependent Society

Our society in the twentieth century has shown a pronounced tendency to "progress" headlong into the future, with little regard for the sanity, health, and happiness of its members, most of whom are struggling to keep up in an increasingly confusing, complex world that is at once too large to grasp and too small for comfort. The key word for the 1980s is "Information" — gobs of it, heaps of it, piles of data and statistics and facts and speculations and premises and deductions and concepts and observations. Technology is simultaneously racing ahead of our ability to use its wonders, and stumbling behind the tremendous obstacles created by both natural and man-made problems. People today are faced with an "information overload" which, though it threatens to overwhelm them, could, if somehow tamed, managed, and understood, hold the secrets to an exciting and marvelous future. At the very least, we must be able simply to maintain in the face of all that is happening in and around our lives.

As educators and information specialists, librarians, particularly school librarians, are faced with the responsibility not only of managing a vast supply of resources, but of giving children and other community members the tools, skills, and confidence to function in today's — and tomorrow's — ever-changing environment. The thought is at once challenging and terrifying, stimulating and exhausting.

Libraries today are evolving into sophisticated resource centers, responsible for gathering, sorting, and dispersing a huge variety of information in all forms, including not only books and magazines, but films, recordings, and, increasingly, computerized data, whether received **online*** via special communications devices and procedures, or printed and distributed as **hard copy**. School libraries, in addition, not only select and distribute resource materials and equipment, but also provide instruction and practice in using library services.

Libraries by their very nature are the logical institutions to provide both the method and the means for coping with the information overload we are all beginning to experience. But doing so will mean profound changes in both the image and the functions of libraries — and in the people who run them. Essentially, libraries have *always* been in the business of information storage and retrieval. What makes things so different now?

In a word, computers. Thirty, even twenty, years ago, computers were the stuff of science fiction, alien and mysterious machines attended by an elite and not entirely trusted class of professionals and technicians. Today they form an integral part of daily life, affecting numerous small and large facets of what we do, see, hear, think, produce, and consume. Computers have made both subtle

---

*The terms appearing in bold type are defined in the glossary (appendix A) of this text.

and dramatic changes in the ways that society and individuals cope with the events and problems of business, science, government, even art. Some large-scale computer applications have been accepted, if sometimes annoying, facts of life for at least a generation (computerized billing and "junk mail" address lists, for example), but the recent trend toward individualized or "personal" applications will almost certainly have far more profound and direct effects on our thoughts, perceptions, and actions. As computers become simultaneously smaller, more powerful, and more pervasive in our society, those who possess the skills to take advantage of them will be better able to function as productive and aware individuals in what might otherwise be an overwhelming and unmanageable world, while those who do not will be left further and further behind.

So what exactly is a computer? At its most basic, a computer is a machine that computes, or performs mathematical processes. Today "computer" means an electronically powered machine that is capable of performing complex series of computations, known as **algorithms**, at very high rates of speed. It is both amazing and reassuring to realize that all of the marvelous, complicated things that computers do derive from one very small, singular feature—the ability to tell if a "switch" is ON or OFF. Is that space on a **Hollerith** (keypunched) **card** light (from light shining through a hole) or dark? Is that tiny area on a disk or tape magnetized or not? ON or OFF. YES or NO. ONE or ZERO. This is why computers are so exasperatingly, unerringly LITERAL-MINDED. Unlike humans, they exist in a world of absolutes where each action is based on whether a given switch is ON or OFF at a particular instant. Every computation, no matter how complex, consists of a series of ON/OFF based actions, which are predetermined for the computer by a *person* known as a programmer. Before a computer can do anything at all, somewhere a human being, or more likely several to many human beings, must painstakingly spell out ALL of the steps necessary to perform each function.

When thinking about this process, it is helpful to picture yourself going through some very basic, everyday routine, one step at a time. For example, suppose you are sitting at your desk reading this book and you wish to look up the word "computer" in the dictionary. What is the first step you would take? The second? The third? Did you say, "Get the dictionary, find the Cs, find 'computer,' read the definition," or something similar? Fine, but you left out most of the steps. A programmer would describe it something like this:

    100   Stand up.
    110   Push back chair.
    120   Move out from between desk and chair.
    130   If you are facing in the direction of the dictionary, go to 190.
    140   If the dictionary is to your left, go to 170.
    150   Rotate 15 degrees right.
    160   Go to 130.
    170   Rotate 15 degrees left.
    180   Go to 130.
    190   Take one step forward.
    200   If you are in front of the dictionary, go to 220.
    210   Go to 190.
    220   Open the dictionary.
    230   If the word at the top of the page begins with "co-" go to 270.
    240   Open to a different page.

250   Go to 230.
260   Look at the first word.
270   If the word is computer, go to 300.
280   Look at the next word.
290   Go to 270.
300   Read the definition.

Complicated, isn't it? And this is what a "higher level" **program** would look like, meaning several levels above the ON/OFF of machine language. Therefore a lot of steps are left out. (Lower your hands to the sides of the chair. Push down with your hands. Raise your body up from the chair. Push the chair back. Take your hands off the chair, etc., etc.)

Fortunately for those of us who are inclined to say "Get the dictionary," a lot of those steps, in fact the great majority of them, are "built in," either in the hardware or the software, when we acquire a computer system. And there are lots of programmers busily seeking ways to free us from executing even more steps, making computers speak languages that are very close to human ones. Like English or French, computer programming languages consist of vocabulary, syntax, and grammar, and follow specific rules. It is quite possible for you to effectively use computers without ever learning a programming language, although some knowledge of programming might be helpful, or even fun. More about that later, but first —

A BRIEF HISTORY OF COMPUTERS

Actually, computers are not such a recent phenomenon. People have been devising calculating tools since they discovered the value of fingers for counting. They carved notches in sticks, drew lines in the dirt, piled pebbles in heaps. Eventually, about 3000 B.C., the first computing device appeared in China. The abacus, which consists of beads strung on wires and uses a "base 5" (as opposed to our decimal, or base 10) system, was practical enough to have stayed in use five thousand years, up to and including the present. School children use it as an aid to comprehending the principles of addition, subtraction, and place value, and merchants in some countries still use it as a practical everyday calculator. The base 5 system and the later, awkward Roman numeral system eventually gave way in Western society to the Hindu-Arabic numerical system, and the mechanical abacus was replaced by the equivalent of pencil and paper algorithms. Knowledge of and ability to perform arithmetic was esoteric and, like reading and writing, reserved to the priesthood and other learned types, much as computers have until very recently been the province of a select, knowledgeable few.

Forty-five hundred years or so after the arrival of the abacus, an Englishman named William Oughtred produced the slide rule, which was the most durable of a number of mechanical calculators invented during the seventeenth century. The slide rule, which incorporated the logarithms developed a short time before by a Scotsman, John Napier, remained a popular tool up until the first battery-powered calculators came on the market. Not long after Oughtred's invention of the slide rule a gear-driven machine capable of performing addition and subtraction was built by an 18-year-old Frenchman, Blaise Pascal, to help his administrator father deal with taxations and other financial matters. His machine was the precursor of (premicroprocessor) automobile odometers. Pascal patented his machine in 1642, and soon after that German philosopher and mathematician Gottfried Wilhelm von Leibniz went Pascal one better and devised the stepped-wheel calculator, which also multiplied, divided, and found numerical roots.

Even before Oughtred and Pascal and their successors, other inventive people had introduced such useful items as clocks and compasses, and there is evidence that a four function calculator already existed by the time Pascal was born. As with most inventions, there was a lot of parallel development, and the credits get hazy. Nonetheless, functional mechanical calculators gained wide use in government and business, though not in education, during the seventeenth and eighteenth centuries.

The next step was automating tools, beginning with the weaving loom — a concept that took three-quarters of a century to develop. Joseph-Marie Jacquard exhibited his loom, which used large punched hole cards to regulate the finished design, at the 1801 World's Fair in Paris. The concept was very similar to the punched paper rolls that manipulate the keys of a player piano.

Other technological and mathematical developments were occurring which would eventually lead to modern computers. These developments included a system of algebraic logic, conceived and developed by George Boole, which became the basis for machine computations; the discovery of the Edison effect, which made possible the invention of the vacuum tube; and the invention by Charles Xavier Thomas of a commercially successful calculating machine. But the technology was not yet far enough advanced to activate Charles Babbage's "Analytical Engine." Working in the early 1800s, Babbage envisioned a programmable machine which included a memory and used punched cards, powered by a steam engine and capable of carrying out sequences of calculations automatically. Though he died before engineering technology could catch up with his ideas, Babbage contributed substantially to the principles used later in functioning computers. While he was working on his "Difference Engine," Babbage met Ada Byron, Countess of Lovelace, who became the first computer programmer. Though her gender prevented her from making her identity public, Ada Byron gave the world a clear and concise explanation of Babbage's engines. At the same time she wrote operating instructions for the machines that were the precursors of today's programming languages, one of which is named in her honor.

Necessity as a stimulus to invention stepped in again when the United States Census Bureau found itself in a bind. The 1890 census was imminent, and information collected in 1880 was still being processed. The bureau needed a faster way to process data or its task would be hopeless. In the American tradition, the Census Bureau held a contest to find a new system. The winner, a statistician from Buffalo, New York, was Herman Hollerith, whose tabulating machine processed data fed into it in the form of punched cards (the familiar "Do not fold, spindle or mutilate" Hollerith cards of a now vanishing era). The first machines were hand operated; operators processed an average of 8,000 cards a day, recording, compiling, and tabulating data on some 63 million Americans. Later the card feeding was done automatically. In the early 1900s a new industry sprang up around tabulating and comparing machinery, giving birth to companies such as the Computing-Tabulating-Recording Company (later known as IBM), the Powers Tabulating Machine Company (which became the UNIVAC Division of Sperry Rand), and National Cash Register.

During the late nineteenth century and the early twentieth century inventors and researchers in other fields such as radio and electronics made technological contributions that would make the concepts of Charles Babbage and others possible beyond their wildest dreams. It wasn't until the 1930s, however, some hundred years after Babbage's work, that serious development of general purpose digital computers began. The Mark I, an electromechanical "Automatic Sequence Controlled Calculator," was developed by Howard Aiken of Harvard University during the late 1930s and early 1940s. The Mark I could be thought of as a link between the "prehistoric" mechanical calculating devices and the first **generation** of true electronic computers, the bulky, light flashing, temperamental "electronic brains." The Mark I, consisting of almost 80 adding machines and calculators controlled by a roll of punched paper, was a considerable improvement on its predecessors, performing up to three additions per second. Operational in 1944, it was quickly and dramatically outpaced by the first generation of modern computers.

The development of the first electronic general purpose computer in the United States, ENIAC (the Electronic Numerical Integrator and Calculator), was financed by the U.S. Army at a cost of some $400,000 during World War II. Operational in 1946, ENIAC, built by J. Presper Eckert and John W. Mauchly at the University of Pennsylvania, is generally considered to be the world's first general purpose digital computer. (Recent evidence, just released from classification by the British government, indicates that England had in operation in late 1943 a computer called COLOSSUS, developed by a group of mathematicians, engineers, and linguists for the purpose of deciphering German codes. Other rumors have it that the Germans had developed a computer or two of their own.) ENIAC and the first generation computers that followed it were large, bulky machines that used vacuum tubes and electronic relays to process and store information which they received via punched cards. They gave off large amounts of heat, consumed a great deal of electricity, and were maddeningly slow by today's standards. Even with their attendant teams of engineers and technicians, the machines tended to be unreliable and difficult to operate. Their memories were quite small (ENIAC could not store programs and actually had to be partially rewired for each new problem it was given to solve). And early computers responded only to **machine language** programs, which were exacting and time-consuming to produce. Even so, ENIAC could perform calculations at a rate a thousand times faster than a human with a desk calculator—an astonishing feat.

The first commercially available computer, UNIVAC I (UNIVersal Automatic Computer), also developed by Eckert and Mauchly, was installed at the U.S. Census Bureau in 1951. UNIVAC used magnetic tape instead of punched cards, and was considerably faster than ENIAC, but presented similar problems with unreliability, difficult maintenance, small memory, and programming difficulties. Most of the computers produced in the 1950s conformed to these early prototypes. During that decade high level programming languages such as **FORTRAN, COBOL**, and ALGOL came into being, and a computer market began to develop, though it was limited to governments and large corporations that could afford the tremendous expense of owning and operating machines that cost hundreds of dollars an hour to run. Even with these limitations, computers began to exert an influence over our daily lives. The new age had begun.

The second generation of computers, which appeared during the early 1960s, was made possible by a 1947 invention out of Bell Laboratories, the **transistor**. Transistors performed much more reliably on a tiny fraction of the power and took up an even smaller fraction of the space required for vacuum tubes, and they gave off far less heat. Computers, along with televisions, radios, and other electronic devices, became much more efficient and less costly in terms of energy and size. Besides transistors, the second generation computers used very small electromagnets for primary memory storage. **Software** (programming) developments kept pace with technology, and other companies like Honeywell, General Electric, and Burroughs joined IBM and Sperry-Rand in what was becoming a billion-dollar industry.

The third generation of computers, identified by solid-state circuitry, became commercially available around 1965. Increases in memory capacity and speed were matched by corresponding decreases in size, price, and difficulty of operation. Minicomputers came into the public realm, in reach of universities, researchers, and small businesses. Programming was taught in colleges, high schools, and even junior highs. And in 1971, the Intel Corporation announced the invention of the 4004, the first **microprocessor**.

The microprocessor incorporated thousands of transistors on a **silicon chip** a fraction of an inch across. In slightly more than a decade, chip technology has advanced to the point where an entire computer — faster, more powerful, and with much greater storage capacity than the "antique" computers of the 1950s — fits onto an area less than a quarter inch wide. The advent of the microprocessor led to the developments which have made computerization so pervasive in the 1980s — the first decade of true "computer dependency." Besides functioning in a variety of devices from traffic lights to microwave ovens, microprocessors have made it possible for individuals to have the resources and capabilities of computers literally in their living rooms.

The implications of this rapid advance are profound, exciting, and disturbing all at once. Four (some say five) generations of computers have emerged in one and a half human generations. The effects on society are more far-reaching than we could expect to cover in a lengthy book, much less this brief overview. For our part, we will look at the effects of the computer age on libraries in general and small libraries in particular.

Until the introduction of the microcomputer, few libraries were in a position to take advantage of computer technology. Those that could were primarily large university libraries which shared computer time with other departments. A number of dreamers recognized the potentials for library computerization, but the size and cost of computers were prohibitive until the late 1970s, when minicomputers and "turnkey" software enabled large and medium-sized public and academic libraries to use circulation, acquisition, and cataloging systems without having to employ staff programmers. During the late 1960s and early 1970s the Library of Congress and the Ohio College Library Center began offering cataloging services which made it possible for libraries to enjoy some of the benefits of computers without owning individual systems. Still, as the flood of information increased, funds diminished, and labor costs rose, manual systems became less effective and more expensive to operate. Microcomputers offer a solution which libraries are just now beginning to explore.

The most common applications of microcomputers so far have been in supplementary roles to larger computer systems, as in the use of **light pens** in circulation, or **intelligent terminals** connected directly or by telephone to a mini or main-frame computer. (For an explanation of the different classifications of computers, see chapter 3.) Microcomputer-based systems have only begun to come into their own since the introduction of **hard disk** storage, which made possible the large database storage needed for even a small collection. It is now well within the capability of even a small library to have a computerized system that is at once independent and interactive, individually tailored to the community being served, and able to access the resources of surrounding larger communities.

In case the idea of an automated library makes you nervous, rest easy. You are not about to be replaced by a computer. Neither are the teachers, if your library is in a school, and neither are the administrators. "Computerization" is not really the same thing as "automation," though the two words are often used interchangeably. Automatic means self-regulating, operating independently of external control, and though computers are used in automation, automation is not what they are about, particularly microcomputers. There is nothing independent about a computer, perverse as it may seem at any given moment. Computers are powerful electronic tools for carrying out actions, according to *human* wishes and human instructions, which if performed by the humans themselves would consume large amounts of time and energy, sometimes prohibitive amounts. Computers do only what people tell them to do, but, given the proper instructions, they can do wonderful things, thus freeing the people they serve to do other wonderful things that *only people* can do.

Some of those wonderful things are happening right now, in libraries of all types and sizes. Since the business of a library is information—collecting it, processing (or sorting) it, and making it available to patrons—it follows that the more knowledge a librarian has about what types and amounts of information are available, and the more easily that information can be accessed, the better the service the library can provide. And since the business of computers is information—collecting it, processing it, and making it available to users—libraries are places where computers can be very, very useful. More than useful; they are fast becoming *necessary*.

Such a thought can be frightening to the uninitiated. And in fact it is wise to approach the idea of computerization with some wariness and skepticism. Simply buying and installing a computer will not cause miracles to happen in your library or anywhere. In order to participate in the "computer revolution" and not be swept away or passed up by it, librarians must make full use of their special skills—analysis, research, and awareness and anticipation of patron needs. They must learn to evaluate and use the capabilities of computers, to understand the limitations as well as the possibilities of computerization. Knowledge, planning, and foresight will mean the difference between increased efficiency, service, and creativity, and frustration, hostility, and wasted money. Many a system sits gathering dust and resentment alongside less esoteric equipment. Maybe there is one in a back room of your school. If so, dig it out and dust it off. It could become your friend.

"Impossible!" you wail. "I'm best at working with people and books, not machines, and besides I'm lousy at math. And furthermore, we just can't afford it."

Well, in the first place, the whole object of computerization is to free people to work with people (and books, and films, and ideas) by taking over the routine tasks that (face it) they are better at doing anyway, and by giving people access to all kinds of information that might otherwise be difficult or impossible to locate. In the second place, computers are becoming easier and easier to use (**user friendly** in computerese), and the necessary skills have nothing to do with being good at math — logic, perhaps, and attention to detail, and patience, but not math. And as for not being able to afford it — in real cost, it is very likely that quite soon not having a computer system will be more expensive than having one, *if* the system is carefully chosen and fully utilized.

This is where a little knowledge (such as the kind available in this book) can save a lot of grief. It is true that there are (some) **turnkey systems** available which you can bring home and use with almost no knowledge of computers. ("Almost" is an important word here. Even with the most automatic of systems, you need to know such mundane but mysterious skills as turning the computer on, loading a program, and backing up data. The days of "plug it in and let it rip" have yet to arrive.) If you get very lucky, you might find a vendor who will magically intuit your needs and sell you just the right turnkey system, and if you are even luckier, that vendor will hold your hand and continue to answer the telephone whenever a problem comes up (which is virtually guaranteed to happen, even with the best of systems).

Such luck, however, is rare. What is more, as every media specialist is aware, there is more involved than simply choosing and implementing a system. The purchase must be explained and justified not only to the purchasing department, but to the school or library board, parent-teacher associations, and other community members. Once the system is in use, the library staff must be prepared to deal with questions and problems of patrons, teachers, and parents. As the coordinator of library services, you are knowledgeable about the resources of your library. If those resources include a computer or two, you had better be knowledgeable about that, too.

This doesn't mean you have to rush out and take a class in **BASIC** or **PASCAL**, or start reading up on **Boolean algebra**. It just means it's useful to have some idea of where computers came from, what they do and how they do it, and how to make them do what you want. This book will give you the background you need to get started, and probably enough to keep you going indefinitely, unless you happen to develop a passion for programming. And once you have your own system, you'll pick up a lot just by using it, through accomplishments and mistakes — yours and other people's. Pretty soon you'll be comparing **BDOS errors** with the best of 'em!

A warning is in order here. Wondrous as microcomputers can be, they are still relatively limited compared to mainframes and minicomputers. In most cases a microcomputer can only be used to perform one task at a time, unlike mainframes and minis which can handle several to many jobs simultaneously. Therefore the dream library with a completely integrated system — including circulation, catalog, acquisitions, etc. — would probably include microcomputers only in a supporting role to a large system, and is thus still beyond the reach of most small libraries.

It is possible, however, and even practical, to introduce computerization a function or two at a time, building and learning as you go, starting with a single microcomputer and one or two software packages. There are several advantages to this approach. In addition to the expense, planning and implementing computerization takes considerable staff time. Limiting the size and number of changes under way at any one time minimizes disruption of library services and lessens staff anxiety. Also, when the changes are small, your mistakes are smaller, less drastic, and more easily corrected. Best of all, you have a chance to tailor your system as it grows, taking into account the reactions of the patrons, the staff, and the community, rather than attempting the impossible task of tailoring the users to a system that may have very little to do with their needs.

We suggest reading the following chapters through to gain an overview of what micros are and what possibilities they offer. Then take the time to do some careful planning. Shop around, ask questions, be skeptical and visionary at the same time. Computerization does not offer automatic answers to all of your problems. Carefully planned and implemented, it can, however, help you place information literally at patrons' fingertips, while freeing you and your staff from time- and energy-consuming routine chores. The effects can go even further, resulting in more creative and innovative services, and more personal interaction with patrons and staff. Even with a limited budget, you and your library can take the first steps into the new information age, and begin to enjoy the benefits of computers as *humanizing* tools.

TIMELINE

Prehistory	People count on fingers and toes, pile rocks, make scratches, etc.
c. 3000 B.C.	The abacus comes into use in China
1614	JOHN NAPIER (inventor of logarithms) produces a device for arithmetic computations using rods or "bones"
1630	WILLIAM OUGHTRED invents the slide rule
1642	BLAISE PASCAL invents a gear-driven adding machine
c. 1694	GOTTFRIED WILHELM VON LEIBNIZ invents the stepped-wheel calculator
1801	JOSEPH-MARIE JACQUARD exhibits his punched-card weaving loom at the Paris World's Fair
c. 1810	CHARLES THOMAS begins mass production of calculators
1812	CHARLES BABBAGE builds the "Difference Engine"
1834	CHARLES BABBAGE builds his "Analytical Engine"
c. 1830	ADA BYRON, COUNTESS OF LOVELACE explains Babbage's engines and writes operating instructions—the first computer programs
1854	GEORGE BOOLE develops a system of algebraic logic
1868	The first practical typewriter is patented
1884	JOHN PATTERSON introduces the commercial cash register
1887	HERMAN HOLLERITH invents a punched-card tabulating machine for the 1890 census
1920	JAMES SMATHERS invents the electric typewriter
1937	HOWARD AIKEN begins work on the Mark I

1937	CLAUSE SHANNON designs electrical switching circuits using symbolic logic to perform addition using relays and switches
1944	MARK I is up and running
1945	JOHN VON NEUMANN introduces the concept of a stored program
1943-1946	J. PRESPER ECKERT and JOHN MAUCHLY build ENIAC
1947	BELL LABORATORIES produces the first transistor
1949	MAURICE WILKS of England designs and builds EDSAC, the first computer to use an internally stored program
1951	UNIVAC is installed at the U.S. Census Bureau
1955	IBM introduces the first large-scale business computer JOHN BACKUS invents FORTRAN
c. 1956	GRACE MURRAY HOPPER invents FLOMATIC (which later becomes COBOL)
1959	TRANSISTORS are incorporated in computer circuitry (second generation)
1963	JOHN KEMENY and THOMAS KURTZ develop BASIC Introduction of time sharing
1964	Use of integrated circuits in computers (third generation)
1965	Minicomputers enter wide use
1971	INTEL develops the microprocessor
1975	Microcomputers enter the marketplace
1975-1976	GARY KILDALL and JOHN TRODORE develop CP/M standardized operating system for microcomputers
1981-	Computer-dependent society

2 An Introduction to Computer Software

FIRST THINGS FIRST

You might think it strange that we are discussing the software—the programs—before the hardware, the physical components of a computer system. At first glance, buying a microcomputer may seem like buying any other type of equipment, such as a movie projector or a tape recorder—compare brands and prices and purchase the hardware, then begin looking for films or tapes. Actually, when choosing a computer system, software availability should be the first consideration. This is because software, the part of your system that actually performs the functions you want to computerize, is not interchangeable among different types of hardware. A program written for an Apple™ will not run on a TRS-80™, or on a Pet™, and vice versa. This is not, so far as we can tell, an actual conspiracy on the part of the computer industry. Rather, it is one effect of the extremely rapid growth of computer technology. Software manufacture, especially, is marked by a large number of "garage" shops, with hobbyists and professionals working feverishly to get their ideas out into the marketplace and onto consumer's computers—often before they are working properly. The number of hardware manufacturers, while not as large, is still impressive.

The amount and diversity of this activity, which is highly competitive, has made it extremely difficult for the industry to agree on any real standardization. With some significant exceptions, such as the **CP/M™ operating system** and the **ASCII code** (both of which are explained later in this book), most efforts to standardize computer components and software have met with resistance from within the industry itself. Sadly, the incompatibility often extends to different products built by the same manufacturer. There are signs that this is changing, but for the present the majority of programs will run only on the specific types of hardware for which they were written.

If this hodgepodge did not exist, it would be quite feasible for you to go out and buy a computer and some peripherals, then find the software you want and implement it. However, at least for the foreseeable future, it is much easier to first find software to fit your needs and then buy hardware that is compatible with it.

There is, of course, one exception to this rule. You may be reading this book because your library has suddenly found itself in possession of a microcomputer and you want to know what to do with it. If so, you will, in a sense, be working backward, and you will have to make your decisions within the framework of limitations presented by whatever type of hardware you happen to have. In this case, you may not be able to computerize your preferred application right away. However, you should be able to choose from several useful functions, any of which can serve as a starting point for building your system. Also, when considering future additions and expansions, you need not be bound into that particular brand. The modular nature of a microcomputer-based system makes it quite feasible to have the software that is best for each particular function, simply by purchasing different computers for different functions.

By themselves, computers are incredibly stupid. Even the most sophisticated, technologically advanced computer is utterly useless without the detailed sets of instructions known as software—the programs, along with related **documentation**—which cause the hardware to perform specific functions. Software is generally divided into two main types, *applications* and *systems*. Applications software is the category with which you, as an **end user**, will be most concerned. It is a program or programs designed to perform a pre-defined series of functions such as inventory control, financial services, etc. Applications software is almost always written in a **high-level language**, like BASIC or PASCAL. These languages are based on English, with vocabularies, syntax, and rules of usage that make them relatively simple for people to understand and use. In order for a computer to use applications software, however, there must be an intermediary program, known as an **operating system**, which acts as a "monitor," controlling the way the computer actually operates to perform the functions specified in the program.

An operating system is one type of systems software that includes any program or group of programs that manages the various components of a computer system and enables it to function. Other types of systems software cause the computer to run more efficiently; these include database managers, **sort**ing packages, and programming and **debug**ging aids. The operating system is an essential element of any computer. Without it, all of the other parts of the system are useless. Acting as an **interface** between the computer and the user, the operating system coordinates all of the elements of the system, including the **CPU**, the **terminal**, the disk or cassette drives, the printer, and so on, by regulating the **input** and **output** functions of each device, and causing each to respond properly to the signals provided by the operator and the software (see figure 2.1). The operating system also acts as a "file manager," keeping track of where data is stored in the system and how much storage is available for additional data. The third primary function of the operating system is providing for the loading and execution of applications programs.

When you purchase a computer, an operating system is generally included with the hardware. Sometimes it is "built into" the **ROM**, or **Read Only Memory** (programs of this type are known as **firmware**); other times it comes on a disk which is loaded into the computer as needed. It may be written in any language, from the 1s and 0s of machine language to a high-level language. The operating system should be flexible, efficient, and fast, and take up as little space as possible in the computer's memory. A disk-based operating system can be much more extensive than one stored in ROM or on tape because of the larger amount of available storage space. It is possible to buy different operating systems for the same hardware. For instance, if you purchase an Apple II and run it with a cassette recorder you will not need to purchase another operating system. But when you add a disk drive you will need to purchase a system or systems such as Apple **DOS** or CP/M. The operating system will determine what software packages will run on your computer.

Figure 2.1. How an Operating System Interfaces with a Computer

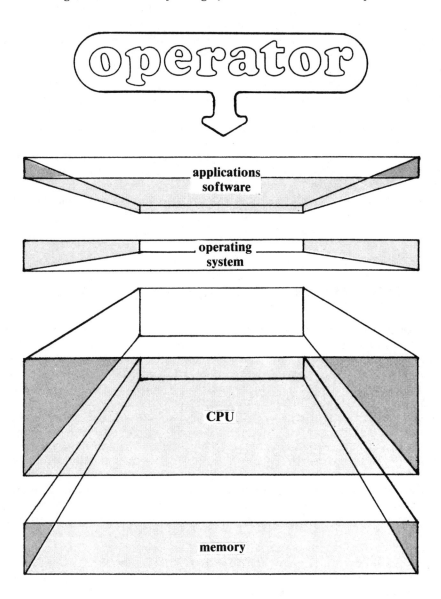

A while ago we stated that software is hardware dependent. This is not precisely so. Specifically, operating system software is hardware dependent, and applications software is then dependent on the operating system. Rather than being written for a particular kind of computer, applications software is written for an operating system, which then interfaces to the hardware. In considering various types of software and hardware, you will need to be aware of the availability of software for each type of operating system, and correspondingly, what types of operating systems are available for each brand of hardware. Some software packages are written for more than one kind of operating system, but most are not. Many programs are now being written for CP/M, which is the closest thing to an industry standard. This is particularly true of business software, such as word processing and file management programs. But for educational applications, you may find a wider range of choice in programs written for the Apple™ or Radio Shack™ disk systems. You may want to purchase one brand of computer and two or more operating systems, running under whichever system is appropriate for a given program.

(Narrative continues on page 30.)[†]

*****

CP/M: TOWARD AN INDUSTRY STANDARD

Though Intel succeeded in producing the first microprocessor, the 4004, in 1970, it was 1973 before the introduction of an 8-bit microprocessor capable of serving in a microcomputer, and late 1974 before the first true microcomputer became available to the general public—or at least that portion of it partial to the kind of projects that appear in magazines like *Popular Electronics.* The first micro, the MITS Altair™, and the competitors that soon joined it in the marketplace used cassette tape as a storage medium and cost well under $1,000. The microcomputer market promptly took off—in all different directions. Though the different brands performed very similar functions, the hardware configurations for each were unique, and each brand was incompatible with every other.

The limited size and speed capabilities of cassette tape storage made micros impractical for uses other than recreational, hobbyist, and some educational applications. But it was not long before several companies introduced **floppy disk** drives, opening up a whole new range of business, scientific, and other possible applications. During this period Gary Kildall, a consultant to Intel, became intrigued with floppy disk drives and developed a file management system which was to evolve into today's BDOS, or Basic Disk Operating System. A colleague, John Torode, designed a disk controller to work with the system, and CP/M, or Control Program for Microcomputers, was born. When they combined all the hardware-dependent features of CP/M into one section, thereby making it modifiable for almost any micro, and began adding "systems utilities" such as a debugger, **assembler**, text editor, and copy program, Kildall and his company, Digital Research™, had a highly flexible and instantly popular operating system. CP/M is compatible with high-level languages such as BASIC, FORTRAN, COBOL, and PASCAL, and since its introduction in late 1975, hundreds of programs of all types have been written for it.

[†]Material set off by asterisks enlarges upon the discussion in the main body of the text.

Versions of CP/M are now available for many different hardware configurations. Although the original version was designed for computers utilizing the 8080 or Z80 microprocessors, recent spinoffs have been designed for other types of microprocessors, and some manufacturers such as Apple offer plug-in boards with Z80 CPUs capable of temporarily "taking over" from the built-in CPUs in order to run CP/M.

Because of the large amount of available CP/M software, the increased ability to "transport" CP/M-based programs between different computers, and the possibilities for networking, computers operating under CP/M have greater flexibility and a wider range of possible applications than those with nonstandard systems. Thus anyone venturing into the microrealm is likely to need at least a passing familiarity with some of the more common features and commands of CP/M, such as:

>**A.** Also known as the "A prompt." When a disk containing the CP/M operating system is inserted into a disk drive and "booted," this symbol appears on the terminal screen to let the operator know that the operating system has been loaded into the computer's memory and is ready to execute commands. The ">A" indicates that the "logged disk drive," or the drive which is currently in use by the computer, is the "A" or primary drive. Unless you direct it otherwise by typing a drive name (indicated by a capital letter, usually A through D) and a colon (:), the computer will "assume" you wish to log on the A drive. When you switch to the B drive, ">B" (the B prompt) will appear, and so on.

TPA. The Transient Program Area, or the portion of the computer's memory which is used to store and execute user programs being run under CP/M.

CCP. The Console Command Processor, or the portion of CP/M which interacts directly with the operator when a user program is not running. The CCP handles functions such as loading programs into the TPA, creation, deletion, and renaming of files, and so on.

BDOS. The Basic Disk Operating System, which handles disk-related operations such as writing to and from disks, allocating disk space, and so on. BDOS is the same for all microcomputers; it is the standardized portion of CP/M.

BIOS. The Basic Input/Output System. Unlike BDOS, BIOS is hardware dependent. It contains the programs that control the input and output devices of each individual computer system—the terminal, printer, disk drive, etc. BIOS is the intermediary between the standardized BDOS and each individual hardware system.

Resident and Transient Commands. CP/M contains several "built-in," or resident, commands which are extremely useful. They include:
DIR: Lists a DIRectory of the files on the current "logged" disk.
ERA: ERAses a file from a disk.
REN: RENames a file.
TYPE: TYPEs the contents of a file to the console device.
SAVE: SAVEs contents of the computer memory as a disk file.

CP/M also makes available several transient commands or "systems utilities" which may be stored on disks and called up as needed. These utilities include such programs as FORMAT, used to **initialize** a disk so that it can receive data; SYSGEN, which installs the CP/M system on a disk; PIP (for Peripheral Interchange Program), used to copy files from one disk to another; STAT, used to determine the amount of storage space taken up by the files on a disk, and several others.

If you purchase a computer system with CP/M, you will probably find yourself making frequent use of the above commands. Many applications programs, such as word processing and file management programs, also make extensive use of CP/M features. Since the documentation furnished by Digital Research™ is not a shining example to the industry, you will probably want to consult other sources such as your vendor, a knowledgeable hobbyist friend or staff member, or one of several books now available (see appendix B) for help in mastering CP/M.

*****

APPLICATIONS SOFTWARE

There are four basic methods for obtaining software for specific applications. Each has advantages and disadvantages. The chart on pages 188-91, compiled by the McDonnell Douglas Automation Company, details these choices very well. Briefly, the methods are as follows:

1) In-house Development
    Requires having available staff with the time and expertise to develop software. It is generally an alternative only for very large institutions or those with a staff member who happens to be a very knowledgeable and energetic hobbyist.

2) Custom Development
    Writing a *very detailed and specific* set of specifications and hiring a programmer or programmers to design custom software to meet those specifications. Once the software is written, there is generally a long period of testing, debugging, and revising before the system is actually up and running. If you have the time, budget, energy, and patience, and are very careful in choosing the programmer(s), this is the way to implement an idea that no one else seems to have developed.

3) Purchased Software
    Shopping for currently available, working software which can be adapted or used as is to meet your needs.

4) Purchased Services
    Hiring a service bureau or data processing service to handle the tasks on their hardware and software. This may involve having a **dumb terminal** or a microcomputer acting as an intelligent terminal on the library premises.

As the administrator of a small library, it is not likely that you can consider buying or designing a complete system which would immediately computerize all possible library functions. Nor, as we discussed in chapter 1, would it be all that desirable to do so. Instead you may plan to computerize many or all of the main functions — circulation, cataloging, overdues, inventory and ordering, etc. — over a period of time, implementing one and letting everyone adjust to it before adding another. If your computerization list includes bibliographic lists, form letters, inventory records, community files, statistical reports, and patron files, you may be able to find a software company that has a variety of packages to perform several or all of these functions. For example, one company may have a word processing program, a file management program, a spread sheet program, a mailing program, etc., with packages that are similarly structured, so that once you become proficient at using one, subsequent programs are easier to learn. The packages may also be combined for some functions, increasing the usefulness of the individual programs.

In shopping for software, you need to be aware of the possibilities for future expansion. This does not mean you must find one manufacturer capable of filling all of your present and future needs. It is quite possible you will find yourself using one type of hardware and a group of software packages to perform administrative tasks, and a completely different system for patron services. One of the greatest advantages of microcomputer-based systems is the potential for customization. Even if you are using only commercially available software, it is possible for you to create a system suitable to the needs of your particular library and capable of growing with it.

Chapter 4 covers specific types of software and their possible applications in small libraries, and chapter 6 explains how to go about determining the requirements for your particular library or media center. For the present we are concerned with general techniques and criteria for finding and evaluating software packages.

One way to begin researching the types and quality of software available is to read reviews. There is a growing number of publications that are partially or wholly devoted to reviewing various hardware and software packages. They are aimed at audiences that include business and professional people, serious hobbyists, less serious hobbyists, educators — and librarians. We have included the most helpful of the current publications in appendix B in the back of this book. As it would be impossible for a mere human to keep up with the volume of material covered in all of them each month, we suggest you examine sample copies and choose several to subscribe to and read regularly. Depending on the size and location of your library, the ages of your patrons, whether or not you are responsible for choosing educational software for classrooms, and so on, different publications will be better suited to your needs. If you are in a school district with a cooperative library system, you might consider having members subscribe to different periodicals, possibly on a yearly rotation basis, or according to special staff interests. Then pertinent information on review sources, curriculum developments, and so on could be shared with less time and money expended by everyone.

In choosing software, the primary concern is the goal you intend to meet by using the program. **If you do not yet have a specific objective or two in mind you are not ready to begin shopping for a computer system.** Books and periodicals can tell you what is available and what is being done in the way of computerization of library and nonlibrary functions, and the applications chapter in this book will give you more ideas as well as techniques for developing objectives for your particular library.

Once you have a purpose for purchasing a system, you can establish some criteria for evaluating possible selections. You will also be able to describe to a vendor what capabilities your system should have, saving both of you large amounts of time and grief. *You must be able to describe your needs in detail.* For example, if you want to have computerized bibliographies or even a computerized catalog, you will need to go to the computer store supplied with information about the number of records you expect to have, the number of characters in each record, the number of ways you wish to sort or retrieve the information, and so on. A program that works marvelously with 500 records could become hopelessly bogged down if asked to deal with 3,000. Some programs—including any that deal with large numbers of records—will require a hard disk to work efficiently, unless you want to spend a lot of time changing disks while searching for data. In evaluating systems, and particularly in reading accounts of other successes and failures, keep in mind that the workability of a system depends upon the basis for judging it. A system designed for high school level could be disastrous in an elementary school, and vice versa. How much relevance does another librarian's experience with a particular system have for you?

A SOFTWARE SHOPPING LIST

There are several criteria that apply no matter what you plan to do with your system. Unless the software meets some basic requirements, it doesn't matter what the vendor or the brochure says it can do, or that it sounds like the realization of your dreams. Developing software is a painstaking, time-consuming, error laden process, and many are the bugs that creep past unwary and rushed programmers. Don't let them get as far as your library. Some questions to keep in mind:

1) Has it been used successfully by someone else?
   The longer a system has been up and running, the more time its creators have had to iron out the problems, to streamline it and make it do what it is intended to do. Unless you want to try alternative number 2 above and go through the test process yourself,* look for software that has been on the market for a year or more. Ask the vendor or manufacturer for a list of users and contact some of them for both pros and cons of the program. Check magazines for reviews, letters, etc., on the program and its competition.

2) Will it run on your computer?
   Or on a computer that fits your hardware criteria, such as price, storage capabilities, etc.? This may seem like an obvious question, but it can be a disappointing experience to get all excited about a program you hear described by a salesman or see in a magazine ad, only to realize that it is not only incompatible with the system on hand, but that the required system is only available by mail order from San Jose and has no service centers within 1,500 miles of you. Ask this question early!

---

*If you are daring, you might save some money by purchasing a program as a test user. Sometimes manufacturers will offer new programs at a special rate to those willing to put up with frequent updates and a few bugs.

3) Have you tried it?
   Most manufacturers supply dealers with demos for hands-on practice.
   The demo may be a limited version of the software, but it should be
   enough for you to try a few functions and get a basic idea of how it
   works. Like dresses or suits, software that looks very good "on the rack"
   can be a big disappointment when you "try it on." This is your
   opportunity to find out if the program actually does what it is supposed
   to do—something you cannot take for granted!

4) Is it "user friendly"?
   Are the screen directions clear and easy to understand? Is the response
   time reasonable, or is it so slow that a user becomes bored and
   impatient, or so fast that he gets flustered? How does it respond to
   operator mistakes? Does a misplaced keystroke spell disaster? What
   kind of feedback does it provide?

   A word here about the two main ways software is controlled by the user.
   Applications programs are classified as either **menu-driven** or
   command-driven. A menu-driven program is one that displays menus,
   or lists of possible functions, on the video display terminal screen. The
   operator selects a number or letter corresponding to the desired
   function, and the computer carries out the selection. Sometimes a
   narrowing down process will take the operator through several menus to
   find a specific command. Menu-driven programs are especially useful
   for novices and operators who have no knowledge of (or interest in)
   programming. If the system is going to be used by library patrons, as in
   an online "card catalog" or information service, a menu-driven program
   is probably the better choice.

   A command-driven program is one in which the computer responds to
   specific commands. The operator must memorize or have easy access to
   the list of commands, and know enough programming to decide which
   ones to use. For those with the ability and knowledge to use them,
   command-driven programs are faster and more convenient. Some
   programs have a built-in flexibility that allows the user to choose
   whether to use menus, commands, or even a combination, displaying
   partial or complete menus upon operator request and otherwise
   responding directly to commands. If you or members of your staff are
   willing to take the time and effort to learn to use it, a command-driven
   program may prove more efficient for administrative applications.

5) How good is the documentation?
   The documentation should include two parts: a user's guide and a
   manual of technical information. The user's guide, especially, should be
   readable and easy to follow, and should tell you everything you need to
   know to use the program. Documentation is perhaps the software
   industry's weakest point. Manuals are usually written by programmers
   who may be too familiar with the program to explain it to a novice, and
   who in addition are programmers, not writers. These documents are also
   often written hastily and are prone to errors and omissions. Many
   dealers will let you borrow a manual to read over before you buy a
   program. This is a good way to become familiar with program features
   as well as to gauge clarity and quality. Even though many sections may

be unclear without a computer there for hands-on trial, you can get an idea of what the program is about, and whether or not you will be able to understand it well enough to use it.

6) What are the manufacturer's policies on **backup**?
One of the more charming features of computers is their tendency to gobble up disks—in other words, to destroy data. This is the first, but far from the last time that we will talk about the importance of backing up your programs and data. Particularly if a program is in daily use, one or more backup copies is essential. Unfortunately, one of the more charming features of software manufacturers is their paranoia about unauthorized copying of their products (more on this later). Some companies trust users to honor the copyright laws and to make copies only as a safeguard, and therefore do not copy-protect their software. Other companies, however, go to great measures to make their programs uncopiable, or almost so. If you purchase copy-protected software, you will have to obtain backup copies. Some companies will send backups when they receive your signed registration. Other companies require more money for backups. Most companies now do require some sort of a licensing agreement in which you agree not to copy the software for use on more than one computer without paying an additional licensing fee.

7) What are the manufacturer's policies on updates?
When you load a commercial program into a computer's memory, usually the first thing that will appear on the screen is the name of the program followed by a number such as "3.2." This number indicates the *version* of the program. Software versions are similar to new editions of books. The first version is numbered 1.0 and usually is distributed only to test users. As the program is improved and debugged, updated versions are issued. Smaller changes are called revisions and are indicated by the number to the right of the decimal point.

Since many working programs are constantly being updated and improved, it is helpful to have the option of updating your copy of a program when a better version comes out. Some manufacturers will replace an old copy with a new version simply for the return of the old disk (this is generally true for test users of new programs); others charge a fee which may range anywhere from a few dollars to the entire price of the program. Your vendor should be able to tell you the manufacturer's policy on updates.

8) What is the availability of knowledgeable help?
Is there a local or an 800 number which you can call for assistance when you run into problems? Even experienced programmers run into difficulties with new software acquisitions. Someone who knows the software and is there to respond to your cry for help is more a necessity than a luxury, especially when you are just entering the confusing world of computers.

9) Does the program accomplish the objective(s) you have established for it?

Just as you set up guidelines for purchases of books, films, and equipment, you will be setting guidelines for purchasing computer software. To answer this question you must have a clear description of what you want to accomplish and be able to translate it into terms of size and speed capabilities, specific functions, and so on. You are also likely to be at least partially responsible for choosing educational software, which requires additional consideration of such factors as type of instruction (computer-assisted, computer-managed, or simulated), sound and colors, response to errors, and so on. The topic of educational software will be covered more thoroughly in chapter 5, The Library as a Computer Resource Center. Chapter 6, Choosing and Implementing a Microcomputer System, also includes methods and criteria for evaluating software in terms of specific needs.

These are general questions to put at the top of your software shopping list. The applications and implementation chapters will cover considerations in looking at specific types of software. Being armed with questions like these will help you hold your own with jargon-spouting vendors, and enable you to choose software that will work for you.

3 An Introduction to Hardware

Although Charles Babbage had the right idea when he began work on his "Difference Engine" over 150 years ago, the limited technology of his time doomed his efforts to failure. All the conceptual developments of computerization would be mere theory without the machinery to carry out functions that are too voluminous, repetitive, or complex for human beings to do efficiently and with good grace. In this chapter we will introduce the workers of the computer system, the infinitely patient, infinitely stupid drudges designed to actually carry out the tasks specified by the programs and the operator—the hardware.

The basic definition of a computer is any device that computes, from an enormous mainframe down to a calculator wristwatch. For most purposes, leaving out calculators and the preprogrammed microprocessors inside appliances, computers are generally divided into three categories by size, capability, and cost. Advances in technology are making even these divisions hazy. Today's microcomputers can outperform the mainframes of ten years ago, and will be outpaced by the micros and even the pocket computers of next year. At present, however, it is accepted practice to refer to computers as one of three types:

MAINFRAMES—fill a room
    —capable of carrying out multiple tasks simultaneously
    —may include as part of complete system minis and/or micros
    —also called "host computers"

MINIS   —fill a wall
    —also able to perform simultaneous multiple tasks
    —may include micros as part of system

MICROS   —fill a desk
    —may perform concurrent tasks for a single user

There are also differences in storage and speed capabilities, with mainframes being capable of handling much more information more rapidly than minis, which can handle more than micros. It is also possible, if both the hardware and software are compatible, for computers to form networks by means of communications interfaces which enable them to "talk" to one another. These interfaces consist of hardware and often software components as well. This ability of computers to communicate, even over great distances, opens up possibilities for users of all kinds. Access to a microcomputer equipped with devices such as a **modem** may also mean access to the resources of a huge mainframe computer system, as well as to other small computers in different places.

All computers, from desk-top micros to whole-floor mainframes, have five basic functions:

1) Input of information
2) Storage of information
3) Processing of information
4) Output of information
5) Control of information

These functions are handled, respectively, by input devices such as a keyboard; storage components such as ROM (Read Only Memory), **RAM (Random Access Memory)**, cassette tapes, and disk drives; the CPU (Central Processing Unit); and output devices such as **CRT**s (cathode ray tubes) and printers, all of which are coordinated and controlled by an operating system such as CP/M.

CENTRAL PROCESSING UNIT

The heart of any computer, from a mainframe to a micro, is the CPU, or Central Processing Unit. In a microcomputer the CPU is a microprocessor, a tiny silicon chip with electronic circuitry etched into it, which holds thousands of bits of information. The terms microcomputer and microprocessor are sometimes (and incorrectly) used interchangeably. A microprocessor by itself is not a computer. Preprogrammed, unalterable microprocessors and memory chips are found in all kinds of devices, from digital gas pumps and automatic cash registers to traffic lights, sewing machines, and electronic typewriters. These devices are not in themselves computers, since they are limited to a specific, limited set of instructions.

A computer's CPU has two main parts: the **control unit** and the **arithmetic logic** unit. The control unit interprets the program commands stored in the ROM and the RAM (see below) and coordinates their execution. It keeps track of the locations and identification of operations and data, moving data to and from the arithmetic logic unit, which performs the actual computer operations—addition, subtraction, multiplication, division, numerical comparisons, and logical functions. Such a sequence of relatively simple operations used to solve a complex problem is known as an algorithm. Microprocessors are able to perform such sequences extremely rapidly, running through several million "program cycles" (getting an instruction, executing it, incrementing the program counter, getting the next instruction, etc.) per second.

In addition to the control and arithmetic logic units, the CPU contains several kinds of **registers**, which are used as temporary holding areas for information currently being used by the CPU. Accumulator registers, for example, store the results of additions, subtractions, multiplications, and divisions, while address registers hold the location of various data items being used in the current program.

The information used by computers is measured in units known as **bits**. A bit is simply an electrical impulse that is interpreted by the computer as a 1 or a 0, the digits used in **binary** (or base 2) **code**, which is the code used for machine language programming—that is, programming that can be directly "understood" by a computer. (This relates to the ON/OFF recognition factor discussed in chapter 1.)

As of this writing, most microcomputers process 8 bits, or 1 **byte**, of information at a time, and can address (that is, use) 64 kilobytes (1,024 bytes, abbreviated "**K**") of memory by using 16-bit address registers. Without getting into complicated explanations of **hexadecimal** addresses and machine codes, this means that the maximum directly addressable internal memory available in a micro with a 16-bit address path is 64K.

A growing number of microcomputers possess 16-bit processors which can handle 2 bytes at a time and have 20- to 24-bit addressing, which allows up to 8 megabytes, or 8 *million* bytes, of directly addressable memory. A few manufacturers have even begun to introduce 32-bit processors. These newer micros actually mimic minicomputers in terms of speed and storage capabilities. As they are very powerful they are likely to become the "workhorse" computers of the next decade. They are, however, comparatively expensive. Hardware prices may be double the price of less powerful machines, while software may cost up to ten times as much for the same application. Unless you are buying on a district level, and/or plan to incorporate an extensive **multi-user system**, you are not likely to need—or be able to afford—the capabilities and memory size of these new "mini-micros" or "micro-minis."

You may, however, find yourself considering a 16-bit machine. If so, pay extra attention to software choices. As with different brands of micros, the 8- and 16-bit processors are not yet interchangeable in terms of the software they can run. Though the 16-bit computers offer certain advantages in terms of memory size and speed, software availability is relatively limited. Also, since most of the 16-bit programs are new, they have a tendency to contain **bugs**. Some manufacturers are getting around this problem by offering micros with dual processors, one of each size. At least one manufacturer is offering a different alternative: a computer with two 8-bit processors, which runs 8-bit programs faster than single-processor machines.

All of the above is one reason why we advise you to choose your software first. Also, just because a 16-bit or dual-processor machine is newer and faster and has a bigger memory, it is not necessarily better for *your* needs, despite all the magazine ads and vendor sales pitches. An 8-bit micro may do everything you need it to do, and as long as your system meets your needs, it is not obsolete.

Another reason for starting with software is that even within the categories of 8-bit, 16-bit, etc., all CPUs are not the same. There are several different "families" within each category, and programs written for one family will not run on a processor from a different family. In fact, software is not necessarily interchangeable *within* a family. Two of the more popular 8-bit "families" are the Z80 and the 65xx. The former includes 8080/8085 and Z80 processors, and is the family for which the CP/M operating system was written. The 65xx series includes the 6502 and 6509 CPUs, which are used in popular home computers such as the Apple. Some computers are capable of running more than one CPU. It is possible, for instance, to plug a Z80 **board** into the Apple which temporarily takes over control of the computer from the normal 6502 processor. For the most part, however, switching CPUs is something you should avoid unless you have competent technical assistance.

What this all means is that you have to make sure your software and your CPU match. You can find this out by checking the documentation for both, or simply by asking your vendor (who should verify the compatibility at the beginning of any discussion on particular equipment). Technical complexities aside, in practical terms this is just another point to check as you shop.

COMPUTER MEMORY

The primary storage unit inside the computer proper contains two types of semiconductor memory which may be addressed by the CPU: ROM, for "Read Only Memory," and RAM, for "Random Access Memory." The ROM is permanently imprinted on a chip; it can be "read" by the computer but not altered. Certain frequently used systems programs are stored as firmware in the ROM. It usually contains the **monitor**, a very basic operating system which goes into effect when the computer is first turned on. If the computer uses a disk operating system, the monitor is responsible for such operations as **bootstrapping** a disk operating system by reading the first sector of a systems disk and loading its contents into the RAM. Many inexpensive personal computers have a built-in BASIC-language **interpreter** in ROM, so that the computer can respond directly to typed commands in BASIC. Since storage space within the computer itself is limited, however, general applications microcomputers have smaller ROMS and rely on disk operating systems for most operating and other systems functions.

(Narrative continues on page 40.)

*****

HOW A MONITOR "BOOTSTRAPS" AN OPERATING SYSTEM

When using a computer with a disk operating system (DOS), your first step is to turn the computer on, then insert a disk into the disk drive and "boot" it. Some systems boot automatically when switched on; others require the operator to push a ‹RESET› button or buttons. This step is known as a "cold boot." You will quickly become familiar with both the word and the action, but what exactly does "boot" mean?

"Boot" is an abbreviation for "bootstrap," and refers to the process by which the operating system is read, or loaded from a disk into RAM. This function is one of the main responsibilities of the monitor in ROM. When the power is turned on and/or the ‹RESET› button is pressed, a short program in ROM is activated, instructing the computer to read information from the first sector of the disk into RAM. The information contained in the first sector tells the computer how to finish loading the operating system into memory.

In the days before the invention of ROM, the operating system had to be loaded manually by keying in switches on the front of the computer to tell it to read a section of magnetic tape. The introduction of an internal memory that could contain a permanent program to handle the initial loading was a big step toward "people friendly" computers. Some unknown figure in computer history decided the process of loading the operating system a portion at a time was comparable to someone "pulling himself up by the bootstraps"; hence "boot" became a basic element of computer terminology.

A "warm boot" is used when exiting from an applications program back to the operating system, or when changing disks. Since part of the system is already in memory, it does not have to be completely reloaded. In CP/M, a warm boot is accomplished by pressing ‹CTRL› C.

*****

Random Access Memory may be changed as well as read. It is usually also **volatile**, meaning its contents are destroyed when the power is turned off or lost. The RAM is the temporary holding area for programs that are being executed, including operating and other systems software and applications programs. For example, the CCP and TPA memory sections used by CP/M (see chapter 2) are both stored in RAM.

Computer memory size is measured in bytes. Technically, a byte usually consists of 8 bits, or electrical impulses, but you will probably come to think of it primarily in practical terms, as in the size and number of files that can be stored on a disk of 130K, or 130 kilobytes. A single **character** of information, whether it is a letter, number, or space, uses 1 byte of the computer's memory. Two kilobytes hold the equivalent of approximately one double-spaced, typewritten page of information.

INPUT DEVICES

Before a computer can do anything, its CPU and memory must have a means of receiving information and **commands**. Bar code readers, scanners, **OCR** wands, **joy sticks,** and keyboards are all input devices. The most common means of input for microcomputers in business and personal applications (other than games) is through a keyboard similar to a typewriter keyboard, with the addition of some special **function keys** such as CONTROL ‹CTRL›, ESCAPE ‹ESC›, and ‹ENTER›. Many keyboards also contain numeric keypads for calculator functions. Some keyboards do not have actual "keys" but have a flat surface which is touch sensitive and labeled to resemble a keyboard. Some computers use touch sensitive screens rather than keyboards; the operator indicates a command or item of data to be used by touching it on the screen. Computers also input information via **peripheral devices** such as modems, and from auxiliary storage devices such as disk drives and cassette recorders.

When the operator "types" a command, scans a bar code label with a bar code reader, or moves a joy stick, the operating system, acting out its role as "traffic cop," directs the information to the various other components. For example, if the system includes a video display unit, the input command would be displayed on the screen. The information is simultaneously relayed to the CPU and any other relevant peripherals, such as the modem or printer.

AUXILIARY STORAGE DEVICES

Auxiliary storage devices are used to store data and programs not in current use by the internal RAM of the computer. The first microcomputers used cassette tapes and tape recorders for auxiliary storage, but tape proved to be extremely limited in its usefulness. In the first place, information could only be accessed sequentially; that is, the tape had to be wound to the portion that contained the needed information. Also, the capacity for data was quite small. The advent of floppy disks and disk drives has made cassette tapes virtually obsolete except for games and limited educational applications. Some home computer systems also provide for auxiliary memory in the form of plug-in cartridges. But for nearly all practical purposes, and especially for library applications, a microcomputer system is incomplete without at least one floppy disk drive. For any applications involving a **database** of any size, such as an online catalog, a hard disk will be necessary as well.

If you already have a microcomputer that uses cassette tapes, you should consider purchasing one or more disk drives for it. Such an investment—probably only a few hundred dollars—could vastly increase the potential usefulness of your current system. Alternatively, you could purchase a different system altogether for administrative applications and use the existing system with the cassette recorder for computer literacy and other types of instruction.

Floppy Disks

Like cassette tapes, floppy disks store data by means of magnetization. The primary advantages of floppies are increased storage space and the ability of the drive read/write assembly to rapidly access stored information, as well as portability and low cost. Floppy disks and disk drives are often compared to records and record players, except that the "record player" can "record" (write) information on the disk as well as "play" (read) it, just as a tape recorder can both play and record sound. The read/write assembly inside the drive looks somewhat like the arm of a record player, and operates like the head of a tape recorder. The arm moves the head back and forth across the surface of the rapidly spinning disk. A felt pad on the opposite side of the disk holds the read/write head against the disk surface (see figure 3.1, page 42).

A disk is a technologically advanced version of the familiar Hollerith punch card. Instead of holes, the bits of information consist of magnetized spots on the disk surface. The disk itself is made of a thin, flexible sheet of mylar material and coated with a magnetic oxide. It is encased inside a protective square jacket which has an access slot for the read/write assembly, a center hole or disk hub, and a timing or index hole (see figure 3.2, page 43). The index hole is used rather like a timing light for a car engine, to determine which **sector** on the disk is being written to or read. Depending on whether it is **hard-sectored** or **soft-sectored**, the disk itself will have one or more holes. As the disk holes pass beneath the jacket hole the computer can determine where it is on the disk.

Whether a disk is hard or soft sectored is one of its four main distinguishing characteristics, the others being size, density, and number of usable sides. A fifth distinguishing characteristic is added when the disk is initialized, or "formatted," for a given disk operating system. Like software, disks, once formatted, are not interchangeable between computers, despite a certain amount of standardization.

Floppy disks come in two sizes: 8-inch diameter and 5¼-inch diameter. (Recently a couple of manufacturers introduced 3½-inch "micro-floppy" disks and disk drives, but as of this writing these are not generally available.) The smaller disks are often referred to as "mini-floppies." Generally, an 8-inch disk will hold more bytes of information than a mini-floppy, but not always. Disks of

Figure 3.1. Floppy Disk Drive and Closeup of Read/Write Assembly and a Disk

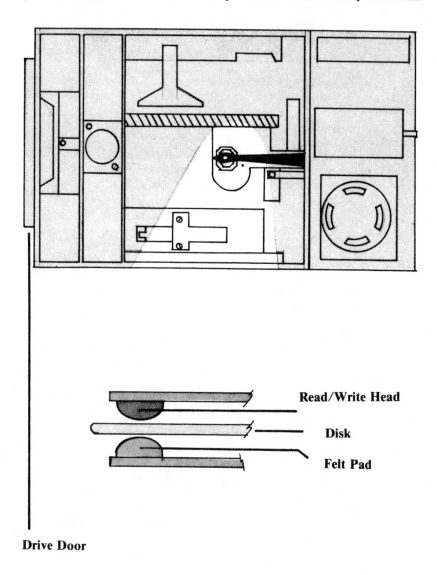

Read/Write Head

Disk

Felt Pad

Drive Door

Figure 3.2. A Floppy Disk

Data is written onto circular tracks which are divided into sectors.

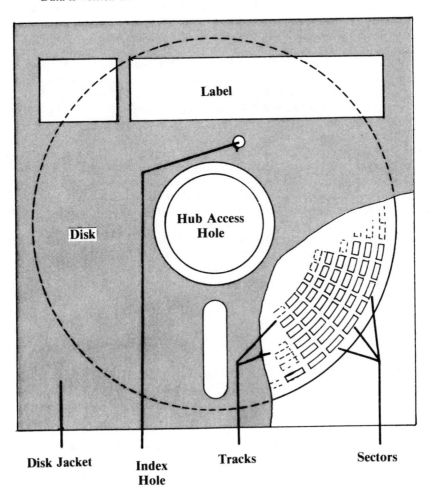

Disk Jacket   Index Hole   Tracks   Sectors

either size may be single density or double density. The information on a double density disk is smaller and closer together than on a single density disk. Therefore both the read/write assembly and the disk itself must be of high quality in order for the "writing" to be "legible." As you probably gathered, a double density disk will hold just about twice as much data as a single density disk of the same size, while a double-sided disk will hold twice as much as one that is single sided. Thus a double-sided double density ("quad density") mini-floppy disk could hold more information than a single-sided single density standard floppy.

Storage space is not the only criterion for choosing a disk drive, however. Double-sided disk drives, in particular, tend to be less reliable, mainly because of the necessity for a second read/write assembly and a more complex inner structure. This, of course, may change as double-sided drives are on the market longer and manufacturers have time to iron out bugs. Disk capacity is one more area where rapid advances are being made; as with any fast changes, however, quality and reliability sometimes suffer.

The other physical disk characteristic does not concern storage capacity, but determines the method used to locate information on the disk. Data is stored on a floppy in binary format (ON or OFF, 1 or 0) by means of magnetic patterns arranged along concentric circles or **tracks**. Each track is divided into segments called sectors. The tracks and sectors have identifying numbers used to locate data on the disk. A hard-sector disk has a ring of holes punched around its center to mark the sectors, with an index hole to indicate the beginning of the first sector. A soft-sector disk uses only one index hole. And just to be different, the Apple II™ ignores sector holes altogether and divides disks into 16 (13 on earlier models) sectors of its own choosing. Eight-inch disk drives are even quirkier in their sector divisions. For practical purposes, you don't really need to be concerned with the whys and wherefores of sectoring. Just make sure to purchase the type of disk required by your system. Computers become *very* obstinate when handed disks they can't read.

The size, type, and number of disk drives a computer uses depends on the **disk controller**, which may be either a circuit board plugged into the computer or a box connected to it with a cable. Controllers are designed for either single or double density disks; a dual disk controller can use a mixture of both. Most micro disk controllers are equipped for up to four disk drive units. It is possible for some purposes to get by with a single drive, but for most serious applications at least two are necessary. Two disk drives make backing up fast and easy (and thus more likely to become a habit), and also provide increased data capacity for such purposes as word processing, where the primary drive contains the disk with the software and the second is free for data files.

For tips on care and handling of floppy disks, see appendix C.

Hard Disks

Although they are a considerable improvement over cassette tape, floppies do not have the capacity to handle large databases (such as those called for in many library applications). They are also quite susceptible to damage (and lost data) from dust, fingerprints, improper handling, etc. The recent entry of the hard disk into the micro market has opened a whole realm of new possibilities for microcomputer applications. Though more expensive than floppies, hard disks offer many times the storage space, operate at a higher speed, and are less fragile.

The type of hard disk used with most microcomputer systems is the **Winchester drive**. Winchester is a generic name, supposedly derived from the sealed cartridge Winchester rifle. Going back to the record player analogy, a Winchester disk drive is rather like taking the turntable and stylus of the record player, complete with a permanent "record," or disk, and enclosing it in an airtight, hermetically sealed protective chamber. The disk is made of a hard but light material coated on both sides with magnetic oxide and rotates at a very high rate of speed (average: 2,400 revolutions per minute). The read/write stylus "flies" on a very thin cushion of air above the surface of the rapidly spinning disk. The distance between the recording head and the disk surface, though less than the width of a molecule of cigarette smoke, prevents wear and tear on both the disk and the head, except in the event of a crash, a disaster we shall cover in appendix C, Caring for Your Computer.

Mini-floppy disks, depending on density, number of sides, and formatting, hold anywhere from 90K up to as much as 600 kilobytes of data, while 8-inch disk capacity ranges from 250K to over 10,000K (a megabyte!). Hard disk storage space ranges from about 5 megabytes (5 *million* bytes) to more than 120 megabytes, while data access speed with a hard disk is two to ten times as fast as with floppies. In physical size a hard disk may use as little space as a floppy drive, and weighs only a few pounds.

A number of manufacturers have recently begun to introduce micros with built-in hard disks. Usually these machines have one floppy and one hard disk drive. As of this writing they are too new to rate in terms of reliability. The present built-in hard disks are also smaller (average 5 megabytes) than would be needed for most library applications, but that, too, may change very soon.

Hard disks also open up the possibility of "networking" both hardware and software in multi-user systems. Implementing a system of multiple microcomputers sharing a hard disk may cost less than buying individual floppy drives for each micro, and offers the additional advantage of allowing users to share common software and data. Such multi-user systems are especially practical when there is to be a large shared database, such as an online catalog or student records which are used by several departments.

If you decide to purchase a hard disk, look for one that has been on the market long enough to have been thoroughly tested for reliability. You will also need to consider factors such as file security—can files be "locked" and "unlocked" so that access may be controlled? A clerk or student aide, for example, might only be able to read certain files, while different staff members might need to both read and edit files for their particular departments. In a multi-user system, there should also be a built-in protection so that two users cannot edit the same record at the same time, since doing so will destroy data. If several users will be sharing a printer and a hard disk, the disk should have **spooling** capabilities, that is, be able to store signals for the printer temporarily if the printer is in use.

Once again we bring up the crucial importance of backup. There are several possible methods for backing up data stored on a hard disk. These include floppy disks, special reel to reel type tape recorders, and even video tape recorders. The floppy method is by far the least expensive, but is also the most cumbersome, mistake-prone, and time-consuming. Using reel to reel or video tape recorders requires additional purchases of interfaces capable of transferring the data, but the initial cost may be offset by considerable savings in time and hassles. Other considerations are the cost of floppy disks and the space and safety problems of storing them. In any case, the cost of a backup system must be figured into the purchase price of a hard disk. You cannot afford the risk of losing precious data.

Adding a hard disk to a computer system also calls for adding a special disk controller and possibly additional cables and accessories. Computer hardware has a tendency to add up, like car options or the "not included" batteries and light bulbs in toys. Make sure the dealer lists *all* the accessories in the quoted price.

Another type of memory you may hear mentioned is "bubble memory." Magnetic bubble memory devices use "bubbles," or locally magnetized areas that move around in a magnetic material. Bubble memory is very high capacity and has been much-talked-about as the storage medium of the future; to date, however, it is not widely available.

OUTPUT DEVICES

Once the computer has received, stored, and processed information, it needs a way to get the results of its work back to the user. This is accomplished through output devices. In most microcomputer systems, the primary output devices are the **video display unit**, or CRT (cathode ray tube), and the printer.

Video Display Units

The video display unit provides immediate feedback to the computer operator by means of screen displays on a cathode ray tube. Screen display characteristics depend on the combination of the monitor quality and the types of signals sent by the **video generator**. Like the CRT in a television set, the video monitor forms images with "dots" of light. The image quality and definition of a CRT screen display depend on its ability to follow the modulation frequency of the signal being received—the higher the frequency, the greater the number of dots, and the sharper the image that can be produced.

High **resolution** screen displays suitable for general text purposes such as word processing require a signal of 15 megahertz or greater. To prevent interference between television stations, TV sets are designed with a "wave trap" which cuts out any signal above 3.57 megahertz. Even if the wave trap is bypassed, few TV sets can handle a signal over 5 megahertz. This means that even though popular home and personal computers are advertised as being suitable for hookup via a modulator with a regular TV set, such a combination has only limited applications.

A variety of specialized monitors capable of receiving the higher frequency signals is available for computer systems.* Besides resolution, other factors to consider in CRT performance include the ability to display both upper and lower case letters, the use of **descenders** (i.e., the tails of y, g, etc., descending below the line), and the number of characters per screen line. These are features that may be hardware or software dependent or both. A good quality monochromatic monitor combined with a video generator that makes it capable of displaying an 80 character screen line, with descenders and clear, sharp characters, is the best choice for uses involving text such as word processing and report generation.

For most library applications, a good quality NTSC, or composite video, monochromatic monitor is completely adequate. Composite video monitors are capable of receiving signals averaging 18 megahertz or better from a video generator inside the computer. The signals contain full-resolution black-and-white and, in color monitors, lower-resolution color information.

Monitors capable of producing high-resolution color graphics are called RGB (for Red - Green - Blue), or direct drive monitors. The higher resolution and color intensity are possible because the monitor receives the signals broken down into the three primary colors of light: red, green, and blue. Color is not likely to be a consideration for library applications, and RGB monitors are quite

---

*The term "monitor" in this case should not be confused with the software or firmware (ROM) monitor inside the computer which regulates computer operations.

expensive. Since television monitors can display at best a 64-character screen line, and produce characters that are fuzzy and difficult to read, they are not practical for any purposes using text. However, for educational programs using low-resolution color graphics, a television set and modulator (which converts video signals to a form suitable for TV set antenna terminals) will probably be sufficient. Since television sets also offer the advantage of being standard equipment in many libraries, a combination of a monochromatic composite video monitor and an ordinary TV set would probably be a practical choice for a library computer system.

A computer that does not contain a video generator transmits signals in bit codes, which are picked up and translated by a video generator outside the computer, usually in the terminal. A terminal is a unit containing a keyboard, video generator, and video display monitor. Contrary to popular usage, the words "computer" and "terminal" are not interchangeable, even though many microcomputer systems now on the market are "all-in-one" packages consisting of a CPU, keyboard, video generator, and CRT in one compact unit which may also include disk drives.

The confusion comes about because these all-in-one computers are also "smart" or "intelligent" terminals. Terminals may be either "intelligent" or "dumb." Earlier definitions of terminal intelligence referred to the capabilities of the terminal in terms of such functions as cursor addressing and sensing (being able to tell where a character is on the screen), ability to utilize special function keys, and graphics capabilities. The newer definition basically refers to the terminal's ability or inability to function as a **standalone** computer. An intelligent terminal contains user-programmable memory; a dumb terminal, though it probably contains a microprocessor, cannot be programmed by the user. A dumb terminal functions as a communications device linking the user and a separate computer, which may be connected to the terminal by a cable, or may be many miles away and accessed via a direct line or a modem.

Printers

Because they are more complex mechanically and have more moving parts, printers tend to be the most costly and the most failure-prone computer peripherals. Like seemingly everything else connected with microcomputers, however, printer technology is striding ahead while prices are shrinking. This is fortunate, because whatever your plans for a computer system, they will almost certainly include a printer.

But what kind of printer? The range of features among printers is tremendous, with a corresponding range in price. Determining which features are necessities and which are extras, or even undesirable, requires a clear understanding of your requirements and the capabilities and limitations of your hardware and software. Choosing one feature, such as "letter-quality" (i.e., typewriter-like) characters, may eliminate the possibility of including another, such as the ability to print graphics, along with tradeoffs in noise, speed, weight, size – and price.

Printers are basically classified by two criteria – the way the characters are imprinted on the paper, and the manner in which the characters are formed. Practically speaking, the two main categories of imprint method are impact and nonimpact. Nonimpact printers form characters on specially treated paper by means of either heat or an electric spark. Though inexpensive initially, nonimpact printers have a high operating cost due to their special paper requirements. The nature of the paper can also make the print difficult or distracting to read. Impact printers, which have a print hammer or wires that strike a ribbon and force it against the paper to form images, are far more common. A third type of printer propels ink onto the paper using tiny jets. Ink-jet printers produce beautiful type, but are, at least at present, prohibitively expensive.

The two primary methods used to form the characters themselves are **daisywheel** and **dot matrix**. Daisywheel printers are used to produce "letter-quality" type. Their name comes from the print element, which has petal shaped spokes radiating from a central hub. At the ends of the "petals" are embossed characters. The daisywheel rotates on a drive shaft between the typewriter-style ribbon and a print hammer. When the proper letter is in position, an electrical signal causes the hammer to fire against the petal, which strikes the ribbon, which strikes the paper and prints the character. Daisywheel elements are usually interchangeable, so that a wide variety of typestyles may be produced.

The primary advantage of daisywheel printers is the production of hard copy that appears to be the work of a prolific and accurate typist. The primary disadvantages are noise, slow speed, low versatility, and high cost, all of which are important considerations in library applications. The "ratatatat" of the petals striking the paper roller can be extremely distracting, especially when two or more printers are in use. Because they print only one character at a time, daisywheels average only thirty to fifty characters per second (cps). This may seem fast compared to a human typist, but when you are printing an inventory list or a series of bibliographies it can be maddeningly slow. Though some daisywheel printers can produce special effects such as boldface and superscripted or subscripted letters, they cannot print graphics designs or vary the size and shape of letters as can dot matrix printers. And finally, they are quite expensive. The cost of a medium quality daisywheel printer could easily be higher than the rest of your hardware put together.

Thimble printers, less common than daisywheels, have a similar print element, except that the wheel is folded in on itself so that it looks like a cup, or thimble, with the characters embossed around the rim. Like daisywheels, thimble printers are slow, expensive, and noisy, but produce good print quality.

There is a third option for obtaining letter-quality printouts, which is to purchase equipment and software to convert an electric typewriter, such as an IBM Selectric™, to work as a printer. Electric typewriters are not as sturdy as printers built for that purpose, however, nor is the setup very fast, making this arrangement impractical for any extensive use. An even bigger problem is the lack of service and support for a system that is the product of at least two manufacturers, neither of which wants to be responsible for breakdowns or difficulties.

Dot matrix printers form characters by arranging dots in a close pattern. The dots are made by a print head containing several fine wires, each of which acts as a tiny print hammer. The arrangement, or matrix, of the wires forms the pattern of the character. The number of wires in the print head can vary from a 5 by 7 matrix to as many as 18 by 18, with a corresponding variety in image quality. Dot matrix printers are faster, quieter, more versatile, and less expensive than daisywheel printers. The main objection most people have to dot matrix printers is the fact that the print looks like it came from a computer and not from a typewriter. However, dot matrix printers have shown a steady improvement in quality. By using more and smaller wires and using overprinting to create denser patterns, they can produce very acceptable copy. Dot matrix printers are considerably faster than daisywheels, averaging 150 to more than 200 characters per second. (Setting the printer to "correspondence" or "enhanced" mode, so that it uses a second pass to overprint and create denser characters, will slow it down considerably. But it will still be faster than the fastest daisywheel.) Dot matrix printers can also be used to print graphics designs, and to vary the size and shape of characters for emphasis and creative special effects (see figure 3.3).

Figure 3.3. A Printer Sampler

Letter Quality

Dot Matrix

Both dot matrix and daisywheel printers are available in what is known as **parallel** or RS-232 **serial input,** which has to do with the way the printer interfaces with the computer. (Interfaces are explained later in this chapter.) Generally, parallel printers are faster, but must be customized for a particular computer, while the slower serial printers will work with any computer having a RS-232 output.

As with other computer components, you need to make certain that the printer you buy is compatible with the rest of your system. Not every printer will work with every computer, and even the units that will work together require both electronic circuitry (the interface) and software (the **protocol**) to communicate with one another. In general, the simpler the interface, the more protocol is required. Both interfaces and protocol generally cost extra, sometimes a lot extra. Be careful to find out what interface card is needed to enable your computer to communicate with the printer you are considering. The interface card is *not included* with your printer; it is a separate item. Make sure you read *both* the printer manual and the interface card manual, and/or have your vendor show you how to install the card and the printer so that the computer sends the printer the proper instructions. Otherwise you may find yourself wondering why your 80 column printer only prints 40 columns. Also, be sure to find out if any special cables, computer modifications, or special driver programs are needed, and how much they cost, before you decide on a particular printer.

As if all this weren't confusing enough, there are a number of other factors to consider in choosing a printer. Besides speed, noise, impact method, and cost, you will need to be aware of such features as:

Number of Characters Per Line. Most dot matrix and daisywheel printers will print either pica (10 characters/inch) or elite (12 characters/inch), or 80 to 96 characters per line. Some dot matrix printers will also print in "condensed" mode, putting as many as 200 characters in a line, or in "expanded" mode, elongating characters so that there are anywhere from 20 to 40 characters per line. Proportionally spaced characters (where an "m" takes twice as much space as an "l," for example) are available with both types of printers, and are generally considered more attractive.

For most library applications you will need a printer that can print at least 80 characters per line; for spread sheets and inventories, etc., you may need as much as 132 cpl.

Ribbons. The type of ribbon (spool or cartridge, nylon or carbon) will affect the cost of operation and print quality. Another consideration is the method of ribbon replacement. Cartridges are easier and less messy than spools, but cost more and may not last as long.

Paper Feed Method and Paper Requirements. Dot matrix printers generally use either "pin" or "tractor" feeds, where special paper with holes on both sides is pulled and/or pushed through the printer on pins. In a **pin-feed** system, the pins are affixed to the ends of the **platen**, or roller, and are therefore of a fixed width, while **tractor feeds** are adjustable for different widths of paper. Daisywheel printers often use the "friction" method, which is like that on a standard typewriter; the paper is held tightly against the platen; as the platen turns, the paper moves. For these printers, optional tractor or pin feeds may be purchased.

The main considerations in paper feeding methods are ease of loading, speed, and registration (positioning of the paper so that the dots or characters strike in the right place). If you will be making multiple copies, the printer should be able to handle the extra layers of paper. If you are going to be using a dot matrix printer to print individual documents, you need to check how easily it accepts single sheets of paper.

There are three types of paper used in impact printers—fanfold, roll, and single sheet. It is also possible to buy fanfold and roll paper with carbon paper between layers of paper. Some printers can be adjusted for any type of paper; others are limited to one or two kinds.

Size and Weight. Some printers are easily portable; others are anything but. Another consideration is storage room for the paper.

Durability and Reliability. A great deal of delicate timing and mechanical precision are involved in getting those hammers and wires to strike in the right places at the right times, to keep the platen turning smoothly and the paper feeding steadily, etc. Also, some kinds of parts wear out faster than others. Daisywheels are available in plastic or metal; platens can be rubber, steel, or plastic. Look for the sturdiest printer available to fit your needs.

Special Features. Again, these will depend on your specific needs and budget. Features such as color graphics are expensive luxuries, and some features, such as descenders (those tails on the y and g), that you might consider necessary are options, not standards. A *detailed* shopping list is important. Options may add to the speed and capabilities of a printer, but they also add to the price, including the cost of the accessories and the software needed to make the printer work with your computer.

Service. Service and support are vital considerations in printer choice. Find out who is responsible for service, the dealer or the manufacturer (if it's neither, look for a different printer), and what the warranties and charges are. Service calls can range from $50 to $200 *initially*, with parts and time over an hour or two costing extra. For this reason, the printer calls for extra care in operation—make sure you read the care instructions in your manual and follow them carefully.

Since features and costs vary so widely, the printer is one of the most difficult and important purchases you will make. Before beginning to shop, make a list of what the printer *must* do, and what you would like it to do, and use the list as a guide. Many of the computer-oriented magazines mentioned in appendix B of this book have frequent articles reviewing and comparing printers. Since the field is changing so quickly, such articles are useful in keeping up with the latest developments in technology and prices. Finally, before you buy a printer, have the vendor hook it up—preferably to a computer like yours and, if possible, with your software—and watch (and listen to) it print.

MODEMS

A modem is a telecommunications device used to transfer information between computers using ordinary telephone lines. The word "modem" is derived from MODulator - DEModulator, for the way the device "modulates" the ON/OFF signals from a computer into two different tones, or frequencies, which can be transmitted over a phone line and "demodulated" on the receiving end. Modems enable computers of different types and in different places to "talk" to one another. This is not quite as simple as it sounds, however. In order to send and receive information via a modem, two computers must be compatible in terms of **baud rate**, or the speed at which the signal is transmitted (see Hertz,

Bauds, and the ASCII Code below), and either use compatible data formats or have interfaces of software and/or hardware that convert the data to usable form. Acquiring the necessary interfaces and equipment can push costs far above the price of the modem itself—in some cases prohibitively far.

One of the attractive features of microcomputers is the promise of access to other systems, but don't let advertisements mislead you into thinking that once you own a modem, you can plug one end into a phone line and the other into your computer and carry on a conversation with the computer in the district media center or your local university. If you plan to access another system or systems with your computer, either by modem or directly by means of a dedicated line, compatibility with the other computers should be one of the important criteria for your software and hardware purchases.

There are basically two types of modems: **acoustic couplers** and direct-connect. Acoustic couplers convert digital data to sound, which is then transmitted through the modem by means of a cradle that holds the telephone handset. Some microcomputers have built-in acoustic coupler modems. Because of their tendency to pick up stray noise through the slight gap between the cradle and the phone, acoustic couplers are not as reliable as direct-connect modems, which plug directly into the phone line. It is even possible to buy telephones with built-in direct-connect modems, or auto-dial modems which allow the phone number to be input from the computer itself, either through the keyboard or from previously entered disk files.

Most modems are "originate-only" devices, meaning they will not automatically answer the phone and hook callers into the computer—for that you need an "originate-answer" modem. If your district has a centralized system for smaller systems to access, that system will probably have an originate-answer modem, with the smaller systems using originate-only modems. Like other microcomputer products, modems are constantly increasing in number and decreasing in price, and are frequent topics for review in current publications. We'll have more to say about intercomputer communications in chapter 5, The Library as a Computer Resource Center.

(Narrative continues on page 55.)

*****

HERTZ, BAUDS, AND THE ASCII CODE

When two people have trouble communicating, they are often said to be on "different frequencies." Similarly, when two computers communicate, they must be transmitting and receiving on the same frequencies for any exchange to take place. Sound frequencies are measured in cycles per second, called **hertz**, after nineteenth-century German physicist Heinrich R. Hertz. Every sound has a certain frequency, or pitch. Middle C, for example, is 261.5 hertz, or cycles per second. A **bandwidth** is the range of frequencies an object can transmit and/or receive. The bandwidth of a good stereo receiver goes from about 20 hertz to 20,000, while a telephone has a range from 300 to 3,300 hertz, and a television can receive signals of several megahertz.

Asynchronous modems (the most common type) transmit computer information over phone lines by converting it to one of two frequencies—one tone stands for "zero," another stands for "one." Each separate signal represents one computer bit of information. The rate at which the signals change from one frequency to another is the baud rate, after French communications engineer Emile Baudot. One baud is one signal change per second. In order for the whole chain of communication to work, all the links must be able to handle the same baud rate—from the sending computer to its modem to the phone line to the receiving modem to the receiving computer. There is a very complex mathematical and technical relationship between the baud rate and the frequency (hertz), which has the effect of limiting the rate at which signals may be sent over ordinary telephone lines to about 2,400 baud. For practical purposes, at the time of this writing, asynchronous transmission (the type you are likely to be using) using standard equipment has an upper limit of about 1,200 baud. The most inexpensive (and therefore the most commonly used) modems have a baud rate of 300 signal changes per second, which is quite adequate unless very large amounts of data are being transmitted.

For extensive communications networks requiring high-volume, high-speed data transmission, it is possible to send information over dedicated lines (that is, leased, permanently connected phone lines), using very sophisticated equipment, at rates of more than 9,600 baud. Such systems use very expensive **synchronous** type modems costing several thousand dollars—more than most microcomputers!

Computers talk to themselves—that is, to their peripheral devices—in the same way as they talk to each other, transmitting bits at certain baud rates. The type of information transmitted, fortunately, is one area where an agreed upon standard prevails. Nearly all microcomputers, as well as some larger systems, use what is known as ASCII code (American Standard Code for Information Interchange), which was created by the American National Standards Institute near the end of the 1960s. A normal ASCII character consists of an 8-bit string consisting of a 7-bit character code and an eighth **parity bit**. There are 128 ASCII codes, each of which may be interpreted in several ways (see figure 3.4, page 54). They may be referred to by a decimal or hexadecimal (base 16) number, or they may represent a character. The codes that have decimal numeric values from 32 to 127 are "printable" characters, with the exception of 32, which represents a space, and 127, which represents "delete." This "96 character set" includes all the **alphanumeric characters** plus about 30 punctuation marks and symbols (such as @ and $). The codes from 0 to 31 represent control characters, for functions such as "backspace," "clear screen," and so on. Control ASCII codes are activated (logically enough) by the use of the 〈CTRL〉 key on a keyboard as well as by imbedded program instructions. The standardization is not quite as prevalent with control functions as with the 96 printable characters—which is one reason hardware and software is not interchangeable, and why transmitting formatted text from one word processor system to another via modem can cause problems.

Although ASCII characters are 8 bits long, the technical process for transmitting them requires extra bits, so it takes about 10 bits to send a character. Therefore, dividing the baud rate by 10 tells you the approximate characters per second rate. A 300-baud modem transmits about 30 characters per second—more than enough to keep up with even the most remarkable typist!

Figure 3.4. ASCII Chart*

Decimal to Octal to Hex to ASCII Conversion

GRAPHIC SYMBOLS: ☐

Decimal	Octal	Hex	ASCII	Decimal	Octal	Hex	ASCII	Decimal	Octal	Hex	ASCII	Decimal	Octal	Hex	ASCII
0	000	00	NUL	32	040	20	SP	64	100	40	@	96	140	60	`
1	001	01	SOH	33	041	21	!	65	101	41	A	97	141	61	a
2	002	02	STX	34	042	22	"	66	102	42	B	98	142	62	b
3	003	03	ETX	35	043	23	#	67	103	43	C	99	143	63	c
4	004	04	EOT	36	044	24	$	68	104	44	D	100	144	64	d
5	005	05	ENQ	37	045	25	%	69	105	45	E	101	145	65	e
6	006	06	ACK	38	046	26	&	70	106	46	F	102	146	66	f
7	007	07	BEL	39	047	27	'	71	107	47	G	103	147	67	g
8	010	08	BS	40	050	28	(	72	110	48	H	104	150	68	h
9	011	09	HT	41	051	29	)	73	111	49	I	105	151	69	i
10	012	0A	LF	42	052	2A	*	74	112	4A	J	106	152	6A	j
11	013	0B	VT	43	053	2B	+	75	113	4B	K	107	153	6B	k
12	014	0C	FF	44	054	2C	,	76	114	4C	L	108	154	6C	l
13	015	0D	CR	45	055	2D	-	77	115	4D	M	109	155	6D	m
14	016	0E	SO	46	056	2E	.	78	116	4E	N	110	156	6E	n
15	017	0F	SI	47	057	2F	/	79	117	4F	O	111	157	6F	o
16	020	10	DLE	48	060	30	0	80	120	50	P	112	160	70	p
17	021	11	DC1	49	061	31	1	81	121	51	Q	113	161	71	q
18	022	12	DC2	50	062	32	2	82	122	52	R	114	162	72	r
19	023	13	DC3	51	063	33	3	83	123	53	S	115	163	73	s
20	024	14	DC4	52	064	34	4	84	124	54	T	116	164	74	t
21	025	15	NAK	53	065	35	5	85	125	55	U	117	165	75	u
22	026	16	SYN	54	066	36	6	86	126	56	V	118	166	76	v
23	027	17	ETB	55	067	37	7	87	127	57	W	119	167	77	w
24	030	18	CAN	56	070	38	8	88	130	58	X	120	170	78	x
25	031	19	EM	57	071	39	9	89	131	59	Y	121	171	79	y
26	032	1A	SUB	58	072	3A	:	90	132	5A	Z	122	172	7A	z
27	033	1B	ESC	59	073	3B	;	91	133	5B	[	123	173	7B	{
28	034	1C	FS	60	074	3C	<	92	134	5C	\	124	174	7C	|
29	035	1D	GS	61	075	3D	=	93	135	5D	]	125	175	7D	}
30	036	1E	RS	62	076	3E	>	94	136	5E	^	126	176	7E	~
31	037	1F	US	63	077	3F	?	95	137	5F	_	127	177	7F	DEL

*The first 32 characters represent control functions; the remainder are "printable" characters.

OTHER PERIPHERAL DEVICES

Although keyboards are the most common general-purpose input device for microcomputer systems, some types of data can be input more efficiently by means of devices such as light pens, **bar code** readers, and scanners. A circulation system, for example, might use a bar code reader, such as those that have become common in grocery stores, to speed up check-out and return operations. Light pens input impulses into the computer by contact with the CRT screen. They are used mainly for selecting menu options or for drawing patterns directly on the screen. Bar code readers and light pens have decreased in price to the point where they may be considered for use in small libraries. Possible uses for these devices will be discussed in chapter 4.

Optical Character Recognition (OCR) devices can "read" printed or typed information by converting reflected light patterns into binary data, and manufacturers are working to develop practical voice recognition devices as well. Another option, more for educational than library applications, is voice capability. Speech synthesizers enable microcomputers to literally "talk back" to their operators. They are relatively new, but are becoming available for a wide range of hardware. Although OCR, voice recognition capabilities, and speech synthesizers are still quite expensive, they have some wonderful applications, particularly for handicapped users. If you serve disabled patrons, they may be well worth the price—which, like the cost of nearly every type of microcomputer hardware, is decreasing rapidly.

Plotters are specialty printers used mostly for scientific applications. They are also quite expensive. A good dot matrix printer will furnish all the graphics capabilities a small library is apt to need, unless it is a high school or college level library with a high proportion of science-minded patrons.

Other peripheral devices protect computers from potentially disastrous power changes. Computers are much more sensitive to power variations than, say, toasters or light bulbs. Hardware components that suffer an undue amount of "voltage stress" may be damaged or even destroyed. At the very least, valuable data may be lost.

Glitch is a term you may come across often in computer talk. Originally used to indicate a short, low-magnitude electrical disturbance, it has come to mean any unexpected and inexplicable problem. A glitch is part of a spectrum which ranges from blackouts due to power failures, such as those often caused by lightning, to the **electrical noise** caused by small appliances, hand tools, powerline switching equipment, etc. In between are voltage dips caused by such events as an office building's air conditioning switching on or off, and **spikes**, or power surges, which are usually caused by equipment failures or changes in the utility distribution network. Even small disturbances can do harm to sensitive computer circuitry.

Powerline conditioners and backup power supplies are two ways of protecting your system against disaster. A powerline conditioner acts as a shock absorber to suppress voltage spikes and noise. **Voltage regulators** can offer further protection against longer and more drastic power drops or surges. Powerline conditioners are generally inexpensive, but vary quite a bit in the amount of protection they provide.

Backup power supplies provide auxiliary power in case of a complete power loss, by means of a battery which may be built-in or supplemental. This type of protection is considerably more expensive than a powerline conditioner, but may be worthwhile if you live in an area prone to electrical storms or other causes of power loss, such as a remote rural district. Backup power supplies may be either standby or uninterruptible. In a standby system, the battery is kept charged by the AC line but does not switch on unless there is an actual power failure, causing a delay of up to a hundred milliseconds — generally not enough to damage most computers. The battery for an uninterruptible system is always switched in to the circuit so that there is no delay at all in the event of a power failure.

PUTTING IT ALL TOGETHER

Buying a computer system is similar to buying a stereo system, in the sense that it may be purchased as a complete package or as a customized set of individual components, or as a combination of the two. There are some significant differences, however, not the least of which is the matter of compatibility. Stereo units such as amplifiers, speakers, and turntables are essentially interchangeable. You can mix and match brands and models with nothing more complicated than some jacks and speaker wire. Getting computer components to work together is considerably more complicated, if they can be made to work together at all.

In order to function as a complete system, the various components must be able to communicate with one another in forms each component can "understand." This is accomplished through interfaces or **ports**, which send and receive electrical signals (bits) to and from the CPU and memory to the various input and output devices. Within the computer itself, a bus structure consisting of a set of electrical conductors transmits the signals between the internal components of the system, such as the CPU and the memory. (A fairly standard bus structure is the S100, so called because it has 100 parallel wires for transmitting signals.) The bus structure and other circuitry and mechanical elements are supported and connected by the **motherboard**.

External components plug into the computer through ports using flat ribbon-shaped or round cables with plastic connectors, containing a number of small metal pins, on each end. One end of the cable goes into the computer, the other into a corresponding port in the peripheral device. For a computer and a peripheral device to "understand" the signals passing between them, it is necessary to have an interface which converts the signals coming through the port to signals that may be transmitted through the bus structure, and vice versa. The interface may be built into the computer, or it may be in the form of a card or board that plugs into the bus structure itself. One requirement for system **expandability** is a provision for adding new or different interfaces, via such plug-in cards, to the bus, in order to accommodate different peripherals or software, such as a modem or a CP/M operating system with a Z80 microprocessor.

Interfaces, ports, and the cables and cards used to connect them are another area of microcomputer technology in which standardization is almost nonexistent, except for some aspects of the physical structure of the devices. What this means is that there is very little conformity as far as which pins and wires carry which signals, which slots hold which interface cards, and which ports can receive signals from which peripherals. Therefore, whenever you are considering hardware additions, memory expansions, or operating system changes, you must acquire not only the components themselves but the correct cables and interface cards for connecting them to your system. This can run into considerable expense, especially if a specialized cable or card is required. Even relatively standard configurations, such as RS-232 ports or S100 buses, can vary enough to cause problems. Make sure your dealer includes everything in the price quotation, *and* shows you how to hook the system up correctly. Unlike a lot of equipment, computer components will allow themselves to be plugged in the wrong way, and you may never know it until it is too late. When plugging interface cards into motherboards or pin cables into ports, be *very careful* to match pins to the proper holes, consulting diagrams if necessary. Otherwise you may do irreparable damage.

Interfaces and ports may be either serial or parallel. A serial port handles 1 bit of data at a time while a parallel port handles 8 bits at once. Most modems use RS-232 serial ports (the most common serial type), and can only interface with computers that have RS-232 ports; printers, on the other hand, may be either RS-232 or "Centronics compatible" (the most common parallel type) interfaced, but will only work with similarly equipped computers. Computers themselves may have either or both types of ports. Therefore you might have an RS-232 interfaced modem and a Centronics compatible interfaced printer connected to the same computer. Some brands of computers use unusual interfaces, such as the IEEE 448. It *may* be possible to convert a peripheral device to use an uncommon type of interface, but it will cost you.

Though the packaging may vary, each microcomputer system will include some form of each of the basic components – CPU and primary memory (ROM and RAM), a keyboard (or other primary input device), a display screen, one or more auxiliary storage units, a printer, and interfaces and ports to connect all of the components together. One system might include everything but the printer in one lightweight desktop unit (it is even possible to buy a system that includes a small printer in the main unit); another may have the CPU, memory, and one or two disk drives in one "box" that interfaces to a separate terminal, which includes a keyboard, CRT, and video generator. Still another system may include the keyboard in the unit housing the CPU, matched with one or more disk drives and a monitor (see figure 3.5, page 58).

With all these different options available, narrowing the choices down to one appropriate system may seem a formidable task. There are, however, some general criteria to aid you in your search:

1) The primary consideration in buying hardware is: will your *software* run on it? It may be the niftiest little computer system on the market, and on sale besides, but if you can't find software for it that suits your needs, there's no point in having it.

2) Unless you have a private computer expert readily available, dealer and manufacturer support are *crucial.* Though a vast amount of hardware is available through mail order at prices that may seem tempting, a local dealer who provides dependable support *after* you have purchased a system will be more than worth the extra cost. Computers are notoriously temperamental, and a bargain stops being a bargain as soon as it develops a mysterious malfunction and no dealer will touch it. Even if your machine runs perfectly, a sympathetic and knowledgeable vendor can be invaluable in choosing a system that is right for your library, and then helping you to implement it.

Figure 3.5. Two Types of Microcomputer Systems

Figure A is an all-in-one system with built-in monitor, keyboard and disk drives; Figure B consists of separate components. The CPU is housed in the unit with the disk drives.

A

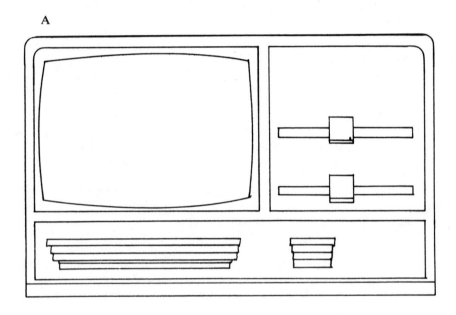

B

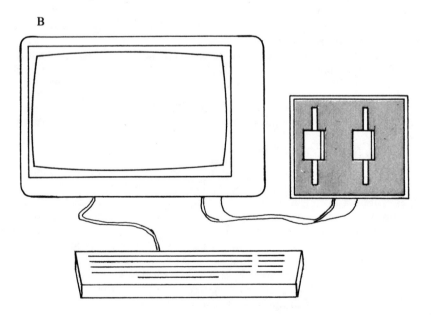

Choose your vendor very carefully. Make sure he sells a variety of software and hardware, so that your choices are not too limited. If you have read about software that sounds appealing, get a list of local dealers from the manufacturer rather than trying to rely on long-distance help. Call and/or visit several different dealers. How willing are they to answer questions? What kinds of warranties do they provide? Can you understand what they say, or do they seem to be doing their best to confuse you with jargon? This book should give you a basic computer vocabulary so that you can talk on an even basis with any dealer who is willing to make the effort to fill your needs. Finally, if you are shopping for a school library, look for a dealer who is aware of and sympathetic to the special needs of educators—and do right by him. Educators have acquired an unfortunate reputation among dealers, who feel—not unjustifiably—that the educational market requires more service and is less willing to pay for it than small businesses or private users.

3) Look for hardware with at least some degree of standardization. What sort of interfaces does it include? RS-232 serial and Centronics compatible parallel ports will give you a wider range of input/output devices from which to choose. Nonstandard interfaces will severely limit you. Similarly, what operating system(s) can the hardware use? Is CP/M™ included or at least available? If not, is the operating system one for which a wide range of software is available, such as Apple™ DOS? What languages can the computer use?

4) Is the system expandable? Can you add memory to increase the primary storage capability? Are there extra ports or room to add them so that you can add peripheral devices as needed? If you anticipate a file-sharing network of computers in the future using a hard disk, can this system expand to include it, or at least be incorporated into it?

5) Is the system durable and reliable? Read periodical reviews and if possible talk to other users (your dealer should be able to furnish names). Has it been on the market long enough for bugs to appear and be solved? Or is it still in the experimental stages?

6) Is the system physically comfortable to use? How does the keyboard feel? Is it in an awkward place, or easy to reach? Some terminals feature detached keyboards which can even be placed on a lap, but you may feel more comfortable with the keyboard right below the screen. If young children will be using the system, a membrane keyboard might be easier to use (and keep clean) than a typewriter style keyboard. Is the CRT screen at a good height, or do you have to bend your head back or forward to see it? Is it wide enough, and easy to read? Some users feel that the newer green- or amber-tinted screens cause less eyestrain; others prefer standard black and white. How large is the system, including peripherals? Will it fit easily into your library, so that everything is easy to reach (including the printer)? Does it need to be portable so that classrooms can check it out?

7) How good is the documentation? This includes all the manuals, instructions, and guides that come with the hardware. Are both a

technical/programming manual and a user's manual included? Is the user's manual written in a language you can understand, or is it highly technical, or worse, just plain garbled? Like software, documentation is often a weak point. Appearances can be deceptive. Expensive printing and lots of pictures do not necessarily mean that the contents are good quality. One good test is to use the manual to guide yourself through some sample procedures (such as initializing a disk) while examining the equipment in the store.

Though the choices may seem overwhelming, you can narrow them down considerably if you know exactly what you plan to do with the system you are buying. One comment is in order here. Because of the extremely fast rate of developments in microcomputer technology, coupled with decreasing prices, many people are tempted to wait for the ultimate micro. Don't. Technical obsolescence and functional obsolescence are not synonyms. The fact that the system you purchase now is likely to be technologically outclassed by a less expensive system six months or a year from now does not in any way decrease its usefulness or its value. Computer evolution may slow down in the next few years, but it will continue for a long time. If you insist on waiting for the perfect system, you will miss out on the wonderful things you could be doing right now. The object is to find the best currently available system to suit your *present* needs.

4 Applications of Microcomputers in Library Services and Management

Until very recently, microcomputers appeared in libraries only in a supporting role to mini- or mainframe-based systems. But since about 1979, the micro has been emerging as a potent library tool in its own right. Even a single microcomputer and some inexpensive software can make a significant difference in the quality and quantity of services a library is able to provide.

The first part of this chapter will describe three types of general purpose software that might be used in libraries: word processing packages, file or database management systems, and spreadsheet and/or accounting programs. The second portion will explore some possible applications of micros, using both general and special purpose software, in the various library subsystems: acquisitions, cataloging, circulation, serials, reference, administration, and, to a limited degree, instruction.

GENERAL PURPOSE SOFTWARE PACKAGES

Word Processing

Word processing is perhaps the single most popular use for microcomputers, both on a personal and business level. Besides being one of the easiest kinds of programs to use, word processing offers features that have a way of transforming even computerphobes into dedicated believers of the "how did I ever live without it" variety. Anyone who knows the frustration of typing an entire page, only to find an error in the middle of it, who equates "updating" bibliographies and inventory lists with redoing them, or who spends hours doing laborious "cut and paste" editing, will quickly learn to appreciate a word processor. Word processing saves time and improves quality, making it easy to produce error-free copy and revise text quickly and easily. The result is more freedom to concentrate on form and content.

Recent developments have made it possible for a microcomputer costing under $2,000 and a software package costing a few hundred dollars to offer features equivalent to those of a "dedicated" word processor costing several times as much. Due to its numerous applications, ease of use, and relatively low cost, word processing software is an excellent starting point for anyone—including a library staff—venturing into microcomputerization. It also provides novices an opportunity to gain confidence in the computer as a familiar, simple-to-use yet powerful tool, easing the approach to other, less verbally oriented functions.

Word processing requires very little in the way of computer programming skills, other than the ability to "format" or "initialize" disks for receiving data, and to use a copy program (such as PIP in CP/M) in order to backup files. Within the program itself, the commands are very brief, usually consisting of the CONTROL ‹CTRL› key and one or at most two other keys; some software takes advantage of special "function keys" so that commands consist of single strokes.

Word processing commands are generally concerned with cursor movement (the **cursor** is the little rectangle or line of light on the screen that marks your position in the text), and with such editing functions as inserting and deleting sections of text. Often the commands are mnemonic, such as ‹CTRL› S for "Save" (a very important command!). Most word processing programs are "menu-driven"—that is, you choose the various commands from a menu displayed on the screen. Some programs make it possible to regulate the extent of the menu display ("helps") as you become more familiar with the commands, leaving more of the screen free for text display (see screen below).

```
      B:SAMPLE  PAGE 1 LINE 21 COL 67              INSERT ON
          < < <        M A I N  M E N U      > > >
   --Cursor Movement--    ! -Delete- !  -Miscellaneous-  ! -Other Menus-
 ^S char left ^D char right !^G char  ! ^I Tab   ^B Reform ! (from Main only)
 ^A word left ^F word right !DEL chr lf! ^V INSERT ON/OFF  !^J Help ^K Block
 ^E line up   ^X line down  !^T word rt!^L Find/Replce again!^Q Quick ^P Print
     --Scrolling--          !^Y  line  !RETURN End paragraph!^O Onscreen
 ^Z line up   ^W line down  !          ! ^N Insert a RETURN !
 ^C screen up ^R screen down!          ! ^U Stop a comman   !
 L----!----!----!----!----!----!----!----!----!----!----!--------R
      Word processing commands are generally concerned with cursor

 movement (the cursor is the little rectangle or line of light  on

 the  screen that marks your position in the text),  and with such

 editing  functions  as inserting and deleting sections  of  text.

 Often  the commands are mnemonic,  such as ^BCTRL S^B for  "Save"  (a

 very  important  command!).  Most word processing  programs  are

 "menu-driven" -- that is,  you choose the various commands from a
```

A sample screen, with menu, from the word processing program Wordstar™. Reprinted by permission of MicroPro™. Wordstar is a registered trademark of MicroPro International Corporation, 33 San Pablo Avenue, San Rafael, CA 94903.

Most word processing programs can be learned in a few hours; some may take two or three days. Generally, the more "powerful" a program is—that is, the more functions and flexibility it offers—the more difficult it is to learn. If you don't have any use for all the extra functions, you might be content with a more limited but easy-to-use program. On the other hand, a willingness to invest the initial time to learn a powerful program could mean extensive time savings and better results in the long run.

Word processing packages are available for almost every kind of microcomputer. Capabilities and prices vary considerably, so it is helpful to have a specific list of features in mind when shopping, preferably divided into "must haves" and "would likes." The computer-oriented periodicals mentioned in appendix B carry frequent reviews of word processing packages, and most vendors have access to demonstration copies you may use to try out the program in the store before you buy. Word processing evaluations seem to be largely a matter of personal perference—the more popular packages all have advocates who will swear that whichever program they use is unequivocably the best.

Since there are so many good packages available, word processing programs are not as hardware restrictive as other types of software. If you want to use word processing in addition to a more specialized function, locate software and hardware for the specialty first, then check to see which word processing packages are compatible with the hardware (including the *printer*). Unless you have a very unusual and unpopular type of system, or have some special word processing needs such as the ability to do sorting operations or customized mailings, you should have little trouble finding a program to satisfy you.

Following are some features to look for in word processing software:

Cursor Movement. Some programs allow the cursor to move in any direction and by varying increments; others are less versatile. Being able to move the cursor up, down, left, or right, a character, word, line, or even screen length at a time streamlines editing.

Word Wrap. This feature frees you from having to press the ‹RETURN› key at the end of each line. The software automatically beings a new line each time a word is typed that will not fit inside the right margin. The ‹RETURN› key is used only at the end of a paragraph.

Some programs have a "right-**justifying**" feature, which adjusts the spacing between words and/or letters to produce a straight right margin like those in books and magazines. If this feature is included, it is useful to be able to turn it off in order to produce a ragged edge for documents such as letters. Some programs also include automatic hyphenization of words at the end of a line. Another useful feature is a paragraph formatter, which automatically indents text to fit a temporary left margin.

Insert and Delete Functions. "Insert" mode allows the insertion of new characters (or of blank lines) without erasing the characters already entered. Some word processors use an insert key to place the computer in insert mode for one key stroke and then return it to standard mode (in which new characters "type over" existing characters). "Dynamic insert" causes the computer to "push" existing words ahead of the new text as it is entered, returning it to standard mode only when given the proper command. This type of command is called a **toggle** because the same stroke or combination of strokes turns the function on if it is off and vice versa.

Programs also vary in deletion capabilities. More powerful programs allow the operator to delete a character, word, line, or part of a line, or even a **block** (an operator defined section of text) at a time.

Search or **Search and Replace.** The **search** function enables the operator to search a file for a given "string of characters," which may range from part of a word to several words. **Search and replace** causes the identified string to be replaced with a different **character string**, either automatically or at operator discretion. These features have many uses, including correcting recurring spelling or punctuation errors, changing abbreviations to whole words, and customizing "boiler plate" documents, such as replacing every occurrence of "John Jones" in a document with "Sally Smith."

Scrolling. Scrolling allows the operator to move through a file a line or screen at a time, often in either direction. This feature allows rapid movement through a text as it is being edited.

Block Movement. Block moves allow text to be maneuvered within or even between files. Special commands are used to mark "blocks" of text, which, depending on software capability, may range in size from a few words to all of the text currently in the computer's RAM. The blocks may then be moved to a different location in the text. If, for example, the contents of paragraph 12 of a document would be more appropriate as paragraph 3, a few commands will accomplish the move.

Some programs allow a block to be copied as well as moved, which is useful where a line or paragraph is repeated several times. It is even possible with some packages to copy a block to or from another file on the disk (or even a different disk). Uses for this feature include easy production of "boiler plate" documents or standardized letters.

Another highly useful feature included in a few programs and available as supplemental software for others is the ability to "merge" files while printing. A common use for the merge function is printing "customized" form letters using a separate data file of names and addresses.

On-Screen Formatting. Not all word processing programs allow the user to see a document's format on the CRT screen. Instead, "imbedded commands" format the material as it is printed. Even with a screen that does not display a full page (and most of them won't), being able to see the text more or less as it will appear in print is very helpful for editing.

Column Mode. This feature allows easy formatting of text in columns rather than paragraphs. Some packages allow columns to be shifted around in block moves.

Footers, Headers, and Page Numbering. Most good word processing programs have provisions for headings (e.g., "Chapter IV"), footers (e.g., "Computer Nut Magazine, Vol. 3, No. 2"), and automatic page numbering. Some will even alternate page numbers on the right and left sides of the page.

Spelling Checks. These are usually separate programs, which may be included as part of a package. A spelling checker will automatically search through text and flag misspellings using its own dictionary, which may be supplemented as needed. Most programs will allow you to create additional dictionaries including commonly used names and special terminology. The nature of the English language places some limitations on spelling checks (Miss steak would pass for mistake, for example), but they can be very useful for correcting recurring typographical errors or misspellings of common words.

The following features may be hardware as well as software dependent:

Upper and Lower Case Display. Any serious use of word processing will require that the CRT, printer, and software all be capable of displaying lower case letters. Sometimes this will mean purchasing additional interfaces.

Number of Characters Per Line. It is possible to do word processing with a screen display of 40 characters per line, but working with a full 80 character display is easier. This also may require an additional interface.

File Limitations. The size limits of files depend on the amount of memory available in RAM and on disk, and also on the software. Some programs limit the size of files to the size of the RAM; others will leave the file on disk, calling it up as it is needed. For practical purposes, you will probably want to limit the size of your files to around 20K (about 10 double-spaced pages), simply because of the amount of time needed to scroll through or save a lengthy file. Documents longer than 20K can be combined after printout. Also remember that in judging disk capacity you must allow enough space for automatically created backup files and editing. A "disk full" message in the middle of an edit can be devastating.

Text and/or Printer Buffer. A **buffer** is a temporary storage place for characters being fed to the screen or printer. This relates to the "baud rate" explained in chapter 3. If the characters are being fed to the printer faster than it can print, it stores them in a buffer until it can catch up. In the same way, a fast typist may outpace the characters appearing on the CRT screen. Software and hardware with inadequate buffering may "lose" keystrokes. Since a side effect of word processing is increased typing speed, this feature should not be overlooked.

Simultaneous Editing/Printing. Some software allows one file to be printing as another is being edited. This capability also depends on the printer.

Print Enhancements. These include underlining, boldfacing, super- and subscripting, double-width characters and other techniques for emphasizing text. Sometimes software adjustments (called "patches") must be made so that the special print commands can be understood by the printer. You may be able to have the dealer set the printer controls up for you.

Highlighting/Reverse Video. This is a combined feature of the software and CRT that allows portions of text (such as a block to be moved) to be set off either by intensity—the marked section appears gray instead of white—or by reverse video—the marked text is black on white instead of white on black.

Function Keys. In addition to the main software, it is possible to purchase programs that designate certain keys (such as the numeric keypad found on many keyboards) as function keys, that is, command keys for cursor movement, etc. This saves the motion of using the Control key in conjunction with other keys for commands.

Electronic Mail. Some word processing packages, when combined with a modem, will transmit formatted or unformatted text directly to a receiving computer, bypassing physical transportation. If you plan to transmit documents to other computers, you will need a program that stores files in ASCII code rather than binary.

Word processing may be used in almost every aspect of library management, from compiling easily updated bibliographies and inventory lists to printing cards and writing year end reports. Though some of these functions may be accomplished even more readily with other types of software, word processing still represents an improvement over manual methods. Specific library word processing applications will be covered later in this chapter.

Database Management Systems

Database management systems form another category of software with a wide range of potential library applications. A database management system is to a filing cabinet what a word processing system is to a typewriter. Just as the word processor streamlines the mechanics of typing and editing documents, a good DBMS streamlines the mechanics of information storage and retrieval, freeing the user to concentrate on form, content, and data relationships.

If the DBMS is compared to a file cabinet, each data **file** is equivalent to a file drawer containing a set of **records**, each of which uses the same format and contains the same categories, or **fields**, of information. An example in a manual system would be a file of student health records, with preprinted forms filled out with information on each student's childhood diseases, vaccinations, etc. The difference is that in a computerized version of the file, records could be retrieved not only by the student name, but by any other field (or piece of information) on the form. This means that during a measles epidemic, for example, it would be possible to obtain within a few minutes a printed list of all students according to whether they had or had not been vaccinated for measles—a process that might take days if done manually.

The effect of this multiple retrieval feature is that in a DBMS one record, for all practical purposes, counts as multiple records. A card catalog, for example, requires as many as eight different cards for a single book, with one card being filed under one or more subject headings, a title heading, one or more author headings, and so on. The same catalog on a computer would require only *one* entry per book, but that entry could be retrieved by any one of several different **keys**—such as subject, author, or title (or publisher, copyright date, etc., for management purposes). A computer "card" catalog is a complex, specialized version of a database management system, which, because of its large storage needs, requires a hard disk system. A simpler, "generic," DBMS may be used with floppy and/or hard disks for a variety of library applications, including equipment inventory, acquisition files, teacher or student records, mailing lists (including printed labels), curriculum catalogs, and more.

In a DBMS, files, records, and keys are all user-defined. Most systems let you design your own forms, tailoring them to suit the particular record type (see screen, opposite page). Once the record format has been designed and saved, the programs allow you to enter, change, or delete data by filling in the form on the CRT screen. The information may then be sorted and retrieved in a variety of

```
        => DB MASTER MAIN MENU <=

FILE NAME :   MT. VIEW INVENT

CHOOSE FROM:

      (1) DISPLAY/EDIT/DELETE RECORDS

      (2) ADD RECORDS

      (3) LIST RECORDS TO PRINTER

      (4) LOAD OR CREATE SHORT FORM

      (5) SET UP OR PRINT REPORT

      (6) FILE MAINTENANCE

      (7) LOAD OR CREATE NEW FILE

      (8) CLOSE FILES & EXIT

  ENTER  YOUR CHOICE (1 TO 8):
```

A sample menu screen from the database management program for the Apple computer, DB Master™. Reproduced by permission of Stoneware, Inc.

different ways. Since each record is entered only once, the chance of errors is considerably reduced.

The user selects the criteria for sorting and displaying records, and for generating reports. Many systems will perform calculations according to user-defined formulas, using the data from one or more fields and storing the results in another field. A business inventory control package, for example, may keep track of the amount on hand of a particular item by subtracting daily sales, **flagging** the item for reorder when the amount reaches a certain level. More sophisticated systems allow manipulation and cross-referencing of data between files. Some systems may even be used to create files for use with other programs, such as mailing or spreadsheet programs.

Database management systems are more variable than word processing systems in terms of programming skill requirements. In fact, a number of them were designed with programmers in mind, and are used as the basis for more complex applications programs, such as accounting packages and online catalogs. Others require no more skills than those needed for word processing — basically disk formatting and backup procedures, and mastery of the specific program's commands (DBMS may be either menu- or command-driven). DBMS also vary considerably in flexibility and capabilities. As with word processing, the more powerful programs take longer to learn, but can be well worth the initial time investment.

Which DBMS is best for your library will depend on what you plan to do with it. Later sections in this chapter will cover some specific uses for database management systems, and the chapter on needs analysis will help you determine your specific requirements. Some general features to consider in choosing a database management system include:

Ease of Data Editing. The system should allow for changes in data within individual fields in a record. Some systems require deletion and reentry of the entire record, even if only one item needs changing.

Ease of Screen Design. Some systems allow you to type in a screen as you want it to appear and then simply save the final version. With others, you are required to visualize the screen as a grid, specifying the coordinates for each field. A few of the less complex (and less powerful) programs do not use screen designs, but simply follow a vertical format, listing the fields.

Another consideration is whether or not the program allows record forms to be edited after saving. With many DBMS, once you have defined a record format, you are stuck with it, so that if you find you need to lengthen or add a field, or that another is unnecessary, you have to start your database over from scratch. Other programs allow you to make changes with relative ease. Some require you to purchase an additional utility program for form editing.

Flexibility of Record Size. The system may allow records of any length up to a given maximum, or it may have rigid size requirements. It also helps to know how records are physically stored on the disk. One program, for example, may store records in 128 byte blocks, so that any amount over 128 bytes requires an entire block, resulting in a lot of wasted disk space. Also, some programs "compress" data by eliminating unused spaces during storage. The way records are stored will determine how many records will fit on a disk.

File Storage. Some systems will allow only one file per disk; others permit multiple files. Some systems even require two disks per file — one for storing program utilities and record formats and one for data, thus increasing the amount of information that can be stored on a disk. Of course, this method also requires two disk drives.

If your proposed application includes files large enough to require multiple data disks, and you will be searching for records by keys other than the primary key (see below), you will probably want a hard disk. Otherwise you will spend a lot of time during searches changing disks.

Ease and Flexibility of Searches. In a DBMS, records are searched according to user-defined **search keys**. When the record form is designed and data is entered, one field — usually the field most likely to be considered in data retrieval — is generally designated as the *primary* key. Most systems store and search records using the Indexed Sequential Access Method (**ISAM**) — that is, the records are stored in alphanumeric order in the file according to the primary key. For example, a file of student health records would probably have students' last names as the primary key field. The records would then be stored in alphabetical order according to last names. When the user asked for a search according to either the primary or another key, the computer would "look" at each of the records in primary key order. (In a SAM, or Sequential Access Method, system, the records are searched in reverse entry order.)

Some systems allow the establishment of permanent or temporary secondary keys. Defining a secondary key causes a second ISAM file of the same records to be set up according to the secondary key order. In the example above, teacher names might be used as a secondary key field. The more ISAM files on a disk, the less space you will have for records, so a program that allows temporary keys offers some real advantages.

A DBMS retrieves information in file records by one or more keys, according to user-defined criteria. In the measles example above, you may wish to find all students in the fourth grade who have not been vaccinated against measles. The search keys would include student names, grade, and vaccination information. The computer would select and display or print the names of all students in grade four whose vaccination record did not include measles.

Most programs will search on a whole or partial match of an **alphanumeric** character string, but the search capabilities vary. One program, for instance, might allow a search for all records with a "city" field that includes the letters "glen." This would mean the records for Forest Glen, Glendale, and Northglenn would all be included. Other programs have more definite requirements — a search for the last name of Smith (where the last name is defined as the last word in the field) would not pick up John Smith, Jr., since "Jr." is the last word in that field. Other search options include ranges of values (such as all the names which begin with the letters M through S), or values with a certain relationship to a defined criterion (such as greater than, less than, equal to, equal to or less than, etc.). A search that includes multiple descriptors or asks for a range of values is called a **Boolean search**.

Flexibility of Report Design. Some systems will simply print out each entire record; others enable the user to design the form (including enhancements such as page numbering, headings, etc.) and determine the content of each report — all fields, one, or several. Reports can therefore be customized for a particular purpose.

Data Security. A number of systems enable you to use passwords to block access to certain information depending on the assigned level of each operator. For instance, a clerk might not be given access to the salary figure on an employee record. Some passwords allow the operator to "read/only" — that is, he or she can view data but not change it. Other levels might include read/write access to certain fields and no access at all to others.

There are numerous possible applications for database management systems within libraries. Several will be covered later in this chapter.

Spreadsheet Programs

The third general purpose program to consider for library use is the electronic spreadsheet, or "calc" program. Spreadsheet programs replace the familiar green ledger sheets just as word processing replaces typewriters and database management systems replace file cabinets—that is, they go far beyond automating everyday spreadsheet functions. They can be used not only for tallying and figure analysis, but for forecasting and "what-if" planning, since changing one variable automatically changes all the related variables. The results of calculations that would take hours and days if done manually are available in seconds.

Though frequently associated with financial planning and budgeting, spreadsheets are not limited to money-related functions. Circulation statistics, collection usage, staff time distribution, service analysis—these are just a few of the areas you could investigate using a spreadsheet program.

As the name implies, spreadsheet programs basically consist of rows and columns, which intersect to form "cells," or memory locations, the contents of which are user-defined. There are literally thousands of locations available. Each location may be filled with one of three types of data: labels, which describe column and/or row contents and are nonfunctional; values, which are variables input by the operator; and formulas or functions, which are calculated automatically from values and/or other formulas in one or more different cells.

To get an idea of how a calc program works, imagine a computerized check register, with columns for the check number, date, payee, amount, and running balance. So far it's nothing special, except perhaps for the automatic calculation of the balance. But now add additional columns for check distribution—categories such as rent, groceries, car expenses, clothing, etc., along with a row that automatically calculates the percentage of income going to each category. You could also add "what-if" and projection columns, calculating, for instance, the practical consequences of buying a new car, or the time needed to save for a Caribbean vacation. Since another feature of spreadsheet programs is the ability to replicate values across a row or down a column, you could view several alternatives at once—how does the picture change if your income increases by 10% each year, or if you save $50 or $100 more each month?

The programs allow you to set up "templates" for various functions, such as the check register example above, or for a monthly budget report, and then use the template indefinitely with only minor modifications (see screen, opposite page). Specific data input is simple and fast, and reports which were odious chores or even unthinkable are easily produced.

Like word processing and database management systems, spreadsheet programs are not "turnkey," that is, they require some time to learn. They are usually menu-driven and require virtually no programming knowledge. Mastering the basic functions takes only a few hours; exploring the more complex capabilities takes considerably longer. The more commands you master, and the more adept you become at manipulating data, the more flexible and useful your spreadsheets will be.

There are a number of spreadsheet programs available. For the most part they are comparable in terms of price and capabilities. Therefore, your choice may depend to a large extent on previously chosen hardware and software. Another consideration in choosing spreadsheet software will be the amount of

```
              PURCHASE ORDER RECORD


     A      B     C     D         M       N

  P.O.# DATE VEND AMT         BUDG.  BALANCE

                                     4000.00
     1      1/3   BTSB 120.00    3%   3880.00

     2      1/10

     3      1/10

     4      1/12

     5      1/15



    21      4/3

    22      4/4
```

A sample screen for handling purchase orders, done on VisiCalc™. Columns E through L would be labeled with amount breakdowns for supplies, equipment, books, etc., possibly further broken down by categories (e.g., fiction, nonfiction, media). Columns M and N show the percentage of the budget used for each purchase and the budget balance. Reproduced by permission of Visicorp.

memory available in your system. If this is your first software purchase and you plan to use it extensively with large files and/or complex formula operations, you will need to choose hardware with a fairly large amount of memory to take advantage of all the potential cell locations. A 64K computer effectively limits the number of cells to about 3,000, no matter what the capabilities of the software. For most uses this should be sufficient—one large library keeps its entire $1.7 million budget in a single spreadsheet file, with room left over.[1]

[1]Michael Schuyler, "Visicalc: Library Uses for a Business Standard," *ACCESS: Microcomputers in Libraries* 2 (Jan. 1982): 9, 17, 27.

Some spreadsheet features to look for include:

Screen Viewing Capabilities. Since any spreadsheet will be too large to fit onto the screen, the CRT acts as a "window" through which you view different portions of the sheet at a time. Useful viewing features include split-screen capability, which allows you to work on one portion of the spreadsheet while simultaneously viewing another portion that would normally be off the screen. Another feature allows you to "lock" certain rows or columns, such as those containing labels, on the screen while scrolling other portions of the spreadsheet.

Number of Memory Locations. Some programs are restricted only by the amount of available memory; others have a fixed number of locations which cannot be exceeded.

Formatting. Flexibility may be useful here. For example, some programs let you define a column width and then automatically make all the columns the same width, while others allow varying widths within a spreadsheet. The program may also allow you to specify the number of decimal places to be displayed.

Ease of Cursor Movement. The cursor may be controlled by using the ‹CTRL› key and/or by various function keys; a "GOTO" command allows the user to specify a cell using screen coordinates and send the cursor directly to it. Other commands allow rows and columns to be inserted, deleted, or moved to another position.

Replication. This function allows a value or values to be copied to another part of the spreadsheet, such as across a row or down a column.

Recalculation. This is the feature that lets you play "what-if" by recalculating all entries that are functions of a value or values that have been changed.

Built-in Functions. These include the arithmetic, logarithmic, trigonometric, and logic functions that are used as formulas for manipulating data. One useful feature not found in all calc programs is an if-then-else function, which allows you to set different conditions for calculating the contents of a cell. For example, *if* the age of an item is less than two years, *then* use the purchase price as its value, *else* subtract N (from another cell) dollars for each year. Other built-ins you may want to look for are: averaging, selecting the highest and lowest values in a row or column, counting, calculating absolute or net present values, and search functions.

File Merging Capabilities. Some programs allow data from one file to be merged onto another worksheet, which allows you to assemble very complex worksheets one portion at a time.

Print Capabilities. Print-out flexibility of spreadsheet programs varies. Some spreadsheet programs are compatible with other types of programs, so that the calc files may be accessed by word processing and/or database management systems and vice versa. This makes it possible to produce printed customized reports. Some systems manage this more easily than others, however — you may need some special programming skills.

MICROCOMPUTERS IN LIBRARIES

In addition to the three types of software described above, a growing number of special purpose packages are being designed specifically for libraries. These include online catalogs, catalog card printing programs, circulation programs, and more. There are also a number of "total system" library packages on the market. These have the advantage of being "turnkey" and relatively easy to use; however, they present several disadvantages, including high initial cost, a lack of flexibility—you have to adapt to the system, rather than building a system that adapts to you—a great deal of room for error, and the trauma to patrons and staff of changing your entire library system at one time.

The concepts presented in this book are aimed at building a flexible, modular system customized to the needs of your library. In the following sections, we will discuss both general and special purpose software as applied to specific library functions and services. The possibilities are of course not limited to the ideas discussed here; new applications are being tried, with varying degrees of success, all the time. The aim is not to be comprehensive, but to offer a wide sampling of microcomputer potential in library management and services. Further information on specific projects and programs can be found in appendix B.

ACQUISITIONS

One major aspect of the acquisitions process, selection, is to a large extent subjective. The remainder of the process consists of routine, repetitive functions such as checking lists, preparing and placing purchase orders, checking for duplications, verifying deliveries, keeping track of back orders, accounting, and so on. Many of these functions could be partially or wholly computerized with a micro, and even the subjective selection process could be aided by access to the sort of information a computer can make available. Computerizing the routine chores of acquiring library materials would make it much easier to concentrate on the content of the collection, due to time savings and *control of information*.

The acquisitions process begins with idea-generating activities such as reading reviews, processing student and staff requests, conducting patron surveys, and previewing materials. These sources are used to build a consideration file, something that varies widely in form and content from one library to the next, from a folder full of notes, flyers, and clippings marked by highlighting, to an organized card file.

Any type of manual file, no matter how well organized, is limited by the method for filing, unless you take the time to make multiple cards for each record. There are any number of valid, but necessarily limited, ways to "key" the file—by subject area, author, title, format, publisher, distributor, etc. So what happens when, for example, you have an author-ordered file and the jobber wants the request in title order? Or by ISBN? Or suppose, as happens occasionally, you suddenly find yourself on Monday with a chunk of funds that must be spent by Friday? To obtain a higher rate of fill, you could order direct from one publisher. Your consideration file, however, is organized by subject, and what's more, you haven't had time to update it since the last order was received.

Now suppose, instead, that your consideration file is on a floppy disk, organized with a database management program according to a screen you designed yourself. You would simply print out a list of items in the file to be ordered from a given publisher, listed according to the priority rating you previously assigned to each item. Instead of settling for rushed, nearly random selection, you use the budget windfall to order the items you need and want most. Sound appealing? It gets better.

As items are ordered and received, you can update the records in the file, so that it is always current. With a moderately sophisticated database management system, you could even transfer the relevant information into a different file of outstanding orders, and then into another of new arrivals, without having to reenter it. Since the data entry screen is your design, it is tailored to fit the requirements for your own library and district. Depending on the way you currently keep your consideration file, the screen might look something like this:

```
          CONSIDERATION/ORDER FILE
AUTHOR_____  CAT_____

  TITLE_____PRIOR._____

    PUB._____YR.___COST_____

    JOBBER_____ COST_____

    OTHER_____

    REQ.BY_____DATE_____

    REC/REVS_____

    _____

    ORDERED___/___  REC___/___ BO__/__

    COMMENT_____  CAN___/___

    _____ DATE__/__/__
```

A sample screen for keeping a consideration/ordering file.

By computerizing this file, you may obtain printouts by any category you wish, such as science, biography, 500s, poetry, film strips, back orders, publisher or jobber, and so on—quite an improvement over folders of clippings or boxes of 3x5 cards!

Caution: when you computerize any function, you will have to become very conscientious about procedures. In this case, for instance, it would be a good idea to keep a category list to ensure that you are consistent, because the computer will be!

If your first software purchase is a word processing rather than a data management package, you could use a word processing "template" form to print pertinent information directly onto preprinted continuous forms. Purchase order information could be typed into the template form and printed out as multiple copies or replicated with a copier. The resulting forms could serve not only as purchase orders but as check-in forms for receiving orders and reordering, and even as cataloging aids. A different template could be used to print file records for a manual consideration file—complete with duplicate records for different access keys. These applications would require a word processing program capable of reading text from one file into another, along with some time to set up the original templates. An even simpler word processing application would be compiling easily updated lists for recent or proposed orders, new arrivals, back orders, and so on. Alternatively, a spreadsheet program might be used to enter orders by categories for budget reports and projections, comparing, for example, circulation statistics with ordering patterns.

You might consider banding together with other libraries to set up a centralized ordering system as has been done in some districts. A single microcomputer with a hard disk and appropriate software could provide complete ordering services, including simple to use check-off order lists and batch ordering for cost savings. A spreadsheet could also be used to organize a centralized ordering system, calculating such information as discount variables and handling time along with making "what-if" projections according to orders and reports submitted by individual member libraries. With careful and cooperative organization, orders for various publishers or jobbers could be coordinated to obtain maximum discounts and minimum confusion, while ensuring that individual libraries retain selection control.

Some jobbers are now offering computerized ordering systems, which might be utilized on a district level once you have developed the batch ordering process. Other possibilities include a networking system using a district mainframe and individual microcomputers equipped with modems and communications software for centralized systems, including acquisitions. (For more information on networking, see chapter 5).

CATALOGING

Cataloging is a high-visibility, labor-intensive function that provides the main means of access to library resources. It also involves several features that make it particularly suited to computerization: large numbers of records containing standardized information that must be accessed by at least three routes (subject, author, and title); repetition; high volume; and continual changes due to acquisitions, losses, damage, and normal circulation. The relatively recent acceptance of a standardized machine readable bibliographic format (**MARC**, or Machine Readable Cataloging) for cataloging materials, along with technological advances in both individual and network computer systems, is changing not only the methods but the objectives of library cataloging services. Functions that might be wholly or partially computerized include: patron access catalogs;

printed catalogs, including complete collections, special collections, specialized bibliographies, or inventory records; catalog card production; and equipment inventories. An increasing amount of commercial software is becoming available for cataloging applications, but much may be accomplished using word processing and database management packages as well.

Library catalogs have two primary functions: to document each item in a library collection with a valid, standardized bibliographic record; and to provide patrons with a means for locating information about specific items. Because they are relatively easy to manipulate, cards and card files have been the accepted format for library catalogs for many years. However, as collections grow and information changes, the disadvantages of card catalogs become more and more apparent. They are bulky, unwieldy, intimidating to patrons, and virtually impossible to keep current.

During the past decade, libraries of all sizes have begun computerizing certain aspects of cataloging via such centralized, large-scale organizations as OCLC (Online Computer Library Center, formerly known as Ohio College Library Center) and RLIN (Research Libraries Information Network), which provide such services as shared cataloging databases, catalog card production, centralized ordering, and interlibrary loan systems. One widely adopted practice is the use of computer-output microfilm (COM) cataloging, which may be purchased through vendors and updated as needed. These services, while making it easier to manage the volume of data, have not really changed the *nature* of cataloging. Micros, however, may have significant impact on the methods by which collection information is made available to both staff and patrons.

Online Catalogs

Perhaps the optimum computer application for a library is an online patron access catalog, and in a small but growing number of libraries, this dream is becoming a reality. The advantages of an online catalog over a card catalog include not only increased access speed and ease of update (thus eliminating or at least reducing backlogs), but benefits such as access to information on nonprint items (including community resources), wider ranges of subject headings and cross-references, and more successful searches by patrons, resulting in increased use of library resources.

As of this writing, out of some 20 to 30 online library catalogs, only 3 are microcomputer based (see appendix B for specific package information). The average cost of the three systems is about $10,000, including hardware and software, which is relatively expensive compared to less complex micro applications, but enormously cheaper than a comparable system using a mini or mainframe. For a new school without an existing catalog, the set-up cost is comparable to that of a card catalog—and the ongoing operational costs are less! Also, equipment prices, particularly for hard disk drives (a necessary component for an online catalog) are still decreasing, and as more catalog packages enter the market, competition should help to lower software prices as well.

The primary criterion for an online catalog, particularly in a school setting, is ease of use. Studies of traditional catalogs have shown that the user success rate declines in proportion to the size of the catalog and increases in proportion to the number of "see" and "see also" references.[2] Another obstacle to catalog use is lack of necessary skills, including spelling and alphabetization, as well as understanding of the concepts of subject, author, and title headings. This problem is not helped by the tendency for catalog headings to be other than colloquial, that is, a search for "Cars" will be unsuccessful if no cross-reference is provided to direct the searcher to "Automobiles."

A computerized catalog, if it is well designed and has a fast response time, will not be any more difficult to use with a large collection than with a small one. The only effect might be a barely noticeable (to the user) increase in response time. Further, the multiple retrieval feature of a computerized catalog makes it possible to include as many cross-references as necessary, with new references added according to expressed patron needs. At least one of the current programs was designed for elementary schools and specifically addresses the lack of skills problem; it is designed to search on parts of words or even a single letter, and to reinforce subject, author, and title concepts as well as encouraging the students to seek help from the library staff when they are having difficulty with a search. This patron-staff interaction is invaluable in building the "see" and "see also" references in the catalog and in evaluating library materials needs. (See chapter 7 for details on this system.)

Along with ease of use, a catalog program needs extensive search capabilities. Patrons must be able to search by subject, author, or title, just as in a card catalog; the entry screen should also include fields for additional subject headings to increase access and facilitate cross-referencing. In addition, it is extremely useful for the library staff to be able to define temporary search keys in order to locate items by publisher, call number, copyright dates, shelf numbers, etc., in order to streamline activities such as inventory, weeding, and ordering. The program should be able to generate reports by any combination of criteria, for both management and patron use. For example, it should be able to generate bibliographies for class projects, or produce a printout of 500s for an inventory.

Editing capabilities are also important. You should be able to make changes as needed, while protecting records from accidental or intentional tampering. Another potential advantage of an online catalog is the ability to receive status information, such as whether a particular item is missing, out for repair, or checked out for a long term project. If the program has "canned fields," that is, a predesigned entry screen, it should include several extra fields for status and other comments, as well as cross-references, extra subject headings, and any special codes or sort keys that might be needed to customize the form for your library. It is possible to introduce variations into a preset screen, as long as you keep records and are *consistent*. For example, if you purchase most of your books through jobbers instead of direct from the publisher, and a vendor field is not included, you could incorporate the vendor name into the publisher field, placing it at the beginning of the field so that the program will sort according to jobber rather than publisher.

Another factor in deciding to acquire an online catalog, if you are not in a new library, is what will be done with the old catalog. If the collection is not large, you may be able to transfer all of the entries to the computer catalog within the implementation period. If, however, the catalog has many entries and/or

---

[2]Joseph R. Matthews, "Online Public Access Catalogs: Assessing the Potential," *Library Journal* 107 (June 1, 1982): 1068-69.

staff time is at a premium, it might be simpler to freeze the old catalog and continue to use it in conjunction with the computerized portion, phasing it out gradually as old entries are either weeded out or entered into the database. Another useful practice during the transition period is to instruct users in the differences and similarities between the two methods, strengthening both manual and computer search skills and concepts.

Backup is another important consideration. Though you will have a computer backup, on either floppy disks or another medium such as video tape, you should also have a hard-copy backup. This could take the form of a printed catalog or a stripped down (one entry per item) card catalog-shelf list.

If you do decide to implement a patron-access catalog, pay special attention to the location and appearance of the lookup station. The station should be visible and easily accessible, with appropriate lighting (bright lights make it difficult to read the screen), space for taking notes, and an attractive setting. Another way to enhance and increase usage is to keep reference aids such as posters, pamphlets, or flashcards nearby. And you will need to devote time to planning and carrying out user orientation, with introductory classes and demonstrations on how to use the catalog.

An online catalog could also be incorporated on a district level. This would necessitate a mainframe or minicomputer, which could be accessed via modems either in conjunction with in-house catalogs or through separate lookup stations in each library. As funds become scarcer, more interlibrary cooperation will be necessary to make maximum resources available to patrons. Such practices as interlibrary loans, the development of union catalogs, and centralized ordering systems may all be facilitated by computerization. It is important to note that programs that might be impossible on a building level may be accomplished collectively for the benefit of all involved.

Printed Catalogs

For primary cataloging purposes (i.e., replacing a card catalog), printed catalogs are simply not cost effective. Paper and binding costs are high, limiting the ability to make updates. Also, printed catalogs are not convenient for patron use. However, for special purposes, printed catalogs can be highly useful. They may be produced using either a word processor or database management program, or a combination of the two.

To produce a catalog with a word processor, staff members would have to manually compile bibliographic and catalog lists. Once entered, however, the catalogs could be easily updated using insertion and deletion capabilities. Possible applications include producing **book catalogs**, such as one of nonprint materials, or another of community resources for staff and interlibrary use, or providing bibliographies for special projects or annual class units.

A good database management package is an excellent tool for cataloging. To a limited extent, such a catalog might be used online, though only for staff purposes and only by trained personnel. This is because the search capabilities are relatively limited in a general purpose DBMS program as compared to a specific cataloging program. Searches not only take longer but are more difficult to perform. However, for gaining control of collection information, and for producing printed catalogs for general use, a DBMS is quite practical. For collections of any size, you will need a hard disk and software that is capable of utilizing it. Therefore, you might start by cataloging a specific part of your collection, such as nonprint, using floppy disks, and add the hard disk components at a later time. If you plan to do this, make sure that whatever hardware and software you buy is not only expandable, but that any files entered on floppy will be easily transferable to a hard disk system.

A DBMS will allow you to set up your files and define records according to field types and lengths, as well as sort and display records by different criteria. If you will be using the system to produce printed catalogs and bibliographies, make sure that it includes a flexible report generator, allowing you to sort and print using specified fields.

Database management systems vary widely in capability, cost, and ease of use. There are even some public domain programs, suitable for use with small files, that would give you an opportunity to work with small-scale, low-pressure projects. For example, a simple subject bibliography form might be used to create materials bibliographies for different grade levels and subject disciplines from the same data file. This might also be a way to increase use of certain materials such as records or study prints, or to correlate your fiction collection with specific study units; for example, a bibliography of historical fiction for the Revolutionary period.

Other possible ideas include a file of important events for each month, gleaned from the back calendars of periodicals; a bibliography of birthdays of important people and the areas of interest related to them; a catalog of your vertical file or poster file; and an inventory of bulletin board materials. These and numerous other creative projects are inexpensive and simple to implement, yet can increase both the quantity and quality of patron and staff services in your library — while demonstrating the value of your microcomputer!

Catalog Card Production

Another easily computerized function that can result in both time and cost savings is catalog card printing. A number of programs are available for this purpose, ranging from simple public domain programs you key in yourself to packages that not only print complete card sets and book labels, but store the data for possible later use in an online catalog or circulation system. It is even possible to print cards using a word processing package, though it may take some time to set up a template, and the printing process will be slower since cards will have to be edited to conform to the different headings.

Specialized card printing programs may be purchased to work with most of the popular hardware types. Printer configurations are somewhat trickier, and you will have to ensure first that the software you purchase can be made compatible with your printer, and second, that the printer itself is capable of handling card stock. Although a letter-quality printer will produce the best-looking cards, it is possible to get very acceptable results with a good dot matrix printer.

A special purpose commercial card printing program may be extremely cost effective if you are currently typing and copying your own cards. Since each item is entered only once, staff time will be significantly reduced, along with copy machine rental or use costs. In addition to cards, most programs will also print card, pocket, and spine labels, and some will print shelf lists as well (see screen on page 80). Some even have sort capabilities, such as alphabetically by call letters or

```
PART OF MENU FROM TELEMARC III

   CARD PRINTING PROGRAM DEMO DISK

PRESS KEY FOR OPTION:

1)ALIGN PRINTER      E) EDIT

2)MAKE A CARD        P) PRINT CARD SET

3)EXIT PROGRAM       R) RECONSTRUCT A CARD


      B) BATCH PRINT CARDS OR LABELS

      M) PRINT MAIN ENTRY CARD ONLY

      S) PRINT SHELF LIST CARD ONLY

      C) SORT AND PRINT MAIN ENTRY CARDS
```

An option/menu screen from the card printing program Telemarc™. Reprinted from Telemarc™ operator's manual, copyright 1983 by Catalog Card Corporation.

numerically by call number; several include built-in or optional AV format modules. If you are using a card printing program as a starter project and plan to implement a circulation system and/or online catalog at a later date, it would be advisable to spend a little more now for a program that stores data in the MARC format—it will save many hours of data entry time in the future. See appendix B for information on some currently available card printing programs.

Equipment Inventory

An equipment inventory using basic hardware and a file or database management system is a relatively inexpensive and low-pressure starting project for the computer novice. There are even some public domain programs available that would be suitable for working with small files. If you are among the many library media specialists who have found themselves with prepurchased hardware and little available funding, this might be a practical and useful way to familiarize yourself with the computer while you figure out what to do next.

If you currently keep your equipment inventory on file cards, you can use the card format as a basis for designing a data entry screen (see screen below). With a database management system, you would then be able to retrieve records and produce reports according to any field. If, for example, you now file records according to equipment description, e.g., projector, overhead; projector, filmstrip, you would still be able to obtain reports organized by descriptions—as well as by other criteria, such as district identification numbers—very useful for coordinating building and district inventories!

```
DIST ID_____  CLASS/SUB_____

DESC 1 _____

     DESCR 2 _____

BLD ID _____  MAKE_____

MODEL_____  SERIAL_____

PURCH __ /__ /__      COST _____ . __

QTY_____  FUND _____  P.O.#_____

VENDOR_____LAMP_____

COMMENTS_____

_____


          EQUIPMENT  INVENTORY
```

A sample screen, prepared on DB Master™, for keeping an equipment inventory.

In setting up database management systems such as this one, it is best to design a form and enter a variety of items—not over 50!—and then evaluate the form before continuing data entry. For example, the most-used fields should be at the beginning of the form for easier data entry. Try out several report formats as well. You may want to keep a separate practice file specifically for testing different formats before trying them on your actual inventory files. Remember that sort time will increase as the volume of records grows, and that cassette tapes and floppy disks are limited as to the amount of data they will store.

Some of the ways this file might be used include: looking up lamp or other part types for replacement; looking up vendors for repairs or warranty replacement; looking up purchase dates for replacement planning; locating purchase order numbers for bookkeeping purposes; locating district identification numbers for comparison with district computer printouts; listing equipment to be serviced during the summer by equipment maintenance staff; and compiling lists of available equipment for staff use.

Another way to computerize equipment inventory is to set up a file using a word processing template. Equipment lists stored on disks would be easy to update using insertion and deletion capabilities, thereby saving retyping the whole list. Even though a word processing program will not sort, rearranging material on a word processor to correspond to specific requirements is much easier than using a typewriter and/or the cut and paste method. Part of an equipment list prepared on a DBMS and printed out might look something like figure 4.1 (pages 83-84).

Alternatively, you could format the list to print on labels to be placed on file cards for a manual equipment file.

With either a DBMS or word processing equipment file, you could catalog equipment as you receive it, making the data entry part of the processing routine. The information could then be updated easily for missing or damaged equipment or long-term check-outs. Yet another possibility is using a spreadsheet program to plan replacement schedules based on life expectancy and budget allocations.

Figure 4.1. Sample Equipment Printout Using DB Master™

```
02-02-83                        TEST LMC REPORT                      PAGE 9

LOCATION     DESCRIPTION              BLD ID        MAKE
   MODEL       SERIAL #      LAMP                 DIST I.D. #

- - - - -  FILMSTRIP - - - - - - - - - - - - - - - - - - - - - - - - - - - -
- - - - - - - - - - - - - - - - - - - - - - - - - - - - - - - - - - - - - - -

LMC-EQUIP      PROJECTOR  OPAQUE       1-80        SQUIBBTAYLOR
               7800045              ELC            31000129-X

LMC-EQUIP      PROJECTOR  OFAQUE       1-80        TAYLOR
   TS-7        7800045              DRS            31000289-X


- - - - -  OPAQUE - - - - - - - - - - - - - - - - - - - - - - - - - - - - - -
- - - - - - - - - - - - - - - - - - - - - - - - - - - - - - - - - - - - - - -

LMC-EQUIP      PROJECTOR  OVERHEAD     1-80        3M
   213         422580               ENX            31000072

LMC-EQUIP      PROJECTOR  OVERHEAD     7-80        3M
   213         422566               ENX            31000073

LMC-EQUIP      PROJECTOR  OVERHEAD     2-80        3M
   213         422495               ENX            31000074

LMC-EQUIP      PROJECTOR  OVERHEAD     8-80        3M
   213         422584               ENX            31000075

LMC-EQUIP      PROJECTOR  OVERHEAD     5-80        3M
   213         422565               ENX            31000076

LMC-EQUIP      PROJECTOR  OVERHEAD     3-80        3M
   213         422567               ENX            31000077

LMC-EQUIP      PROJECTOR  OVERHEAD     4-80        3M
   213         422568               ENX            31000078

LMC-EQUIP      PROJECTOR  OVERHEAD     6-80        3M
   213         422574               ENX            31000079


- - - - -  OVERHEAD - - - - - - - - - - - - - - - - - - - - - - - - - - - - -
- - - - - - - - - - - - - - - - - - - - - - - - - - - - - - - - - - - - - - -

LMC-EQUIP      PROJECTOR  SND FS VR    1-80        DUKANE
   28A63       895696               DDK            31000102


- - - - -  SND FS VR - - - - - - - - - - - - - - - - - - - - - - - - - - - -
- - - - - - - - - - - - - - - - - - - - - - - - - - - - - - - - - - - - - - -

LMC-EQUIP      PROJECTOR  VIEW/SLIDE   1-80        BELL&HOWELL
   799B        0028187              DDM            31000130


- - - - - - - - - - - - - - - - - - - - - - - - - - - - - - - - - - - - - - -
```

(figure continues on page 84)

Figure 4.1 (cont'd)

```
02-02-83                    TEST LMC REPORT                        PAGE  11
LOCATION     DESCRIPTION           BLD ID     MAKE
    MODEL        SERIAL #      LAMP          DIST I.D. #

LMC-EQUIP       RECORDER   TAPE,CAS   CL 4-81     SHARP
    EDUCATOR    10500510                          B-136

LMC-EQUIP       RECORDER   TAPE,CAS   CL 5-81     SHARP
    EDUCATOR    10500594                          B-137

LMC-EQUIP       RECORDER   TAPE,CAS   CL 6-81     SHARP
    EDUCATOR    10500595                          B-138

LMC-EQUIP       RECORDER   TAPE,CAS   CL 7-81     SHARP
    EDUCATOR    10500596                          B-139

LMC-EQUIP       RECORDER   TAPE,CAS   CL 8-81     SHARP
    EDUCATOR    10500597                          B-140


- - - - -  TAPE,CAS - - - - - - - - - - - - - - - - - - - - - - - - - - -
- - - - - - - - - - - - - - - - - - - - - - - - - - - - - - - - - - - - -

LMC-EQUIP       RECORDER   VIDEO      1-80       PANASONIC
    NV9300      GOHA60089                         31000105


- - - - -  VIDEO - - - - - - - - - - - - - - - - - - - - - - - - - - - - -
- - - - - - - - - - - - - - - - - - - - - - - - - - - - - - - - - - - - -

LMC-EQUIP       RECORDER   VIDEO/VHS  VTR 2-80   QUASAR
                01820079                          31000110


- - - - -  VIDEO/VHS - - - - - - - - - - - - - - - - - - - - - - - - - - -
- - - - -  RECORDER - - - - - - - - - - - - - - - - - - - - - - - - - - -
- - - - - - - - - - - - - - - - - - - - - - - - - - - - - - - - - - - - -

LMC-EQUIP       STATIONS   LISTENING  1-12, -80  TELEX
    753-01                                        B-007-1

LMC-EQUIP       STATIONS   LISTENING  13-10,-81
                                                  B-007-2


- - - - -  LISTENING - - - - - - - - - - - - - - - - - - - - - - - - - - -
- - - - -  STATIONS - - - - - - - - - - - - - - - - - - - - - - - - - - -
- - - - - - - - - - - - - - - - - - - - - - - - - - - - - - - - - - - - -

LMC-EQUIP       SYSTEM 80             1          BORG WARNER
    SYSTEM 80   618126            DNF             B-101

LMC-EQUIP       SYSTEM 80             2          BORG WARNER
    SYSTEM 80   615723            DNF             B-102

LMC-EQUIP       SYSTEM 80             3          BORG WARNER
    SYSTEM 80   615723            DNF             B-103


- - - - - - - - - - - - - - - - - - - - - - - - - - - - - - - - - - - - -
```

CIRCULATION

A quick analysis of your current circulation system will, if your library is at all typical, indicate that check-outs, check-ins, and especially overdues, are among the most labor-intensive, least rewarding, and most difficult to maintain of library functions. This, along with the inherent suitability of such tasks to computer capabilities, probably explains why microcomputers are presently being used more for circulation systems and subsystems than for any other library application. Numerous turnkey systems are available for most of the popular types of micros (including several CP/M-based systems) at very reasonable prices.

The actual range of price and capability is considerable, from a very simple overdue program for about $30 to a complex and sophisticated multiple station system costing more than $30,000 (which does include hardware). Most of the programs are clustered toward the lower end of the scale, and are capable of taking on a large part of the circulation burden using basic hardware (a disk drive and a printer are necessary). Another option is designing a circulation system in-house with a database management system — perhaps using the expertise and enthusiasm of one or more students.

"Standalone" circulation systems, that is, those that do not include a cataloging component, are generally absence-based systems, tracking only items that are checked out. Depending on the program's sort, screen-search, and print capabilities, field and record lengths and quantities, and the amount of staff and/or volunteer time available for data entry, circulation computerization may range from producing regularly updated overdue lists and notices to keeping track of collection activity according to any number of criteria, including titles, patron names, dates due, classroom numbers, and teachers names. A number of programs will print not only overdue notices, but letters and bills for appropriate distribution (see screen, page 86). If the circulation system is part of or includes at least a basic catalog component, it may also provide a means for amassing statistics on collection usage (by grade, class, season, subject, etc.), ordering, unit planning, inventory, and other purposes. In addition, anyone looking up an item using the catalog component would immediately know its status — checked out, missing, in for repairs, etc.

Circulation data entry may be via keyboard or by some variation of a bar code system, using a bar code reader. While easier to operate, a bar-code based system can be very costly, both initially and operationally. Barwands or other readers are quite expensive, and you must also be able to obtain or produce bar code labels of sufficient quality. Also, you will have to encode your entire collection, labeling book spines, card pockets, and cards — a time-consuming task. There is also the problem of determining a numbering system. If you already use accession numbers or another type of unique identification number, you could use those — except that you would then have to special order or print the bar code labels and match them to each item. Alternatively, you could use sequential labels, attaching them as items are checked out. This would necessitate creating a new cross-reference file in your database, which would take up additional storage space. Also, if the number were to be used as a search key, you would need a separate record for each copy of multiple items. Sequential labels, possibly on library cards, would be used to identify patrons as well. Although it is not as fast and is somewhat less accurate due to human error, a key-in circulation system is considerably less expensive. In the near future, bar-code technology,

```
THE OVERDUE WRITER                              /
---------------------


    (1)  ENTER CHECK-OUTS


    (2)  CREATE OVERDUES/BILLS


    (3)  PERFORM RECORD SEARCH


    (4)  PRINT


    (5)  END PROGRAM




    /                                           /
```

Sample option/menu from the Overdue Writer™. Reproduced by permission of the Library Software Company.

like that of other microcomputer peripherals, is likely to improve while decreasing in price, making such a system a more viable alternative—one criterion for choosing a particular keyboard-based circulation system now might be whether it offers the possibility of conversion to a bar code system later (see figure 4.2).

A standalone circulation system that tracks only absent items will not require a hard disk; some systems use different disk storage arrangements to increase the number of records per disk. For example, one disk might be used to store only item identification numbers and patron identification numbers. A search by patron number would produce a list of item numbers. A second disk containing titles and identification numbers could then be inserted to obtain a list of titles currently held by a particular patron—whose name could be found by inserting a disk containing patron names and numbers. This could be very useful, for example, when a student is leaving the school and you want to ensure that all items checked out by him or her have been returned.

Figure 4.2. A Typical Bar Code

4 2 1 3 8 5 7 9

While methods such as the one described above involve more disk switching, they allow a large number of records to be stored on each disk, and increase access speed. Such a system also makes data entry easy—only the patron and item identification numbers are entered. Such a system should, however, contain some sort of safeguard against errors, such as requiring double keying of numbers which are then tested to see if they match.

Whatever the method used, volunteers or student aides could handle data entry either as items are checked out or in **batch** form. This is one application which might be used by a library that has to share its computer with other departments, or as a secondary application, since batch data entry, and even printing overdue lists and notices, can be managed in an hour or less per day. To save even more time on circulation procedures, many libraries are adopting a system whereby items are due only one day a week, or even one day a month.

In choosing a circulation system, you will have to consider such factors as the amount of staff/volunteer time available for data entry, the number of titles the system should be able to handle, and the type and amount of information you will need. A system could function quite well with as few as four or five fields: patron, author, title, date due, and, for a school, teacher. One "canned" program using these fields, for example, only allows screen searches by student, title, and teacher, and printouts only by teacher. There are ways around such limitations, however. By placing the date due in the "teacher" field, the author in the "date due" field, and the teacher in the "author" field, you could search by patron, date due, or teacher, and obtain printouts by date due (an automatic overdue list!).

Using a database management program, an in-house system could be designed using the above fields, perhaps using numbers to identify patrons and items, thus decreasing data entry and access time and increasing the number of records per disk. If item cards are then filed in numerical order by date due, a title disk is not even necessary, since the title can be found in the card file as quickly as by disk switching. Overdue notices may be printed and sent out by item number as many times as necessary without reentering the information, except for the addition of a fine the second or third time a notice is sent. Libraries that have tried variations of this system report a much higher rate of return—for whatever reason, patrons seem to respond more quickly to "computerized" notices!

The more fields per record, and the more search keys that are allowed, the more flexible and informative a circulation system will be. However, more fields also means more data entry time and more disk space used. If you have the staff or volunteer time available, you may find the extra statistical information well worth the software and time investment. For instance, it would be useful to have fields for indicating reserved items, along with the next borrower in line.

Other considerations are whether the program allows record editing (many programs require complete reentry for changes or renewals), print out capabilities (while classroom lists might be suitable for an elementary school, they would not work in a secondary school where students change rooms and teachers, and where their library selections sometimes involve sensitive subjects such as drugs or pregnancy and therefore should be confidential), and flexibility to adapt to your particular system.

An "ideal" system would combine an online catalog with an online circulation system, with the status of every item and every patron constantly updated by fast, easy, and accurate data entry, and reports obtainable by a wide range of criteria. Even though such a dream system may be outside your present financial and time budget, it is a goal that may be approached in steps. At the very least, you can save considerable time, increase the rate of item return, and decrease the amount of paperwork involved with both regular circulation and interlibrary loans by computerizing the most burdensome of your circulation tasks.

SERIALS CONTROL

Serials control is yet another library function that is high volume, routine, repetitious, and difficult to maintain. Computerization may be applied to any or all of the following serials control activities: check-in or inventory; circulation statistics; interlibrary loan; union catalogs and periodicals lists; subject bibliographies; routing slips/comments; subscription maintenance; and financial record keeping. These functions are available in several turnkey systems, or you may design your own system using database or file management programs and/or, to a lesser extent, word processing and spreadsheet software.

In considering whether to automate some part of serials control, you should consider the staff time that will be needed to maintain data entry on a daily or weekly basis. (Once the system is implemented, this could be accomplished with student or parent volunteer aides.) Timing is more critical with periodicals than with equipment, books or nonprint media. Therefore, if you handle many periodicals, you may want to wait to implement any extensive computerization of serials control until after you have successfully computerized other library functions. You could, however, begin by putting a list of periodicals received by your library in a word processing file to be printed and distributed to staff members and interested patrons. The list could then be easily updated as subscriptions are added or expire.

Check-in

A file management or database program could be used for keeping track of periodical check-in and inventory using an entry screen similar to standard check-in cards:

```
TITLE_____  FREQ_____

ORDERED_____SOURCE_____  TERM_____

SUB.COST_____.__   IND. COPY___.__

YR____  MO.1___  2___  3___  4___  5___  6___
          7___  8___  9___10___11___12___
YR____  MO.1___  2___  3___  4___  5___  6___
          7___  8___  9___10___11___12___
YR____  MO.1___  2___  3___  4___  5___  6___
          7___  8___  9___10___11___12___
YR____  MO.1___  2___  3___  4___  5___  6___
          7___  8___  9___10___11___12___

CATEGORY_____COMMENT_____

COMMENT_____DATE_____


            PERIODICAL RECORDS
```

A sample screen for managing periodicals.

As with any file or database management project, you should set up a trial screen, enter several items, and try some different report formats to evaluate your screen. (Remember that when designing a screen you should decide which fields will be used most and put them at the beginning for easier data entry.) The record format above could be used to generate reports for inventory, weeding of outdated issues, subscription renewals, and missing issues. It could also be used to produce printed individual library and union catalogs of periodicals for staff use and interlibrary loan programs.

Other fields could be added for routing purposes, so that as soon as an issue is checked in it may be sent to the first person or department on the routing list. Routing slips could be printed either from the data file or using word processing, with space included for comments—a good way to increase staff communications.

Another file could be used for circulation control, either according to borrower name or by the name of the periodical. For example, a record form might contain fields for the name of the periodical, the issue date, volume and number, the name of the borrower, and the due date. Reports could then be printed to determine overdues, current locations of specific issues, circulation statistics (a big aid in ordering), and other useful information.

Other possibilities include the production of topical bibliographies using either a file or database management program or a word processing program, and using a spreadsheet program to compare last cost, current cost, and circulation statistics for doing budget projections and ordering, or simply to keep records of expenditures for periodicals.

The approach you take to computerizing your serials control will depend to a large extent on your current methods. Some of these systems will be relatively time-consuming to set up, but could result in considerable time savings for the staff and increased cost effectiveness in periodicals expense and usage.

REFERENCE

The bulk of our discussion on reference will occur in the next chapter, The Library as a Computer Resource Center, which covers networking and accessing databases. Within an individual library, however, there are several ways in which micros and one or more general purpose software packages can aid the media specialist's role as a reference librarian. Particularly in a school setting, many questions tend to come up again and again. (No doubt you can think of several with little effort.) These questions and the answers could be computerized using either a word processing or a file management program. The material could then be retrieved either through periodically updated printouts or even through searches performed by the patrons themselves — which would be excellent practice for later development of more sophisticated searching skills. If you are fortunate enough to have an online catalog, it could incorporate many reference questions/answers. Setting up a computerized reference file will take some skill and familiarity with the computer; therefore, this would be a good project to undertake after you are somewhat familiar with both the hardware and the software.

One reference tool familiar to media specialists but largely unknown to patrons is the *Sears List of Subject Headings*. The guide is a natural tool for locating "see" and "see also" headings; patrons should be taught how to use it along with the card catalog and *Readers' Guide*. If a copy is then kept near the catalog (card or online), many reference questions could be answered without staff assistance.

Outside resources may also be part of your reference file. Community speakers, field trips, local media, etc., are valuable supplements to your collection. A community resources file would be an excellent district cooperative project. Different libraries could specialize in different types of resources, such as speakers or field trips, and/or in different subject areas, such as ecology, history, and oceanography. Information could then be shared by means of periodically circulated printouts or even, if the same type of hardware is used districtwide, on disks. Other useful possibilities are union catalogs of serials and community resources.

ADMINISTRATION

By administrative tasks we mean report writing, budgeting, record keeping, and any other task that does not fall clearly into one of the other categories described in this chapter. Every media specialist must deal to some extent with externally oriented functions, whether they have to do with accountability—to a school principal, district media center and district purchasing committee, parents and others—or, as in the case of a small rural or specialized library, with more autonomous management tasks such as payroll. By acquiring one or more of the three types of general purpose software, you will be able to accomplish more in less time, provided you do not become so enamored of data accumulation that you bog down in a pile of useless information. Many of the applications of general purpose software have already been covered in the sections on each type, so this section will give just a brief overview of specific computerization possibilities.

Letter Writing. Form letters, in particular, are virtually painless to produce if you have a word processing package. Add a mailing list program and you can "customize" each letter with the appropriate name and address, as well as print envelopes and/or mailing labels. Parent and/or teacher or patron newsletters, announcements, overdue notices, equipment requests—all these and more may be kept in "template" files and modified or updated as needed. Incidentally, a letter-quality printer is *not* a requirement. More and more missives are being sent out with the telltale serrated edges and instantly recognizable characters of dot matrix printers. Actually, since they let everyone know that their writer has a computer, dot matrix printed letters are beginning to amount to a status symbol!

Reports. The bane of every administrator, report writing can be streamlined and even enhanced using word processing, database management, or spreadsheet programs singly or in combination. Report writing is directly related to the keeping of:

Statistics, all kinds of which may be collected and analyzed with the aid of your micro. There is a danger, however, of getting carried away and compiling more data than anyone can possibly use—as a certain relative of ours discovered when he was an assistant postmaster in California. He had assigned a certain monthly report to a clerk to fill out so that he could sign it and send it on. One month he happened to notice that none of the figures had any relation to the columnar headings. A little research showed that about six months before the form had been changed. No one had noticed, from the clerk who continued to put in the figures in the original order to the higher-ups who supposedly used the reports! There is probably no way to avoid doing reports that someone else has ordered and which make little sense. These can be gotten out of the way less painfully with a computer. For your own use, however, stick to data that you can analyze and *use.*

This also holds true within individual records, whether they are part of an overdue system, an equipment inventory, or a patron file. While records must be designed with enough space in each field and enough fields for all the pertinent information (including some "spare" fields for afterthoughts), the space need not be filled just because it is there. The only exception to this is a key field which is needed for sorting. For example, if you are currently sending out overdue lists once each quarter and including prices in the list, computerizing your overdue system would require you to have a price field in each record. With the files on a computer, you would be able to make weekly lists—but there would be no need to include prices except once each quarter. Entering the prices every week would be needless data entry and wasted time.

Budgeting. This is one area in which spreadsheet programs are especially useful. As we stated earlier, there are several comparable programs available, all of which allow you to design your own templates to adapt to your own systems of budget planning, ordering, etc. For an independent library with more complex accounting needs, a general purpose small business type accounting package may be more appropriate. Such packages usually include several modules, such as payroll, accounts payable, accounts receivable and so on, so that you could purchase only the modules that are applicable. Note: Accounting packages are very popular with program writers these days. Be sure to check out any prospective purchase very carefully using the criteria described in chapters 2 and 4.

AV and/or Film Management. Specialized programs are available to aid in AV cataloging and distribution (see appendix B), or you could use word processing and/or DBMS packages to keep records of AV activity (particularly useful where several libraries share materials).

Collection Profiles and Materials Retrieval. There are a number of formulas for testing text "readability" by analyzing such factors as sentence length, word length, number of different words, number of "personal words" ("you," "me," etc.), and number of modifiers. While useful, these formulas require arduous counting and calculating—tasks at which humans balk and computers shine. A number of programs are available that take advantage of this—some of them free, except for the time involved in typing them into the computer and storing them on tape or disk. These "freebies" are found in a number of computer and/or education magazines (see appendix B). Although many such programs are aimed at helping writers evaluate manuscripts, they are equally useful for evaluating reading levels, and some of them are geared specifically to that purpose. There are also commercial programs available, at least one of which will display the results graphically. Or, if you are at all interested in programming, you might try writing one yourself.

Since evaluating a particular text requires typing a portion of it into the computer, readability programs offer student aides or would-be typists (perhaps recruited from a business class?) the opportunity to practice typing and build your collection readability profile at the same time. The profile could then be used as part of a materials retrieval system that includes other criteria such as topic, media type, publisher, and so on, either using a commercial package (see appendix B) or one designed in-house. This could be especially helpful in matching curriculum objectives with library materials and activities, in evaluating collection strengths and weaknesses according to patron needs, and in making purchasing decisions.

These are just some of the ways in which micros can ease the administrative load. Depending on your system and the talents and interests of you and your staff, you will probably discover — or invent — more. Even if you are purchasing a microcomputer system for a specific primary purpose, it would be wise to purchase and become familiar with at least one general purpose software package, even if you must "steal" computer time at lunch or after school to do so. If you are undecided as to which type of package to buy first, we suggest word processing. Virtually any library administrator will be able to discover a number of tasks that can make a word processor indispensable in very short order.

LIBRARY SKILLS INSTRUCTION

This section will address only software and applications related specifically to library skills instruction; general educational software will be covered in chapter 5. By "library skills," we mean not only the traditional skills — how to use a card (or online) catalog, how to locate materials, how to use indexes, etc. — but the newer and increasingly important skills needed to search online databases, particularly the very large and varied databases accessible through services like DIALOG™ and The Source.

The two types of skills have several significant similarities and differences. Sitting down at a microcomputer, "logging on" to a database, and conducting a "search strategy" is closely related to tracing a topic through various references and cross-references in encyclopedias, the *Readers' Guide*, and a card catalog, except that the information is much more comprehensive, current, and faster to access.

Online bibliographic searching is becoming an increasingly common method for obtaining information in both the public and private sectors, for business, government, education, and personal use. (The nature of online database searching will be discussed more thoroughly in chapter 5.) In order to search effectively, information seekers will need to know how to develop search strategies, how to use database catalogs to choose databases and descriptors, and how to use search program commands.

These are all skills that can and should be taught alongside traditional library skills. One effective method is hands-on training using an actual database, which might be an online catalog, or a locally administered database on the district or state level. There is also at least one program* that uses diskettes provided by sources such as ERIC — such a program might provide a less expensive alternative for skills acquisition than learning "online."

As of this writing, the amount and especially the quality of software aimed at developing traditional library skills is still quite limited; however, there is quite a bit of work in progress, most of it by professional librarians working in conjunction with programmers or writing programs themselves. Programs that teach and/or reinforce such skills as the use of periodical indexes, almanacs, and card catalogs, and concepts such as classification are becoming available. Several programs include workbooks or worksheets and many incorporate colorful graphics. The effectiveness of the programs varies considerably; previewing is *strongly* suggested. Library skills instructional software should be evaluated using many of the same criteria as for other types of instructional programs (see chapter 5). Appendix B contains a list of currently or soon-to-be available programs.

---

*"Microsearch." See appendix B for details.

5 The Library as a Computer Resource Center

"The application of microcomputers in the classroom is no longer coming ... it is here, and the implementation of microcomputers for instructional purposes should be an integral part of the total instructional system ... microcomputers, their peripherals, and their software are a part of educational technology and as such should be treated as any other component of educational technology in a school media program. It is understood that computers and their peripherals will be located in, maintained by, and circulated from the media center in the same manner as 16mm projectors, video cassette recorders and other audiovisual equipment.

Computer software ... and the accompanying documentation will be housed in the media center and catalogued for retrieval by students, teachers and administrators in the same manner as other audiovisual software.

The media professional will be computer literate, have an understanding of computer logic, and be able to demonstrate the use of the microcomputer to students, teachers, guidance counselors, and administrators as they now demonstrate the use of other audiovisual equipment."

—From a position paper by the
Minnesota Educational Media Association[3]

INTRODUCTION

The widespread introduction of microcomputers into schools, homes, and businesses cannot help but influence the role of the library media center. First, as the supply of information grows and budgets shrink, libraries will come to rely more and more on each other and on other sources, such as online databases, to give patrons access to the most complete, current, and reliable information available. Computers offer the only viable and practical means of tapping into that vast information bank and coordinating and managing resources. In addition, as the quotation above shows, media centers and media specialists will be expected to take a leadership role in preparing students and community members for a society in which computers will be an integral part.

Recognition of the growing influence of computers has spawned a new movement in education and the media—the drive to promote **computer literacy**. Hazily defined, often hastily implemented, and approached with everything from enthusiastic abandon to defensive hostility, computer literacy programs have become the educational fad of the 1980s. If computer-related

---

[3]Minnesota Educational Media Association, "Position Paper," *CMC News* 3 (Fall 1982): 4.

education is not to go the way of New Math and other ill-fated experiments, planning, knowledge, and forethought must take precedence over wishful thinking, ignorance, and impetuousness. Computers *are* here to stay, and some knowledge about them and skill in their use will be requirements for success in many career fields and even in private life.

Those who oppose the idea of computer literacy programs (though not necessarily the idea of computers themselves) have used several analogies meant to illustrate the silliness of learning about computers in order to use them. For instance, in order to use a bicycle, a car, or a telephone, students would have to acquire "bicycle literacy," "automobile literacy," and "telephone literacy." First they would learn the history of the bicycle (car, telephone), then all the parts and how they work, and *then* a few students would be able to try going for a ride or making a call. Actually, some knowledge of the workings of a bicycle or a car is useful for becoming a skilled, responsible, and safe vehicle operator—it is handy to know how to change a tire, or to talk knowledgeably with a mechanic—and driver education and bicycle safety programs bespeak society's recognition of the need for people to learn at least minimal operating skills before venturing out on the road. Also, anyone who has spent much time on the telephone can understand the (mostly unmet) need for teaching telephone skills. It may also be argued that it is very important for people to understand the influence and uses of automobiles, telephones, and even bicycles in society. Similarly, some working knowledge of computers is useful for operating them, as more and more people will be expected to do in both their working and private lives, and knowledge of computers as they affect society is desirable from both an individual and a societal point of view.

Whether it is called "computer literacy," "computer awareness," or something else altogether, the need to achieve it on a widespread basis is becoming more and more apparent. Perhaps the best definition is the one contained in the Minnesota Education Media Organization position paper quoted above: "A computer literate person may be defined as one who knows what a computer is—and what it isn't; why computers exist and how they influence people's lives; how computers are being used; what computers do and what they cannot do."[4]

Most definitions seem to concur that computer literacy includes some ability to operate microcomputers, but there is considerable debate on whether it also includes the ability to program. Like drawing, or music, or writing, programming is a specialized skill best performed by people with certain personality characteristics and at least some measure of talent. Though most people can learn programming basics, proportionately few will be interested in pursuing it further, and fewer still will make it a career. Added to this is the fact that the costs involved in teaching every student to program would be enormous—one estimate places the equipment bill for the United States alone at a billion dollars, and that figure does not include software or instructor costs.[5]

It is equally unrealistic to expect, as some have predicted, that every student will have a microcomputer by 1990, or even 2000, or that computers will replace teachers, or, for that matter, librarians. A realistic approach to the need for education *about* computers and the possibilities of education *using* computers

---

[4]Ibid.

[5]Jerry L. Patterson and Janice H. Patterson, "Teaching Computer Literacy in Schools: The Promise and the Reality," *Educational Computer Magazine* (July-August 1982), p. 19.

will have to take into account many factors, including the technological, financial, sociological, and even psychological capabilities and limitations of schools, libraries, educators, administrators, and students. It is also crucial that the old-fashioned but still important basics of reading (*especially* reading!), writing, arithmetic, history, etc., do not get lost in the rush to become computer literate. Voice capabilities aside, any individual who cannot read will be very limited in his or her ability to use a computer.

COMPUTER-RELATED SERVICES

Given all these considerations, how can media centers promote computer literacy and fulfill their new role as computer resource centers while still providing—perhaps even expanding—the necessary traditional services? Some possibilities were discussed in the last chapter, such as using microcomputers to lighten administrative burdens, leaving more time and energy to devote to patron services, including instruction about and with computers. In addition, library media centers might offer any or all of the following computer-related services:

Maintain and Circulate Computer Hardware

Computer equipment is in many ways like any other type of audiovisual equipment, from slide projects to video cassette recorders. Unless a school is affluent enough to place one or more micros in every classroom, or is able to dedicate space and staff to a full time computer center, the library media center is the logical location for any equipment intended for general use. Many computers are in fact portable enough to place on carts for check-out to individual classrooms. In the case of a public library, security reasons will probably preclude actual check-out of equipment to patrons. A number of libraries now offer coin-operated computers for public use. (See appendix B for a list of vendors and users.) Or, if your budget allows, computer time could be made available to anyone who has a library card and has taken an orientation class covering basics such as how to turn the computer on, how to insert disks and boot the operating system, etc.

If only one or two computers are available to serve an entire school or community, schedules and priorities will have to be carefully planned. You certainly could not teach every student to program. The possibilities would then be to limit use of the computer either to gifted and talented students, and/or to remedial or educationally handicapped students, or to find an application such as an online catalog, which would allow everyone to use the computer and gain some idea of its capabilities. Lunch hours and after school time could be used to provide access to those willing and eager to learn more, perhaps through a computer club. If the *primary* purpose in acquiring the computer is to promote computer literacy, you could either incorporate computer awareness classes into regular library instruction, or circulate equipment to classrooms for special teacher-conducted units, with the media center acting as a coordinator. (See the section, "Arrange Interlibrary Loans …, on page 103.)

Maintain and Circulate Software

Computer software may be cataloged, shelved, and checked out like films, tapes, or other software. However, extra precautions will be necessary due to the special vulnerability of disks. A noncirculating backup collection is essential! Documentation should be circulated with the disks—standard three-ring binders work well, with special plastic pages, obtainable through computer supply catalogs and vendors, for holding disks. It is also a good idea to "write-protect" disks by covering side notches with special tabs made for that purpose (usually included in boxes of new disks). Other considerations in circulating software include precautions against illegal copying and ways of ensuring safe and prompt return of disks. These are problems that are just beginning to be addressed by media specialists, and as yet there are no clear answers. One approach, of course, is to limit software use to library or school premises. Other possibilities include security deposits, or special library cards which can only be obtained by signed agreements to care for disks properly, refrain from copying them and return them promptly. As more libraries begin to acquire and circulate software collections, more methods will be tried; we expect that this will become a frequent topic in professional journals and computer periodicals in the near future.

This brings us to something that is already a frequent and controversial topic of discussion—copyright. As with other media, the area of computer software copyrights is a touchy subject, particularly when applied to educational products. Like video and sound recordings, computer software is often very easy to duplicate, and the prospect can be very tempting. Software *is* expensive, often costing more than the hardware needed to run it. It may seem difficult to accept that a floppy disk containing one program can cost anywhere from $100 to several thousand—until you try to write a program to do the same thing. Like books and films, computer programs take time, expertise, and money to produce. In chapter 2, we gave you some idea of the "chain of command" involving the little silicon chip inside your computer and the seeming ease with which the various devices execute user-designated functions. Computer programming is incredibly complex, as you can discover by taking even an introductory programming course. Try to write a program that successfully computes the square roots of a list of variables, or alphabetizes a list of names, and you begin to appreciate the effort involved in developing a program that acts as a chess partner or prints an itemized inventory for a small business.

From the viewpoint of software manufacturers, educators are crying for good software, but have not indicated much willingness to pay for development costs. Like everyone else (except institutions such as schools and libraries), software companies are in business for more than the satisfaction of creating good products. At the same time, schools and public libraries, handicapped by lack of funds, find it difficult to offer the kind of compensation that results in competitive products. Educators and software developers alike are attempting to find ways of establishing pricing methods that are fair to both, including sliding scales for multiple use.

In the meantime, be aware that unauthorized duplication of software is a clearcut violation of the law, and that you have a legal and moral obligation to uphold the law and work as well as you can within it. Stealing software, though it may seem a justifiable way to cut expenses, will ultimately result in fewer and poorer quality available programs.

Because software is easy to copy, vendors may be reluctant to allow previewing. Some have partially solved the problem by offering demonstration disks that contain sample program functions; others have 30-day return policies. Some programs have built-in "time bombs" that cause the program to fail after a certain number of transactions or records have been entered.

There is a growing supply of software that is considered to be in the public domain and available to anyone who wants it. A good portion of this software, which is available through programs such as Softswap (a source of teacher-tested and evaluated software: see appendix B) and in various periodicals, consists of educational programs. These sources can be used to build your software collection for the cost of disks and postage, but commercial software must be acquired through legitimate channels—that is, bought and paid for. Another consideration is that no service is available for pirated programs—if you run into trouble, you're on your own.

Perhaps the current debate will lead to some mutually beneficial policies. In the meantime, you can help by adhering to the law and working with fellow media specialists, educators, and vendors to create consistent standards for development, evaluation, and pricing of computer software.

Provide Evaluations and Information on Hardware and Software

Just as you now locate filmstrips, records, books, and periodicals to meet specific objectives, you may be expected to locate and evaluate computer equipment and programs, both for library and general use, and to provide instruction. Major sources for descriptions and reviews of computer-related products are periodicals and current users. In the case of software, if at all possible, try to obtain preview privileges, either by trying demo programs or by purchasing programs that have some sort of return policy.

In the previous chapters, we discussed a number of criteria to consider in choosing hardware and software. If, as is likely, you are asked to help evaluate instructional software (also called **courseware**), you will need to consider some additional factors. The educational software market is still very young, and is going through severe growing pains. Finding quality educational programs can be even more difficult than locating other types of software. It would be a waste of money and hardware to purchase software that is no more effective than an inexpensive workbook or that, as is quite possible, actually has more negative than positive results. The information below will provide some helpful guidelines for choosing instructional programs.

Computer-Assisted Instruction, also known as **CAI**, generally falls into one of four categories: Drill and Practice, Tutorial, Simulations, or Games. Programs range from what are essentially mechanized workbooks to sophisticated exercises requiring complex problem-solving skills and strategies. In Computer-Managed Instruction (CMI), the programs include some means for evaluating student progress, ranging from displaying a score on-screen for each program session, to keeping cumulative records for each pupil by name. Some programs allow the instructor to regulate each student's progress by giving him or her access to certain lessons each time the program is used, or offer some other means of controlling the interaction between the computer and each individual. CMI programs may also provide for printouts of scores and evaluations.

Before beginning to shop for instructional programs, the involved teachers and administrators, including the media specialist, should develop a clearly defined set of objectives for computerized instruction. Which students will be involved and to what extent? Is the focus to be remedial, accelerated, standard, or a combination? What will be the program goals? Do they meet an existing curriculum need? Is computerized instruction an appropriate way to achieve them? How will the program be evaluated? Once armed with the answers to these and other questions, you will be able to study periodicals, catalogs, and vendor suggestions for software that might meet your objectives. Remember to consider each program in the context of the way it will be used. What is exciting and appropriate for a fifth grader might be boring and silly to a high school freshman.

A large part of the evaluation process will be subjective, based on the evaluators' perceptions of curriculum objectives, student needs, and computer capabilities. The primary criterion, of course, is whether or not the program achieves the intended objective — that is, does it teach what you want it to teach in a way that encourages, motivates, and reinforces learning. Beyond that, these are some features to watch:

Error Response. Screen messages such as "That's not it, dummy!" (they do exist!) or buzzes, bells, or beeps do not encourage learning. Audible responses have the added disadvantage of advertising to anyone within hearing that the user has made a mistake. A simple message such as "No, that's not it. Try again." is quite sufficient for a drill and practice program. Tutorial programs should allow students to reinforce necessary concepts without belittling them. Any kind of insulting, derogatory, or sarcastic response should automatically eliminate a program from consideration. On the other hand, some programs actually encourage wrong answers with clever graphics or sound effects. These, too, should be avoided.

Feedback and Rewards. Look for programs that give positive reinforcement through screen messages, graphics, or combinations of the two. (Although sound effects can be fun, they can also be extremely distracting to others in the vicinity. If the program does use sound, make sure it can be turned off if necessary.) Many programs can provide personalized responses by having the student type in his or her name at the beginning of the session. Messages such as "That's great, Jeff! Now try this one," are exciting and motivating. Tutorial programs should let the student progress at a rate that is challenging but not frustrating, while games and simulations should give users clear and understandable responses to their actions.

Content Validity and Presentation. An astonishing number of programs contain factual, grammatical, and spelling errors. Watch for them! The manner of presentation also affects a program's effectiveness. The sequence in which information is presented, patterns, etc., should reinforce what is being taught by more traditional methods. This can best be judged by someone accustomed to teaching at the level the program is designed to reach. Programs are more likely to be effective if one or more experienced teachers had a part in their authorship — even the best-intentioned and most creative programmers do not necessarily know what constitutes effective teaching methods. A program may be very clever and creative yet have serious defects which are only apparent to someone with actual classroom experience. Alternatively, some teachers may prefer to write their own programs, using an "authoring program." These are basically preformatted instructional programs that allow a teacher to write the content, including potential user responses and the appropriate program actions. No programming knowledge is necessary to use authoring programs; the only language needed is English. Another idea that has proven successful for at least one school district is to have older students write programs for younger ones. This is a great way for different students to be learning about computers and with computers at the same time!

Program content should also be evaluated on ethical and "humanizing" grounds. Racial, ethnic, and religious prejudice, whether blatant or subtle, has been known to crop up in programs. If at all possible, the program should encourage cooperative behavior and reinforce positive social skills. At the very least, it should not reinforce negative ones.

Ease of Use. Instructions should be clear and easily understandable. Students should be able to use the program by following screen instructions without having to consult a manual, although accompanying workbooks may be useful. The level of difficulty should be appropriate for the potential users. A program for first graders, for example, should not contain a lot of text.

Documentation. This should be geared to the instructor rather than the student, and contain instructional objectives, activity suggestions, explanations for teacher use of student evaluation tools, and so on.

Response Time and User Control. Too short a response time can be frustrating and discouraging; too long a time results in boredom and impatience. Also, the user should be able to control such factors as the rate of screen advance rather than trying to match a built-in pace.

Bombproofing. The program should not **bomb** just because a user inadvertently presses the wrong key. This could be devastating, especially for a first-time or timid user.

Use of the Capabilities of the Computer. Graphics, **interactive** one-on-one responses, and unending patience are computer fortes and should be utilized as fully as possible.

Consistency. This should be in all of the above factors. It would probably be helpful to all staff members to set up a software evaluation file, which could range from a simple card file, to a looseleaf notebook, to a database management file using the media center microcomputer. If standardized forms are provided (see appendix E for examples), staff members could be encouraged to evaluate different software packages and contribute their findings to the file.

Provide Computer Reference Material and Resource Information

Reference material may take the form of books, periodicals, pamphlets, video or cassette tapes, or names, addresses, and phone numbers of organizations or individuals to contact for advice and information. (See appendix B for a list of suggested resources.) Whether or not you have a micro in the media center, you could set up a "computer corner" with reference material and resource information for patrons, teachers, and administrators. You might also hold information sessions, including demonstrations (provided by local vendors?) and guest speakers. Many people are more than willing to talk about their experiences for the benefit of interested audiences.

If such activities seem too time-consuming and/or expensive for your staff and budget, consider banding together with other libraries in the school district or community to plan for and provide computer-related services. Interlibrary loans are another excellent source of reference material, as are the newsletters being published by a number of national and local educational, library services, or computer-oriented groups (see appendix B for list).

Provide Access to Online Databases

This may be one of the most valuable computerized services a secondary school or public library could provide. You may already be using, either independently or through a district media center, the services of one or more of the three bibliographic utilities set up expressly for libraries: OCLC, RLIN (Research Libraries Information Network), or WLN (Washington Library Network). Their services range from search-only access to bibliographic records (RLIN) to extensive acquisitions, cataloging and interlibrary loan assistance (OCLC). In order to utilize the services, you must have a company-provided terminal and either a dedicated line or access through a **dial-up** utility and be able to pay access, use, and service charges. In the case of OCLC and WLN, you must also be able to contribute new records to the database. These costs are in most cases beyond what small libraries can afford to pay. Cooperative memberships, such as on a district level, are one solution. A second and growing possibility is access to dial-up databases via microcomputers, using modems and dial-up utilities. More and more services are becoming both available and affordable not only for small libraries and businesses but for home users as well. Concurrently, the ability to conduct online searches is becoming a valuable skill.

Database services vary widely in the types and amounts of information they make available. Those oriented toward home use, such as The Source and CompuServe, are related mainly to entertainment, travel, and finances, providing airline schedules and reservation confirmations, stock market information, movie reviews, and the like. By contrast, the large information systems such as DIALOG™, a subsidiary of Lockheed Corporation, and BRS offer access to bibliographic, and in some cases statistical, information on literally thousands of subjects. Many of the databases include abstracts as well, and for an extra charge it is possible to have entire articles printed offline and sent to the user as hard copy. Alternatively, located items may be obtained through interlibrary loan.

Online database searching offers considerable advantages over traditional manual search methods:

1) The resulting information is much more comprehensive. At last count, for example, DIALOG made available more than 150 different databases, covering a tremendous range of subjects and types of information. Most of the information is bibliographical, much of it including abstracts; a growing number of databases contain statistical and factual information. Sources include not only books, newspapers,

and magazines, but government documents, professional journals, and research reports.

2) The information is *current*. One of the most up-to-date printed indexes, the *Readers' Guide*, is a good six weeks behind; online databases are updated continuously. In such fast-moving fields as science, medicine, and politics, recent developments can be of major significance. Online databases offer immediate access to information on current thought and events.

3) Access to information is very *fast*. Most online searches may be conducted in 15 minutes or less. The better the search strategy, the less time it takes, which is one reason good search skills are so important. Using a Boolean search strategy with AND and OR and NOT delimiters takes a fraction of the time needed to sort through printed indexes. For example, you could access all the information in a particular database concerning women in business between 1930 and 1950 in the United States, France, and England with one command. This, incidentally, is why the cost of database access may be deceiving. Sixty dollars an hour may sound high, but a search rarely takes that long. Also, many databases may be accessed for considerably less than $60 an hour.

4) Information may be multilingual and international. References will only be limited to English if you specify the limitation!

5) The information will be as *specific* as you want it to be. The Boolean search strategy mentioned above narrows and refines your search criteria to very distinct and manageable limits.

In order to use an information service, all you need are a microcomputer and the software to allow it to "talk" to the database computers, plus a modem and the services of a dial-up utility such as TELENET™ or TYMNET™. Some services charge a one-time membership fee. For each search, the user pays a connect charge, and in some cases a royalty fee, which goes to the producer of the database. Though the charges, which are given at an hourly rate, sound high, most searches take only a few minutes and therefore are not as expensive as they might seem. Also, in many cases discounts are available, depending on how much an organization or group will be using the service. Dial-up utilities, now available in many cities, allow you to dial a local number and access the database at a rate which is considerably less than standard long distance charges. The current reorganization of the phone company, along with technology advances and the growth of competitive services, should bring rates even lower over the next few years.

Most of the information services will provide database catalogs upon request. Some sample databases include "American Men and Women of Science," "America: History and Life," and the "Foundation Directory." Search strategies vary somewhat between services, so it is wise to take advantage of the training sessions the services offer—they are likely to be more cost effective than learning online.

Online databases, with their rapid access to current and comprehensive information, are already beginning to replace printed resource guides. More and more sources such as ERIC (Educational Resources Information Center), *Books in Print*, and *MicroSIFT* (an educational software directory and evaluation guide) are "going online." In the not-so-distant future, many libraries will be expected to provide online access just as they have provided *Readers' Guide* and other printed indexes in the past. As the need for information grows, more and more people will be willing to pay for it. If interest is high enough, it would not be difficult to set up a system in which users pay the connect charge, dial-up charges, and any royalty fee for each search, either at the time of the search or through some sort of regular billing process. With enough users, such a system would actually cost the library very little beyond initial membership fees, if any, and administrative costs, which could be defrayed by adding a slight service charge, or by using volunteers such as computer club members.

Other uses of microcomputers as communications devices include "electronic bulletin boards," electronic mail services, and community newsletters. These may be general message services, such as those offered through several database services, or aimed at specific groups, such as educators, the disabled, or people seeking career and job information.

See appendix B for information on specific information and computer communications services.

Arrange Interlibrary Loans
(including materials located through database searches and computer-related materials)

As rising costs and budget restrictions place more limits on the size and scope of individual library collections, interlibrary loans are becoming more and more essential for providing quality patron service. In addition to the loan assistance provided through information services such as those listed above, many libraries are discovering the rewards of networking on local, state, and national levels. The 1980 *Directory of Library Networks and Cooperative Library Organizations* lists over 600 different groups whose participants are "primarily or exclusively libraries ... [engaged] in cooperative activities that are beyond the scope of traditional interlibrary loan services ... [and] extend beyond reciprocal borrowing [and operate] for the mutual benefit of participating libraries."[6] Activities include acquisitions, cataloging, consulting, equipment sharing, research, warehousing, and more. You might begin with small-scale, localized activities such as exchanging (computerized?) bibliographies of special collections or popular topics with other libraries in your area, or "stretching" limited computer equipment and software by having a centrally located computer lab. Such cooperation can potentially expand the quality and quantity of services each library may offer to an almost infinite degree.

Provide Patron and Staff Instruction
(concerning computers and contribute to computer-related curriculum development)

This could range from simple orientation classes as a prerequisite for using the media center's computer to a complete K-12 computer literacy program. The type and depth of instruction will depend upon who will be using the computers

---

[6]*Directory of Library Networks and Cooperative Library Organizations 1980*, Washington, DC: National Center for Education Statistics, 1981, p. vii.

and to what extent, and your community or school district's computer-related educational priorities. You may want to have open classes for parents or other community members in evenings or on weekends, perhaps using some of the more able and enthusiastic students as instructors (see Sponsor Computer Clubs, below). By charging nominal fees for such sessions you could even raise money for additional hardware and software purchases! Some topics and skills to cover include:

a) history, capabilities, and limitations of computers

b) hardware use

c) software use

d) programming

e) information retrieval via computer, including database searching skills

A great deal of instruction can take place without actually using computers. Keyboarding skills, for example, may be taught using standard electric typewriters, or even cardboard mockups, for all or part of the instruction, at considerably less expense. If typing tutorial programs are used, students could practice on the typewriters and use the computer for taking tests.

Similarly, basic programming skills can be taught using activity books and classroom instruction, with computers, if available, being used only for the final testing of student solutions. Other techniques that have been used successfully include printed practice "keyboards" and exercises in which students act out various computer functions.[7]

The development of full-scale computer literacy curriculums goes considerably beyond the scope of this book. However, since media specialists should be involved in such planning at both school and district levels, we have included a number of resources on the subject in appendix B. You will find these particularly useful if budget and staff restrictions cause the media center to do double duty as a computer center.

Sponsor Computer Clubs

Computer clubs are an excellent way not only to increase computer usage and awareness, but to enlist volunteers for such projects as holding classes for parents and community members, tutoring, writing programs, and raising money for more equipment and software. Some of the sharpest and most creative programmers around are seventh and eighth grade students who spend every possible moment in front of a microcomputer. Why not utilize their talents and enthusiasm? It's quite possible that they could write programs for use in the school or library, and then market them! Tutoring programs in which students teach parents, other students both older and younger, and even teachers, have proven enormously successful in several schools and could work equally well in public libraries. In addition, computer club members could use their skills and the library's or school's computer(s) to raise money. Other ideas include public awareness campaigns, with open houses and demonstrations, community

---

[7]Barbara Feddern, "Playing Computer, a Computer Literacy Activity for the Elementary Grades," *The Computing Teacher* 9 (Oct. 1981): 57-59.

newsletters, and career exploration. Computer enthusiasts tend to be quite self-directed—you might find that the staff time investment for sponsorship could reap some surprising and serendipitous rewards!

Provide Computer-Related Services to the Handicapped

future possibility

Microcomputers offer special advantages to the physically handicapped. For example, touch sensitive screens and/or keyboards are easier to manipulate than pencil and paper. Voice synthesizers, braille keyboards, and other features may be incorporated into micros to offer new capabilities and open new vistas for those who lack speech, vision, or hearing, or have limited movement. Considerable work is being done now to utilize the special properties of micros to supplement the abilities of physically and learning disabled children and adults and to teach them the skills they need to become productive and self-sufficient members of society. Information on technology-related (including microcomputer) services, products, and programs for the handicapped is available through a number of sources, including at least one online electronic bulletin board and a semimonthly newsletter (see appendix B for details). Topics range from computer-assisted instruction for the deaf to computer-driven wheelchairs to special computer input devices for quadriplegics. These and related projects represent some of the most exciting and promising applications of micros, and if your library or media center serves disabled students or community members, you should subscribe to one or more of the pertinent information services.

Provide Information on Community Resources

another function

This could be a good computer club or class project. It could be anything from an online community bulletin board to regular printed lists or newsletters giving information on all sorts of resources, including local media, clinics, support groups, museums, business leaders, workshops, jobs, and special events. A school library media center could even offer this service to the public at a slight charge (another fund-raising possibility)—or instead of charging money, why not "charge" a contribution to the resource list?

Although the computer age will place new demands on nearly everyone in our society, it will also open up wonderful opportunities for increasing our knowledge and capabilities to a degree we are just beginning to visualize. Libraries and media centers can and should be leaders in bringing new resources within reach of their patrons, not only by making those resources accessible, but by providing the skills and knowledge necessary to use them.

6 Choosing and Implementing a Microcomputer System

Probably the most common—and potentially disastrous—"microcomputer mistake" is buying a system without knowing how it is going to be used. Before you even begin to shop for software and hardware, you need to decide whether and how computerization will work in *your* library, keeping in mind that your main objective is to provide the *most needed* services to patrons using available staff, time, and materials. Careful planning at this stage can mean the difference between a computer that sits useless and idle, and one that quickly becomes indispensable. This applies even to any hardware and/or software you may already have—some ways of using it will be more effective than others. In this chapter we will discuss analyzing the needs of your particular library, choosing hardware and software to fit those needs, and incorporating the computer into your present system as smoothly as possible.

DETERMINING YOUR NEEDS

The computerese term for "needs assessment" is "systems analysis." It starts with a careful examination of *current* methods with respect to time requirements, efficiency, and appropriateness for computerization. As you analyze your library, you will probably find that some existing manual methods are quite satisfactory, or require only minor reorganization. Other functions, however, will probably stand out as strong candidates for computerization.

To promote user acceptance of the new system and to justify expenditures to the administration, it would be helpful if the initial project(s), at least, offers high visibility and direct user benefits, that is, somehow makes life easier and/or more satisfying for staff and patrons. Therefore a good place to start your analysis is with the people who will be affected by the change. A formal or informal survey of potential users will help you to discover who is most interested in using the computer, for what purpose(s), and how often, the existing degree of familiarity with computers, and the amount of staff and volunteer time that will be available for computer-related activities, such as data entry, orientation classes, or monitoring of users. Besides offering useful information, such a prepurchase survey can contribute to building a higher acceptance level for the coming changes.

In addition to the human factor, you will also have to consider space needs. Is there room in your library or office for a "computer corner"? What about noise? Perhaps some physical reorganization will be necessary. If so, now is the time to start planning for it. Space availability may turn out to be an important factor in your decisions as to who will use the system and for what purpose(s), and it may also affect your choice of hardware.

Yet another primary consideration in deciding what to computerize is the amount of time and energy you will be able to invest in the selection and implementation process, *including training time.* Although, done properly, computerization will save at least some, and probably a lot, of time once it is in effect, the transition process itself can be very time-consuming. Development time can be anywhere from a few days to several months or even years, depending upon the task(s) involved, the availability of suitable software (which may need to be adapted), the degree of difficulty involved in learning to use the system, and the amount of data to be entered.

A good way to begin your analysis is to keep a log of daily activities. How much time do you spend doing what? If you have other staff members or aides, have them keep logs as well. To make logkeeping easier, use a tally sheet like the sample log on pages 108-109. It is actually a simple spreadsheet, with various activities labeling the horizontal rows, and 15-minute or half hour blocks forming the columns. Each sheet represents a day. By duplicating the sample or a similar spreadsheet, you can keep a log simply by checking the appropriate boxes. It would also be useful to project a year-long tally sheet, breaking down major activities such as ordering and taking inventory.

As an added indicator, we have placed an extra column at the right edge of the sheet headed "C.U." for "Caught up?" You will probably find that certain tasks (such as filing) always have "No" in the "Caught up?" column. These may be just the sort of tasks that could be handled more efficiently with a computer, leaving your time and conscience free for patrons. There are also two additional columns for subjective ratings of the "reward value" of each activity on a scale of 1 to 10, from both a patron and a staff point of view ("Value-P" and "Value-S").

After two or three weeks, you should be able to tell roughly the relative amounts of staff time spent for each type of activity, which functions are the most difficult to maintain, and which activities are most rewarding for patrons and/or staff. Now you may begin to analyze each activity to determine whether it is a suitable candidate for computerization.

You may want to create another chart at this point, with cells defined by the various activities on one side and computerization criteria on the other. Or make a checklist, with a separate copy for each activity. The questions you should ask about each activity include: whether the task is the sort that computers do well (remember that computers excel at tasks that are repetitive, quantitative, routine, voluminous, simple, logical, and straightforward, and that require accuracy and precision);[8] whether software is currently available to perform it; how visible the system would be; what user benefits it offers, both direct and indirect; time and cost estimates for computerization; how well or how poorly the current method for the task works (including cost effectiveness); and how much resistance there might be to changing it.

Once you have evaluated each activity according to the above criteria, you should be able to list several tasks that look like good prospects for computerization. Now is the time to begin thinking in terms of long range planning and implementation. As we stated earlier, you are more likely to be successful if you build your system in steps, completing each transition before beginning another. Eventually you may wish to incorporate several or all of the

---

[8]William T. Cound, *Colonet, Microcomputers in Libraries,* Denver: Colorado State Library Network, 1982, pp. 1-4.

Sample Log

Activity	8:00	9:00	10:00	11:00	12:00	1:00	2:00	3:00	4:00	5:00	Evening	Caught up?	Value-P	Value-S
Processing:														
Books														
Media														
Periodicals														
Equipment														
Circulation:														
Check-in/out														
Overdues														
Inventory														
Weeding														
Shelving														
Ordering														
File Maintenance:														
Cards														
Vertical														
Poster														
Picture														
Catalogs														
Patron Assistance:														
Students														
Teachers														
Instruction:														
Group														
Individual														

Production:														
Video														
Photos														
Tapes														
Slides														
Lamination														
Transparencies														
Equipment Maintenance														
Mending														
Reports														
Scheduling														
Stories														
Special Activities														

eligible functions into your computer system, but to start, pick one or two that are relatively simple and low pressure. For example, unless you have a lot of assistance, avoid a task that requires daily upkeep, such as circulation. This will give you and everyone else time to become familiar and comfortable with the computer. You may want to designate primary and secondary uses for the system: for example, a computer might be used for instruction or networking in the morning, for administrative tasks in the afternoon, and for computer club projects in the evening. If other media specialists in the district are considering computerization, individuals or teams might tackle different applications, sharing experiences with the group as a whole. This approach could also be used, for example, to develop standardized district forms for inventory and file management systems.

Besides the ideas offered in the preceding chapters, you can find many suggestions in educational, library, and computer periodicals, as well as by talking to people who have already had some experience with library computerization. (Some possible contacts are listed in appendix B; there are bound to be others in your community or nearby who would be happy to share their experiences.) It is also a good idea to invite input from staff members, from patrons, and from the community. Besides offering suggestions, people may wish to get involved in fund-raising activities to help in computer purchases (see appendix D). The acceptance level for the new system is also likely to be higher if people feel they have had a part in its acquisition.

Once you have decided what function(s) you want to computerize, it's time to get specific. The better you are able to define for the vendor (and the budget committee or purchasing department) exactly what you need in terms of volume, speed, accuracy, response, and specific functions, the more likely you are to get it. If, as is likely, you are purchasing your system through a bid process, knowing how to ask for what you want becomes even more important.

Begin by analyzing the method you are currently using for the task(s) involved. A good way to do this is to use a favorite tool of programmers—the flow chart. A flow chart is simply a diagram of a process, broken down into steps. The steps are placed in different-shaped boxes according to type, for example, rectangular for a definitive action, or diamond-shaped for a decision (always Yes or No). Figure 6.1 is a simple flow chart for checking out a book. Depending on the outcome of a decision box, the process either returns to an earlier step or skips ahead. Flow charting requires you to be very specific and detailed about the process you are describing, and also provides a graphic illustration of the feasibility of computerizing it. You may find yourself "going to" one of the preliminary selection processes described earlier if the application you chose is not really suitable, or if you discover that making a simple change or two in your current method would actually be just as effective as computerizing it. If the application you wish to implement is something altogether new, such as one of the networking systems described in chapter 5, rather than an automation of a current function, use a flow chart to describe the way the system should work.

The second step, using the flow chart analysis from step 1, is to prepare a written statement describing *exactly* what you want the system to do, how it will be used, and by whom. The object of this statement is to give everyone, including you, the vendor, your administration, and the purchasing department, a precise view of the objectives and goals of the computerization project. Clearly defined

Figure 6.1. A Simple Flow Chart

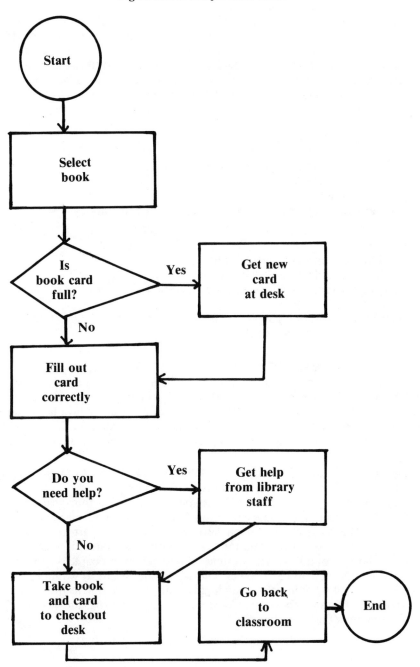

written objectives will also give you a tool for evaluating your progress later. If part of the objective is to become more cost effective (which may include salary savings due to less clerical time, etc.), be specific about the expected savings, some of which may be long term. Include a list of the expected benefits to patrons, such as increased staff availability, increased access to resources, and so on. You may want to include a cost comparison of traditional methods versus computerization. A sample comparison of a card catalog versus an online catalog for a new school, including a list of patron benefits, appears below:

To: Mr. V. I. Person and the Board of Education
From: Meade A. Specialist
Date: May 5, 1983
Regarding: Computerization of the Modernview Card Catalog

PURPOSE:
1. Developing a more efficient media management system
2. Promoting student computer literacy
3. Making the entire media/library collection readily accessible to teachers and students
4. Saving time for library staff, teachers, and students seeking information (less than 3 seconds to find a title or subject)

WHY LOOK AT A COMPUTER?
Considerable time and resources are required for organizing a new library. Rex O. Mend of the State Library has advised us to computerize our card catalog now, since it would be cost effective, excellent software is available, and the system is working well in Success Elementary in Nexttown. If we were not creating a new library collection this procedure would not be as cost effective.

WHAT ARE THE COSTS OF A COMPUTERIZED CATALOG PROGRAM COMPARED WITH A TRADITIONAL CATALOG?
These costs are for 4,000 library volumes purchased over a four-year period and 1,950 other media, including educational kits, filmstrips, magazines, prints, films, etc. The costs are based on current salaries of a part-time aide and a librarian, and do not reflect inflation. The 1983 summer salary is $7.00 per hour, and the average contracted school time salaries for both people is $11.50 ($7.00 per hour for the aide and $14.00 per hour for the librarian). It would appear that the librarian will be doing more cataloging than the aide due to the limited time the aide would be available on the Modernview Library Program. The $11.50 per hour estimate is therefore low.

	Four Year Costs for Conventional Card Catalog Setup	**Four Year Costs for the Computer Catalog Setup**
Summer 1983 1,000 titles	6 books/hr @ $7.00/hr 166 hrs = $ 1,162.	30 books/hr @ $7.00/hr 33 hrs = $ 231.
750 media	3 media/hr @ $7.00/hr 250 hrs = $ 1,750.	30 media/hr @ $7.00/hr 5 hrs = $ 380.
Winter/Spring 1984 1,000 titles	6 books/hr @ $11.50/hr 166 hrs = $ 1,909.	30 books/hr @ $11.50/hr 33 hrs = $ 380.
500 media	3 media/hr @ $11.50/hr 167 hrs = $ 1,920.	30 media/hr @ $11.50/hr 17 hrs = $ 196.
Winter/Spring 1985 1,000 titles	6 books/hr @ $11.50/hr 166 hrs = $ 1,909.	30 books/hr @ $11.50/hr 33 hrs = $ 380.
350 media	3 media/hr @ $11.50/hr 116 hrs = $ 1,334.	30 media/hr @ $11.50/hr 11 hrs = $ 127.
Equipment to do Cataloging	Card Catalog Furniture and Cards = $ 2,000.	Microcomputer, Hard Disk Printer, Training = $ 9,445.
TOTAL	Conventional System Total = $15,227.	Computer System Total = $11,441.

EQUIPMENT NEEDED
1. 48K microcomputer
2. Hard disk drive
3. Floppy disk drive
4. TV monitor
5. Printer
6. Software

UNIQUE ADVANTAGES OF THE COMPUTER CATALOGING PROGRAM
1. Arouses natural curiosity about computers.
2. The computer lists subject/title/author indexes, and provides many more cross-referencing suggestions than do most catalogs.
3. Requires less skill in alphabetizing, spelling, and filing which makes many more opportunities available for research to elementary school children.
4. Computer stores an inventory that can be retrieved as printed lists.
5. The computer system eliminates the need for multiple cards and prevents filing backlogs.

6. In addition to library uses the system can be used to keep track of all school textbooks, workbooks, and other instructional materials in the building.

7. Instant catalog changes are possible.

8. No cards to file or withdraw.

9. All holdings (books and materials) are integrated into a single catalog. Includes articles from periodicals, poster file, and pamphlet file, which is not possible with a card catalog.

10. Cost of maintaining the catalog is more predictable and not as dependent on extra aide time or money available.

11. Makes more time available for helping users, teaching students, and creative use of media instead of tedious typing and filing tasks.

RECOMMENDATION

We purchase necessary equipment to place Modernview Library materials into a computerized program since the program is financially sound, administratively efficient, and educationally beneficial to the entire curricular program.*

Next, list your requirements for hardware and peripherals, including any special features, such as color graphics capability or letter-quality printing. The list should be divided into two parts—*must haves* and *would likes*. Do the same for software. Include the number of records the system must be able to handle, the size of the records, the average frequency of usage for each record, the response time and speeds needed, and the degree of accuracy required. (Refer to chapters 2, 3, and 4 for some general and specific criteria for hardware and software choices.) It may be helpful to prepare comparison charts, using your required and desirable features as criteria to evaluate various hardware and software choices. (Sample comparison charts may be found in appendix E.) If your research (reviews, interviews with experienced users, etc.) and preliminary evaluations indicate specific equipment and programs you think may fit your needs, include them as suggestions. You may feel very strongly that a certain brand of hardware or a specific program is what you want. If so, go ahead and include it as a requirement, but keep in mind that there may be products your dealer knows about that have not surfaced in your research and that might be ideal for your purposes. If a vendor does recommend a product you have not heard of, you can use the comparison charts to evaluate it.

The next section of your specifications is the part that protects you from unpleasant surprises. It spells out the obligations of the prospective vendor with respect to accountability, delivery and installation, experience, references, service and support (including training), system compatibility, and equipment and software guarantees. The list should include:

1) Demonstrations

The vendor must be able to demonstrate the hardware and software in a school or library setting at your request. In the fast-moving and highly competitve microcomputer industry, many manufacturers have ideas that outpace their capabilities. *See it work before you buy.* Better yet, use it

---

*Based on a proposal submitted by Dr. Clark L. Milsom, Principal, Skyview Elementary, Windsor, CO.

yourself. Also, keep in mind that many demonstration programs are abbreviated versions, and as such handle less data but at a faster speed than the actual program. This is especially true in the case of database management systems. If you can, get specific figures on what differences to expect.

2) References

The dealer should furnish a list, with contact names and phone numbers, of customers in the educational or library field, whose needs are similar to yours. Once you have this list, use it. Most people are quite willing to share their experiences with you, both good and bad. If the vendor is unwilling or unable to furnish references, find a different vendor.

The dealer should also be able to verify that the hardware and software have been in use by at least five educational or library customers for a minimum of three months. The exception to this would be customized software or a test site project for which you are prepared to deal with the debugging process. In the latter case, verifying the dealer qualifications and references is especially important.

3) Equipment

If you have made any suggestions as to specific brands and models, the vendor should ensure that the equipment named in the actual bid is equal or superior. In any case, it must be capable of running the software (which ideally has been chosen first). Also, any necessary cables, interfaces, or other special equipment must be included in the original bid price. Surprise add-ons could prove very costly.

The above also holds true with respect to delivery and installation costs. State that all necessary services must be included in the package price, whether specified or not. Your specifications should indicate the location or locations and a fixed date for delivery, with a penalty clause for late delivery.

In addition, if you have plans for future expansion, such as to a multi-user system, find out if the dealer is capable of providing those services and products as well. Otherwise, you may find yourself caught in a bind between or among dealers, with no one willing to accept responsibility.

4) Training and Follow-up Assistance

The dealer should provide a minimum of two hours of on-site staff training in basic use and maintenance of the system, with the cost of further training, if needed, specified in the bid. You should also have telephone access to someone qualified to answer the inevitable questions about the software. (Though this service should be available, and is one of the primary reasons to buy from a local dealer rather than through mail order, it should not be abused. Manuals are included for a purpose!)

If your project is ambitious and/or staff members have little or no experience with computers, you may wish to investigate the option of a short term "handholding contract" providing intensive support during the early stages of implementation.

5) Service Contracts and Warranties

Accept bids only from authorized dealers, and specify that all equipment must be factory-approved and warranted for a minimum of 90 days, with free repair or replacement. You may wish to require an extended service contract for up to a year, possibly even including training of district service personnel, and availability of loaner equipment if necessary.

In reviewing the bids, remember that cost is not the most important consideration. For this reason, you must be prepared to defend your vendor choice to the budget committees and/or purchasing department. We hope we have given enough emphasis to the crucial importance of dealer support in purchasing a computer system. Microcomputers are particularly vulnerable to bargain backfires, and what seems like a good deal could become very costly all too soon. One way to help bring costs down is to buy "in bulk," with a district (or even several) ordering en masse. This, of course, would require careful cooperative planning, but could result in considerable savings.

Though all of this may seem like a long, complicated process, in the long run (and perhaps sooner) it will save you both time and money, not to mention irritation. If you are working with prepurchased hardware and/or software, use it as a starting point for your specifications, incorporating it into your comparison charts to guide you in choosing potential applications as well as software and peripherals. You may have to use extra thought and imagination in order to turn a potential white elephant into a wise and rewarding investment. It is highly probable that an already-purchased computer will by its very existence be justification for additional purchases, such as disk drives or a printer, if it is of little or no value otherwise. Also, remember that just because your library already possesses a certain type of computer, all future applications are not necessarily limited to that type. The nature of microcomputers can allow for an effective system consisting of several independent subsystems, which may use different types of computers altogether.

IMPLEMENTING YOUR NEW
COMPUTER SYSTEM

Now that you have planned for and selected a microcomputer system and outlined one or more proposed uses for it, how can you ensure that it will be used as effectively and beneficially as possible? What are the pitfalls to avoid, and the steps to take to ease the transition for staff and patrons alike? How will you evaluate the progress of your program in terms of cost effectiveness and improved services? And how do you determine the possibilities and directions for growth?

The first thing you should realize is that the implementation process is bound to take longer than you think it will, even if no significant problems develop. Therefore, it would be wise to double or even triple your original estimates for completing each step, at least when setting up time frames for the benefit of administrators, staff members, patrons, and parents. If you purchase a circulation system in September and hope to have your entire collection online by the time school reopens in January, *plan* for a completion date sometime in April. This will prevent a lot of unrealistic expectations and resulting tension. If you should finish by January, wonderful! — consider it a bonus and go on to the next step. You might even set up two time tables, one ideal and one based on everything you can imagine going wrong, and see where you come out.

We *strongly* advise you to keep a computer journal, beginning no later than the date your system is delivered and installed. A day-by-day record of computer events—what you or someone else did and how the computer responded, procedures, problems, accomplishments—will be enormously useful for maintaining consistency, as well as debugging and troubleshooting. Also, in the case of staff turnover, new members will have a basis from which to start. A system that is known by only one person is utterly useless if that person should happen to leave. Keep the journal by the computer and encourage users to make entries in it—including subjective responses! If your computer is being used by both staff and patrons, you might want to keep two journals, one for staff and one for general use. This would be an excellent way to evaluate progress and plan for future computer projects.

You should do some preparation before the computer's arrival. This includes setting up a "computer corner" in the library or an office, deciding who will be using it and when, and doing some preliminary training and orientation. User preparation is extremely important! You will no doubt encounter a full range of attitudes toward the new acquisition, from enthusiasm to timid curiosity to outright resistance. With luck, at least one staff member (yourself?) will fall into the enthusiastic category; this person or persons will probably be the best choice(s) for getting the project underway. They should attend training sessions offered by or arranged through the vendor, and be given access to manuals and any other information that will help them to feel at ease with the computer when it arrives. If possible, they should take an introductory programming course through a local college or adult education program. Also, try to recruit student, patron, teacher, and/or parent volunteers, either people who have computers at home or at work and therefore have at least some experience with micros, or who are highly motivated to work with them. Don't try to do the whole project yourself if you can get help! Note, however, that at this stage you need people who are self-starters and able to learn a lot on their own. Later they can help everyone else play catch-up.

During the preparation phase you should also give noninvolved patrons and staff members notice that a change is coming. This "publicity campaign" could be anything from printed announcements or newsletter articles to orientation classes giving a brief overview of computers in general and your new system in particular. Include a list of benefits, but don't get carried away. Unrealistic expectations could mean trouble if the system does not live up to its advance billing.

Once the computer arrives, those staff members who will be primarily responsible for its use should spend some time getting acquainted with it, perhaps taking it home overnight or on weekends. As soon as one or two people are comfortable with it, they can start implementing the first application. This process will depend on what is being computerized. If it is a cataloging or circulation system, the initial stages will consist primarily of data entry. If you are developing your own inventory system using a database management system, the first step (after learning the basics of the program) will be to design some screens and begin setting up files. (Note: In any program that involves data management, whether specific or general, it is a good idea to enter 25 or 30 items and try generating some reports before entering any more, in order to discover any problems as early as possible.) If your first program is a word processing package, you could begin by sending out a "computerized" newsletter announcing the new arrival.

The idea is to start with something simple and low pressure, until you are sure there are no serious hardware or software problems and involved staff members are familiar with basic procedures. Make sure you allow plenty of time for the initial training period. This is liable to be the most frustrating phase of computerization, since everyone is dealing with something new and strange on top of trying to keep up with what is probably already a heavy work load. Patience is the key! Once you get to the "How did we ever live without it?" stage, it will be worth all the frustration.

If you are computerizing an existing function, such as circulation or cataloging, do not be in a hurry to retire the old system. In most cases the transition should be fairly gradual, with the manual method and the computer method running parallel until the new system is "up" and operational and necessary data entry is complete. Besides giving everyone time to become familiar with the new system, this ensures that you have a backup in case something goes wrong. For instance, you might start an online catalog by entering only new acquisitions for the first month or two, keeping the card catalog for your existing collection. Then, once you are sure the system is working and as time permits, you can begin entering items from the card catalog, taking the opportunity to weed as you go. Depending on the size of your collection, this process could take anywhere from a few months to a few years.

In the beginning, at least, do not attempt to upgrade your system at the same time you are computerizing it. Get the basics first and add the frills later. For example, if you are computerizing your overdue system, and your present method lets you send out notices two weeks after books are due, don't plan to start sending notices the *day* books become overdue instead—at least not right away.

 If patrons are going to be using the computer, the next step will be some sort of orientation program. Orientation can begin even before the computer is ready to use, with demonstrations, descriptions, and class exercises such as "playing computer." At some point, however, each user should have some hands-on experience in the basics of operation—turning on the computer, inserting a disk or cassette, loading a program, etc. The peer-tutoring method works well here. You or another staff member can instruct two or three especially interested students or patrons who in turn will serve as instructors. Orientation sessions could be held on a class by class basis, or, in the case of a public library, once or twice a week (more often with volunteer tutors). Even though everyone who uses the computer will have to go through the orientation, you will probably want to have staff or volunteer monitors available whenever the computer is in use.

Orientation classes are one way to help overcome "technophobia," which is more likely to afflict staff members than patrons. There are a number of reasons for this fear of computers, ranging from nervousness about breaking the computer to fear of being replaced by it. In the first instance, it may be helpful to draw analogies between computers and more familiar equipment such as movie projectors or tape recorders. Selecting and running a program is not so different from selecting and showing a film. In each case, a specific objective is involved, and a specific process is necessary to achieve the objective. Inserting a disk into a drive is actually less complicated than inserting film into a projector. Demonstrations and hands-on trials help to overcome fears of breaking the computer by striking the wrong key, etc. Fear of replacement, or simply a resistance to change, is harder to deal with, and may, in fact, be manifested as overt hostility. For these people you will need to stress the benefits of the computer as a *tool* while making its limitations very clear. If you have involved people from the beginning, your chances of problems at this stage will be lessened.

In order to cut down on staff time and increase user-independence, it is a good idea to have some sort of user's guide at or near the computer station. Include such things as the basics of machine operation, a program catalog, a glossary, and perhaps a bibliography of resource material. Alternatively, you might "decorate" the area around the computer station with posters or flashcards depicting the various steps of operation, such as inserting a disk, along with terminology and things to remember, for example, "Don't touch the shiny part!" captioning a picture of a disk.

Early in the implementation process, make a list of definite rules for using the computer, and keep a copy at the computer station. Include which periods the computer is to be used for each purpose, the number of persons who may be at the computer at any one time, the length of time each person is allowed to use the computer during one session, allowable noise levels, rules for scheduling, and so on. The actual rules structure will depend on your computer priorities and the amount of time available (you will soon find there is never enough). Sign-up sheets are one way to handle scheduling, with limits on the number of times each person may use the computer during a given period of time. Or computer time may be scheduled by class. If you have an online catalog or other type of database searching service, time limits may be set according to whether or not others are waiting to use the computer. You will also need to set rules for disk space usage, printer use, and so on, if these are factors.

If the computer is to be available for general patron use, you will have to decide whether to allow game playing. This is a subject of some debate. Some people feel that games increase the noise and general commotion level and serve no useful purpose, while others believe that they serve as motivation for students to learn more about computers. They may also be used as "rewards" for accomplishing more instructional tasks. If you do decide to allow games, be prepared for more scheduling and noise problems. You might want to limit game playing to lunch or after school hours, or only allow educational and/or user-written games to be played.

Another consideration is the matter of security. Hardware is best protected with locks (including bolt-down equipment or lockable carrels), sign-up or sign-out sheets, and staff monitors, just as you protect other types of equipment. In the case of software, your best protection is a backup collection, *including documentation*. If possible, keep master copies of software in a place other than the library.

Smooth implementation is a matter of planning, patience, and realistic expectations. Ideally, you have purchased a system from a local vendor who will be able to help you through the initial get-acquainted process and deal with any bugs or unusual problems that come up. You are paying for this service, so take advantage of it—but don't abuse it. In summary, think ahead, take your time, involve others, and have fun! Good luck, and welcome to the Computer Age!

7 A Case Study: One Librarian's "Micro Conversion"

Being married to a computer professional has meant that computers have had a slightly more than average impact on my life. Until about 1977, however, that impact consisted mostly of late night phone calls and interrupted vacations due to various computer crises. When the first microcomputer kits came out in the mid-1970s, we naturally had one in our basement. Within a year the original kit was replaced by a more complex and capable machine, but computers had not yet captured my interest.

During that same period, the district where I worked as a library media specialist had acquired the use of a mainframe computer and building inventories. Unfortunately, the system took several years to get into working order, during which time teachers and administrators at building level had to deal with its growing pains. The printout lists we received came in no definable order. One cassette recorder might appear on page 1 and another on page 15. Other items appeared more than once, with different identification numbers and different descriptions. Further, the printouts were organized differently every year.

I was becoming increasingly frustrated trying to reconcile the district lists with my own inventory reports, until I thought of a practical use for my husband's grown-up toy. At my request, he wrote a program that allowed me to store my equipment inventory records and retrieve them in multiple ways. Instead of writing and organizing file cards, I was bringing home records and entering them into the computer using a fill-in screen. Once entered, the inventory items could be retrieved by any field and printed out in easy-to-follow lists. The success of what was a relatively simple program had a radical effect on my ideas both about computers and about library management.

In the fall of 1980 I became library media specialist at a brand new elementary school, under a principal who was eager to incorporate microcomputers into the library from the beginning. Our objectives were twofold: first, to make library resources readily available to both staff and students, and second, to give every student an opportunity to actually use a computer and learn to regard it as a useful tool. The method we chose was ambitious—more so than we realized at the time. Rather than purchasing a traditional card catalog system, we elected to put our library's catalog on a microcomputer.

Putting a collection of more than two or three thousand items on floppy disks was just not feasible. At that time, however, hard disks had just come onto the market, and increased storage availability made a mirocomputer catalog a real possibility. The school district had already purchased several Apple computers, which meant we were in the position of finding software to fit our existing hardware. An exhaustive search, however, did not turn up anyone who had written a catalog program for an Apple or any other micro. Since the district did not have an in-house programming staff, we decided to use Software Acquisition Method Number Two, and find someone to write a custom program to our specifications.

Fired by dreams of an accessible, easy-to-use, and always-current catalog, I wrote out the functional specifications, with technical assistance from my "in-house" consultant-husband. The proposal was put out for bid and awarded to a local computer dealer who hired a leading Apple programmer to write the catalog. Although it was a custom program, the dealer recognized its marketing possibilities, and proposed a contract giving us the software at a volume price if we would agree to serve as a test site. The software was to be written, delivered, and tested in several phases.

What followed was one of the most intensely frustrating, exciting, and rewarding periods of my library career. Though being a test site meant dealing with all the inevitable bugs, delays, and difficulties, it also meant being part of the discovery and development of something totally new and different and exciting. The major obstacles I had encountered in my 10 years as a library media specialist were the lack of time left over from routine clerical and management duties, and the reluctance of students and staff members to acquire and use library skills. Therefore, I found the idea of an accessible, easy, and even fun to use system exhilarating enough to boost me through the difficulties of implementing it.

We received the first portion of the program, for manual data entry, that October, and my aide and I began entering our collection, typing information from shelf cards into a fill-in screen on the computer, and storing the data on floppy disks (see screen, page 122). (A second data entry phase arrived later in the fall, which enabled us to transfer information directly from the district OCLC catalog to our own.) At that time my only experience with microcomputers had been using the equipment inventory program, plus a 10-hour dealer-taught course on "How to Use the Apple"; my aide had no computer experience at all. Both of us were average typists; we found we could enter about 50 records an hour.

During that first semester we did not have a card catalog. Few new schools do, since setting up a traditional card catalog, with the large amounts of filing involved, is also a lengthy process. By December, the "look-up" portion of the program had arrived. We transferred our floppy disk data to the hard disk, and when the students returned to school after Christmas we introduced them to our "card catalog," which by then had been christened "Computer Cat."

Although the catalog was new to the students, the computer was not. During that first semester everyone was introduced to the computer and had an opportunity to use it. We labeled all of the components (and left them labeled), for example, monitor, keyboard, disk drive, etc. Two copies of *The Computer Alphabet Book*, by Elizabeth Wall, taken apart and laminated, became giant flashcards for teaching computer vocabulary. Each student learned how to turn on the computer and monitor and boot a disk, and how to do two simple programs, writing either his or her own or teacher's name across the screen in different ways (see screens, pages 123-126). Little "Apple reminders" posted behind the computer reminded students that "HOME" clears the screen, "NEW"

(Text continues on page 127.)

```
ACCESSION NO. __  _____        NO. VOLS. __

LOCATION _____                 STATUS_____
MEDIA TYPE___
CALL. NO. _____
              ___

    AUTHOR_____

    TITLE_____

      PUBLISHER_____
      COPYRIGHT_____    PURCH__ /__(MMYY)

      COST $ ____.__         FUND ____

    SUBJECT  _____
    -OR      _____
    COMMENT  _____
    --       _____


   (RETURN) = AHEAD     (ESC) =BACK
   CTL-F  = FILE NOW    CTL-E = END MODE
```

The data entry screen from Computer Cat™.

```
10 PRINT "  MICROS ARE IN  "

20 GOTO 10

RUN
```

The screens on pages 123-126 show two simple programs and the resulting screens. Note the difference made by adding a semi-colon to the PRINT command.

```
MICROS ARE IN
MICROS ARE IN
MICROS ARE IN
MICROS ARE IN
MICROS ARE IN
MICROS ARE IN
MICROS ARE IN
MICROS ARE IN
MICROS ARE IN
MICROS ARE IN
MICROS ARE IN
MICROS ARE IN
MICROS ARE IN
MICROS ARE IN
MICROS ARE IN
MICROS ARE IN
MICROS ARE IN
MICROS ARE IN
MICROS ARE IN
MICROS ARE IN
MICROS ARE IN
MICROS ARE IN
MICROS ARE IN
```

```
10 PRINT " MICROS ARE IN " ;

20 GOTO 10

RUN
```

```
MICROS ARE IN  MICROS ARE IN  MICROS ARE
N  MICROS ARE IN  MICROS ARE IN  MICROS
 IN  MICROS ARE IN  MICROS ARE IN  MICRO
RE IN  MICROS ARE IN  MICROS ARE IN  MIC
 ARE IN  MICROS ARE IN  MICROS ARE IN  M
OS ARE IN  MICROS ARE IN  MICROS ARE IN
CROS ARE IN  MICROS ARE IN  MICROS ARE I
MICROS ARE IN  MICROS ARE IN  MICROS ARE
N  MICROS ARE IN  MICROS ARE IN  MICROS
 IN  MICROS ARE IN  MICROS ARE IN  MICRO
RE IN  MICROS ARE IN  MICROS ARE IN  MIC
 ARE IN  MICROS ARE IN  MICROS ARE IN  M
OS ARE IN  MICROS ARE IN  MICROS ARE IN
CROS ARE IN  MICROS ARE IN  MICROS ARE I
MICROS ARE IN  MICROS ARE IN  MICROS ARE
N  MICROS ARE IN  MICROS ARE IN  MICROS
 IN  MICROS ARE IN  MICROS ARE IN  MICRO
RE IN  MICROS ARE IN  MICROS ARE IN  MIC
 ARE IN  MICROS ARE IN  MICROS ARE IN  M
OS ARE IN  MICROS ARE IN  MICROS ARE IN
CROS ARE IN  MICROS ARE IN  MICROS ARE I
MICROS ARE IN  MICROS ARE IN  MICROS ARE
N  MICROS ARE IN  MICROS ARE IN  MICROS
 IN  MICROS ARE IN  MICROS ARE IN  MICRO
```

clears the computer for a new program, "PR#6" boots a disk, and so on, and cautioned them to "Hold the disk by the label" and "Read directions first!"

The children went through the computer introduction by the peer tutoring method. Each class sent two students who went through the flash cards and sample programs with me; the first two taught the next two, who taught the next two, and so on until everyone had had the opportunity to type something into the computer and see it on the screen. The entire school, from first through sixth grades, went through the mini course, including learning disabled children.

Even though we had not finished entering the entire collection, everyone was encouraged to use the computer catalog when school resumed after the holidays. For orientation, the computer was hooked up to a 19-inch TV monitor and the students sat on the floor and watched as each classmate searched on the computer, wrote down a call number, and went to the shelves to find the corresponding item (see screens, pages 128-29). The fact that data entry was incomplete actually turned out to be an advantage, since it acquainted students with an important part of the system—"I don't find anything on.... Please ask your librarian." The resulting student and staff input has proven immensely valuable in building the cross-reference, see, and see also section of the catalog.

The summer and fall of 1981 were spent adding nonprint media, vertical file items, and a collection of leased media to the catalog. A Computer Cat search on a given subject therefore turns up not only all applicable books, but filmstrips, records, and vertical file items as well. The catalog may even be expanded to include community resources. One district that later purchased the program, for example, added locally available speakers on given subjects. For small neighboring schools and/or public libraries, multiple collection catalogs with location codes could facilitate interlibrary loans.

Computer Cat has features that make it especially suitable for use by elementary students who are just developing spelling and alphabetizing skills. The program will conduct a search on an entry as brief as one letter, so anyone who is unsure about spelling can type in only as much of the word as he or she knows, for example, DINO for dinosaurs, and receive a response. Students who are unfamiliar with the keyboard are encouraged to find the first three letters of the word before starting to type. Besides reinforcing basic skills, the program seems to encourage students to read subject headings more closely.

Even during the first semester it was in use, Computer Cat produced some unexpected benefits. For example, the program reinforces the concepts of subject, author, and title, which are ordinarily difficult for students to grasp. A student typing in "Seuss" for a subject search discovers that the computer cannot find any books under that subject and that he or she should consult the librarian, who will explain that "Seuss" is an author and not a subject heading. In the same way, a search for books by "Beverly Cleary" instead of "Cleary, Beverly" would lead back to the librarian and the realization that an author search is conducted using the last name first (see screen, page 130).

Among the more helpful services a library may provide are bibliographies on various topics. In the past this meant manually compiling, typing, and running off dittoed lists—a painstaking and time-consuming process. Also, although bibliographies could be recycled from year to year, it was difficult or impossible to keep them current. With Computer Cat, obtaining a complete and current bibliography on any subject requires nothing more than doing a quick subject search and having the program print the results. This makes it possible for

(Text continues on page 131.)

```
LOOKING FOR SUBJECT PETS


A #PET STORIES
B PETS &...
C HAMSTERS...
D CAPYBOPPY


   _ _ _ _ _ _ _ _ _
  _____


S PETS-VF (636,)
T #HAMSTER WHO HID, THE

PUSH THE LETTER OF THE ITEM YOU
WOULD LIKE TO SEE OR (SPACE)
TO KEEP LOOKING
```

An option screen from Computer Cat™. Selecting option "D" results in the display shown in the screen opposite.

```
ITEM D


599.3       CAPYBOPPY
PEE
            BY PEET, BILL

            PUBLISHER HOUGHTON MIFFLIN

            COPYRIGHT 1966


SUBJECTS
            CAPYBARAS
            PETS

(SPACE) SEE THE LIST AGAIN
ANY LETTER A TO T SEE THAT ITEM
(CTRL) AND P TO PRINT THIS
(ESC) START OVER
```

An onscreen "catalog card" from Computer Cat™.

```
LOOKING FOR SUBJECT CLEARY

I'M SORRY, BUT I CAN'T FIND ANY

ITEMS ON CLEARY


PLEASE ASK THE LIBRARIAN




PRESS ANY KEY TO CONTINUE
```

An unsuccessful subject search leads to the librarian.

teachers to obtain printed bibliographies on as little as a day's notice for subject units or special class projects. The bibliographies can be distributed for research projects, and/or kept in teachers' unit files for annotation and year-to-year updates. In addition, bibliographies on most-requested subjects may be printed and kept available in the library for patron use.

Computer Cat can be used to print other types of "bibliographies" as well, for ordering and inventory purposes. Information on items can be retrieved by any field, including publisher, copyright date, and price (see screen below).

```
                    EXECUTIVE MODE
     LOCATION                  STATUS
     MEDIA TYPE
     CALL NO      599.3
                  PEE

     AUTHOR    PEET,BILL
     TITLE     CAPYBOPPY
     PUBLISHER  HOUGHTON MIFFLIN
     COPYRIGHT  66       PURCH 6/81
     ACCESSION #81-171  COST $ 7.20

     SUBJECTS:

        CAPYBARAS
        PETS




     C)CHANGE    D)DELETE   P)PRINT
```

A Computer Cat™ record shown in the "Executive mode." Note the additional fields, as opposed to the standard "catalog card" shown on page 129.

This feature makes the system marvelous for preventing duplications and weeding out obsolete items. In addition, the library need not close down for inventory, since items may also be listed in shelf order. We set up a continuous inventory system, section by section — the 600s in January, 700s in February, and so on. A printed shelf list may be easily checked against shelves and charge tray without any interruption in service. (The only exception to this is Easy Fiction, where the turnover is very great; this section is best done the last week or two of school.)

Another service I always wanted to provide and never seemed to have time for is an extensive cross-reference system. The first cross-reference to go on Computer Cat was of course "CARS—See subject AUTOMOBILE" (see screen below).

```
LOOKING FOR SUBJECT CARS

A   SEE SUBJECT 'AUTOMOBILE'
B   SEE ALSO 'VEHICLES'










PUSH THE LETTER OF THE ITEM YOU
WOULD LIKE TO SEE

(ESC) TO START OVER
```

A "see, see also" screen from Computer Cat™.

The number of cross-reference entries grew steadily in response to student and staff requests. Computer Cat also allows data to be entered in such a way that a given item may be retrieved by several subject headings, so we were able to introduce some nontraditional categories into our catalog. The new subject headings included such topics as "Newbery – 19___," "Caldecott – 19___," "Encyclopedia Brown Series," "Raggedy Ann Series," and "The Chronicles of Narnia." When we received a series of books for our professional collection for art instruction, cataloged under the single subject heading of "Handicrafts," we added the second heading of "Art" to each book entry, since "Art" is the heading most teachers would use to look up that type of book. Similarly, "Guidance," which is not a preferred Sears heading, was incorporated into records for items cataloged under headings like "Emotions," "Feelings," or "Behavior." Other subject headings were added to help students as teachers taught various units. If a teacher wanted a certain book listed when a student looked up "Environment," for example, "Environment" was added as a heading for that book. Making such additions to Computer Cat takes seconds. A single modification to one record has the same effect as pulling and changing an entire series of catalog cards.

I received a graphic lesson in the literal-mindedness of computers after we had entered about 4,000 items. We had entered authors' names without spaces between the comma and the first name (e.g., "Cleary,Beverly"). The OCLC formatted entries, however, inserted a space after the comma. The result was that a search by "Cleary,Beverly" missed all the OCLC entries, and one by "Cleary, Beverly" missed the manual entries. We also entered "Mys and Detective Stories" where OCLC used "Mystery and Detective Stories," with similar results. Consistency is *very* important when working with computers, and the only way for humans with their fickle memories to practice consistency is to *document*—abbreviations, identification numbering sequences, dates, problems, everything. This becomes even more important when there is a staff turnover, in order to save newcomers from starting over from scratch!

Computer Cat is still growing. A circulation component is being added this year which will use a bar code system like that used in many grocery stores. Also, as other libraries purchase and implement the system, they are finding new ways to use it. Though the format of the program is fixed, it is wonderfully flexible, since it may be used for any type of media, as well as other resources and even equipment inventory. It is also possible to add a networking peripheral to the hard disk drive so that it may be used with several microcomputers simultaneously. The multi-user system allows one or more patrons to use the "look-up" feature while a staff member edits, does data entry, or prints lists for ordering, inventory, or bibliographies.

Both students and staff members have become more informed about and intrigued by computers. A second Apple was added during the first year for instructional purposes, and a number of teachers check it out regularly for classroom use. During the second year the catalog was in use (1981-1982), the students renamed it "Kitten on the Keys." The name inspired the assistant principal, who was taking a programming class, to write a program that used an animated kitten to lead students through the three search methods—subject, author, and title. We now use her program to instruct new students in the use of our catalog.

I am still growing as well. Many of my frustrations that first year came from ignorance about computers—the sort of ignorance we have tried to dispel in this book. Programs will appear to "hang" for a variety of reasons, most of which are simple to detect and solve, *providing you know what to look for*. Static electricity, power problems, a printer not being available when the computer is ready for it—these are all minor problems once they are understood. I have experienced some intensely frustrating times attempting to "unhang" a computer that was spewing garbage across the screen or onto a printout for no apparent reason. But I have also had the intense satisfaction of seeing children eager for a turn at the catalog, of watching students simply "browse" until they find something new that catches their interest, of handing teachers bibliographies on every conceivable subject. Through the conception, testing, and success of

Computer Cat I have realized many facets of my "dream library," and become aware of other possibilities I had not even considered. I have come to regard computers not as cold, impersonal, and incomprehensible machines, but as marvelously capable and flexible tools that can be used to realize human goals.

Figure 7.1. The Author Demonstrates Computer Cat™ for Two Young Pupils

FURTHER READING

Articles about Computer Cat have appeared in a variety of publications.

Newspaper articles include:

Denver Post, Neighbors-Boulder Valley Section, Mar. 11, 1981. "School Children Handling Computer Technology."

Rocky Mountain News, Sept. 18, 1981. "Library Computer Saves Time, Prevents Frustration."

Magazine articles include:

"Apple Replaces Library Card Catalog," *Apple Education News* 3 (Jan. 1982): 8.

"Behind the Scenes Interview," *ACCESS: Microcomputers in Libraries* (July 1981): 7 + .

Costa, Betty. "An Online Catalog for an Elementary School Library Media Center," *School Library Media Quarterly* (Summer 1982): 337-46.

Costa, Betty, and Marie Costa. " ' Card' Catalog on a Microcomputer — So Easy a Child Can Use It!" *Catholic Library World* (Nov. 1982): 166-69.

Costa, Betty, and Marie Costa. "Microcomputer in Colorado — It's Elementary," *Wilson Library Bulletin* (May 1981): 676-78 + .

Costa, Betty, and Marie Costa. "The Microcomputer in the School Media Centre," *Review* (June 1982): 23-24.

Costa, Betty, and Marie Costa. "Microcomputers in Libraries," *Technicalities* (Oct. 1981): 16.

Durbin, Hugh. "There's a Computer in Your Future," *Ohio Media Spectrum* 34 (Spring 1982). This article was Mr. Durbin's description and evaluation of his visit to Mountain View to observe Computer Cat. Mr. Durbin is the Director of Media Services for School Libraries for the Columbus Public Schools, Columbus, OH.

Gonder, Peggy Odell. " ... But Try Them Instead of Dewey Decimals," *Education USA* (Oct. 12, 1981): 52.

Malsam, Margaret. "A Computer First for an Elementary School: Microcomputer Replaces Card Catalog," *Educational Computer* (Sept./Oct. 1981): 40-42 + .

Malsam, Margaret. "The Computer Replaces the Card Catalog in One Colorado Elementary School," *Phi Delta Kappan* (Jan. 1982): 321.

Matthews, Joseph R. "Online Public Access Catalogs," *Library Journal* (June 1, 1982): 1068. Includes Mountain View's Computer Cat as one of "20 online public access catalogs in North America."

"School Uses Microcomputer to Replace Card Catalog in Library," *Small Computers in Libraries* 1 (May 1981): 1.

News items include:

AEDS Bulletin 7 (Apr. 1982): 16.

American Libraries (May 1981): 293-94.

Electronic Learning (Mar./Apr. 1982): 12-13.

Media & Methods (Sept. 1981): 2.

Personal Computing (Dec. 1981): 99-100.

School Library Media Quarterly (Summer 1981): 219.

T.H.E. Journal 8 (Sept. 1981): 16.

APPENDICES

Appendix A: Glossary

Acoustic coupler — a **modem*** that works by converting digital data into sound waves for transmission over ordinary telephone lines.

Algorithm — a process for carrying out a complex operation by breaking it down into a hierarchical sequence of simpler operations; e.g., multiplying 67 times 308 by performing a series of additions: $308 + 308 = 616$, $616 + 308 = 924$, $924 + 308 = 1232$, etc. All computer operations are carried out using algorithms.

Alphanumeric character — a character that is machine processable; includes alphabetic upper- and lowercase letters A through Z, digits 0 through 9, and special characters such as $=$, $/$, $*$, $< >$, #, etc.

Applications software — programs written to perform specific functions, e.g., inventory control, word processing, etc.

Arithmetic Logic Unit — the portion of the **CPU** that performs arithmetic and logic operations.

ASCII code — American Standard Code for Information Interchange, developed by the National Standards Institute for transmitting information between computers and computer components; consists of 8 binary characters, a 7-bit character code and a **parity bit**. There are 128 codes, 96 of which represent "printable characters"; the remainder represent control functions.

Assembler — a program that converts nonmachine language programs to **machine language** so that they may be used by a computer.

Assembly language — a "low-level" programming language resembling **machine language** that uses mnemonic rather than numeric instructions.

Asynchronous transmission — data transmission in which the time interval between characters varies according to the speed at which they are sent; uses start and stop elements to identify individual characters.

Authoring language — a programming language used for designing instructional (**CAI**) programs using English commands.

Backup — a procedure for copying a data file or software in order to have a reserve copy in case the original is lost or destroyed; also procedures and/or equipment to use in the event of power loss or other equipment failure.

Band — referring to data communications, a range of frequencies.

Bandwidth — the difference, in **hertz**, between the highest and lowest frequencies in a band.

Bar code — a system for automatic identification of items, such as books in a library or grocery items in a supermarket, by means of printed bars of different widths which represent numbers; the code is read by a light-sensitive peripheral device similar to a **light pen**.

---

*Note: Boldface terms appearing in definitions are found elsewhere in the glossary.

BASIC — Beginner's All-purpose Symbolic Instruction Code: a high-level, relatively simple-to-use algebraic programming language, which is very widely used for all types of computers, especially micros.

Batch processing — a method for collecting and executing programs in groups, or batches, then returning the results to the users; usually performed in a computer center to which the users have no direct access.

Baud rate — the rate at which signals change from one frequency to another; one baud equals one signal change per second.

BDOS, BDOS error — Basic Disk Operating System, the disk-handling component of the **CP/M operating system**; it is standard for all microcomputers using CP/M. A "BDOS error" is any error arising when the computer cannot read or write to a disk; causes may range from a drive door being open to a disk being full to a data wipeout.

Binary code — the basic code used by computers. In binary arithmetic, there are only two digits, 1 and 0. Therefore, the equivalent of 2 in base 10 (decimal) would be 10 in base 2 (binary), decimal 4 would be binary 110, 5 would be 101, and so on. In binary code, all data is broken down into **bits**, which are represented by either 1 or 0.

Bit — abbreviation for binary digit (1 or 0); also used to refer to the signals sent between computers, or between computer components. Generally, 8 bits equals 1 **byte**.

Block — in word processing, a user-defined section of text, ranging in size from part of a word to an entire file, which may be manipulated as a single unit.

Board — a card that plugs into a computer's bus structure and that contains the circuitry for one or more functions, such as interfacing with a peripheral device or substituting a different CPU for the built-in microprocessor.

Bomb — a dramatic program failure; as when an operator accidentally presses the wrong control character while entering data and the screen fills up with **garbage**; good programs should be well-protected against this possibility.

Book catalog — a catalog in book rather than card form.

Boolean algebra — a system of symbolic logic similar in form to algebra but dealing with logical rather than numeric relationships. Named for its creator, George Boole.

Boolean search — a search method using logical delimiters to specify the search object; e.g., all scientists who were born before 1920 AND were women who worked in either medicine OR physics. Using AND in a search restricts the possibilities (the object must satisfy both criteria); using OR expands them (the object may satisfy either criteria).

Bootstrap — the process by which an operating system is "loaded" into the computer's **RAM** from a disk, usually abbreviated to "Boot."

Buffer — a temporary storage area for data that is being transmitted between devices with different operating speeds; e.g., a printer that cannot input and use data as rapidly as a computer can send it.

Bug — a mistake or malfunction in computer software or hardware.

Byte — a group of **binary** digits, or **bits**, that are treated as a single unit by a computer; usually a byte consists of 8 bits. Also used to designate a group of bits which represent a single coded character.

CAI — Computer Assisted Instruction. Individualized instruction using a computer to provide a preprogrammed sequence of instruction, which a student may follow at his or her own rate, and which is interactive and responsive to a user's individual needs.

Character — a letter, digit, punctuation mark or symbol which may be stored and/or processed by a computer or its peripherals.

Character string — a connected sequence of characters which is treated as a single data unit.

Chip — a very small piece of silicon containing integrated circuitry, including transistors, diodes, and resistors, with electrical paths consisting of thin layers of gold or aluminum.

COBOL — COmmon Business Oriented Language, a **high-level language** used mainly for business applications.

Command — a coded instruction that causes a computer to do something.

Command-driven — a program that requires the operator to input commands rather than choosing options from a menu (see also **menu-driven**).

Computer literacy — nontechnical, use-oriented knowledge of computers and their role in society.

CONTROL key — usually abbreviated CTRL on the keyboard; often indicated by ‹CTRL› in user's guides; used in conjunction with other keys to input commands for applications programs.

Control unit — the portion of the **CPU** that interprets program commands stored in **RAM** and **ROM** and coordinates their execution.

Courseware — instructional software, which includes instructor materials such as teaching objectives, course outlines, lesson plans, related activities, etc.

CP/M — Control Program for Microcomputers, a flexible, standardized **operating system** that runs on many types of microcomputer hardware and permits programs to be written and used on different machines.

CPU — Central Processing Unit, consisting of a **control unit**, an **arithmetic logic unit**, and several **registers**; the computer component that interprets and executes program commands. In a microcomputer, the CPU circuitry is etched on a **microprocessor chip**.

CRT — cathode ray tube, an **output** device that displays data visually on a screen similar to that of a television.

Cursor — a marker that indicates positions on the **CRT** screen, varying in appearance from a line to a small rectangle, may or may not "flash."

Daisywheel printer — a printer that uses a rotating flower-shaped print element containing characters on the ends of the spokes, or "petals"; when the proper character is aligned with the paper, a small hammer strikes it, pressing it against a ribbon to imprint the character image on the paper.

Database — a collection of data used or produced by a computer program; also a collection of related information, in machine-readable format, which may be numeric, bibliographic, factual, etc.

Database service — a service providing remote, online access via dedicated terminals and/or microcomputers and modems to a variety of **databases**.

Debug — to eliminate **bugs** (i.e., mistakes or malfunctions) in computer software or hardware.

Descender — a character image that is displayed on a **CRT** screen or by a printer so that any "tail" (e.g., of a "y" or "g") extends below the base line.

Dial-up access — use of a dial or push-button telephone to initiate a station to station telephone call, as between a library's microcomputer and **modem** and a **database service** computer.

Disk controller — the **interface** between a computer and a disk drive.

Documentation — the technical information, manuals, user's guides and accompanying instructions included with **hardware** or **software**.

DOS — Disk Operating System, an **operating system** that is loaded into the computer from a **floppy disk**.

Dot matrix printer — a printer that forms characters consisting of close patterns of small dots by means of a head containing several fine wires that act as individual print hammers.

Dumb terminal — a **terminal** without independent computing capabilities, for communicating **online** with a computer at another location.

Electrical noise — small power variations caused by such devices as small appliances, hand tools, powerline switching equipment, etc.

Electronic mail — a method for sending messages via computer, usually through a network that uses a mini or mainframe computer accessed via **modems** or direct lines by either **intelligent terminals** (including microcomputers) or **dumb terminals**.

End user — the person(s) or organization who uses an applications program and the hardware needed to run it.

Expandability — the ability to add memory, **peripheral devices**, or capabilities to an existing system using plug-in **interfaces**.

Field — in database management systems, a single data item within a **record**.

File — a collection of related data stored and processed as a unit.

Firmware — program instructions or data that is permanently stored in the **ROM** of a computer.

Flag — a method for marking a record or file for later attention, e.g., errors detected by a spelling check program within a word processing file.

Floppy disk — a flexible magnetic disk used for secondary or auxilliary storage of data; provides fairly high capacity and easy access of information at low cost.

Form feed — the automatic progression of a continuous sheet of paper through a printer so that the next line of print will begin on a new page.

Format — the way that data is arranged, e.g., on a **floppy disk** being used by a specific computer.

FORTRAN — FORmula TRANslator, a **high-level language** used mainly for scientific, mathematical, and engineering applications.

Function key — a key on a keyboard that acts as a single-stroke command for applications software.

Garbage — meaningless characters or information.

Generation (computer) — a way of classifying computers according to technological development: First generation computers used vacuum tubes, were bulky, slow and unreliable; second generation computers used transistors and were somewhat faster, etc.

GIGO — Garbage In, Garbage Out; i.e., if the input data is wrong ("bad"), the output data will also be wrong.

Glitch — originally used to indicate a short, low-magnitude electrical distrubance; has come to mean any unexpected and inexplicable problem.

Handshake — an exchange of information between a CPU and a peripheral device that verifies that communications have been established before actual data transfer begins.

Hard copy — a printed copy of output data.

Hard disk — a rigid, as opposed to flexible, storage disk, which provides higher capacity and faster access speed, but at a greater cost, than **floppy disks**.

Hard-sector — a method for marking **floppy disks** into sections by means of punched holes to indicate the **sectors**.

Hardware — the physical components of a computer system.

Hertz — in measuring signal frequency, the number of cycles per second.

Hexadecimal — a number system using base 16; numbers greater than 9 are indicated by the letters A through F, e.g., decimal 168 is equivalent to hexadecimal A8.

High-level language — a machine-independent, procedure- or problem-oriented programming language, usually with English-based commands and syntax.

Hollerith card — a punched card with 80 columns and 12 rows; characters are represented by holes punched in specific column/row positions according to a special code, which is also named after Herman Hollerith, inventor of the punched card tabulator.

Initialize — in the case of a disk, to prepare it to receive data according to a specific computer's **format**.

Input — introduction of data via a **peripheral** device into a computer's internal memory.

Intelligent terminal — a **terminal** with built-in computer processing capabilities.

Interactive — a system in which each input entry elicits a response, as in games or instructional programming.

Interface — the connection between two components that converts the signals from one so that they may be "understood" by the other.

Interpreter — a **systems program** that translates programs written in **high-level languages**, one statement at a time, into machine instructions and then executes the instructions before going to the next program statement.

I/O — abbreviation for Input/Output, including devices, techniques and processes.

ISAM — Indexed Sequential Access Method, a method for retrieving data stored by a database management system, according to a user-specified **key** or keys.

Joy stick — an input device, often used with graphics (as in games), with a stick that is manipulated by the operator to control **input**.

Justification — alignment of characters, as in word processing, where margins may be flush on both sides of the text; or as in database management or a spreadsheet application, where one character may be flush with either the leftmost or rightmost position in a field.

K — abbreviation for kilobyte, or 1,024 **bytes** of data.

Key — in database management, a **field** used to identify a record or **sort** the records in a file (see also **search key**).

Light pen — an **input** device resembling a pen which is used to "write" directly onto a **CRT** screen or to "read" predefined patterns from the screen.

Log on — to initiate a terminal or computer session, either by turning on the computer and loading a program, or by establishing contact with a remote computer, as for a database search.

Logged disk drive — the disk drive currently in use by the computer.

LSI — Large Scale Integration, placing many (over 100) integrated circuits on a single silicon **chip**; very large scale integration places 1,000 or more circuits on a single chip.

Machine language — the most basic programming language; it can be "understood" and used by a computer without further interpretation.

MARC — MAchine Readable Catalog records which conform to a national standard for communication of bibliographic information, established and used by the Library of Congress.

Menu-driven — a type of applications program that displays a list of command options called a "menu" on the terminal screen; the operator indicates his/her choice by pressing the appropriate key, and the command is executed.

Microprocessor – a "computer on a chip," which may serve, alternatively, as the **CPU** in a microcomputer, or as a preprogrammed control device for an appliance, traffic signal, business machine, etc.

Modem – abbreviated from MOdulator-DEModulator, a communications device that converts computer signals (**bits**) into tones that can be transmitted over telephone lines (modulation) and also converts incoming frequencies received over a telephone into signals the computer can use (demodulation).

Monitor – a video display unit or **CRT**; alternatively, a control program usually built into the **ROM** of a computer.

Motherboard – the assembly inside the computer that connects all the circuitry, interface cards, etc.

Multi-user system – an interconnected system with multiple **online** access which may be provided either by microcomputers or **dumb terminals**. In the first case users share one or more common devices, such as hard disks or printers, and a common database; in the second the terminals also share one or more **CPU**s; also called a network.

OCR – Optical Character Recognition, the process of converting human readable data to a form suitable for computer input by means of a device that recognizes light reflected from printed characters.

Online – in direct communication with the **CPU** of a computer, either through a physically connected **peripheral device** or through remote access using a **modem** or a **dumb terminal**.

Operating system – a type of **systems software** that serves as a controller for all the operations of a computer.

Output – transfer of data from a computer's internal memory to a **peripheral device** for display or transmission.

Parallel input/output – simultaneous transmission of **bits** using individual, parallel wires.

Parity bit – an extra **bit** added to the group of bits composing a character, word, or byte to ensure that the number of bits is always either odd or even; parity bits thus establish a consistent bit pattern within the system and make it possible to detect errors and loss of bits.

PASCAL – a general purpose, **high-level language** used on both large computer systems and micros.

Peripheral devices – Input/Output (**I/O**) and secondary storage devices (e.g., disk drives and terminals) connected with the **CPU** by circuitry and/or cables.

Pin-feed printer – a type of printer with pins for feeding paper affixed to the **platen**; it is capable of accepting only one width of paper, as opposed to an adjustable **tractor feed printer**.

Platen – on a printer, a roller or other backing against which the paper rests as the print head strikes it to form a character impression.

Plotter – an output device for graphing data with an automatically controlled pen; the two main types are drum plotters and flatbed plotters.

Port – an **Input/Output** channel through which a **peripheral device** can communicate with a computer.

Powerline conditioner – a device that acts as an electrical shock absorber to suppress voltage **spikes** and **electrical noise**, which may cause system damage or loss of data.

Program – a sequence of instructions that cause a computer to perform a specific task; programming is the process of designing, writing, and testing such instructions.

Protocol – a set of rules or procedures, usually software-defined, for governing the exchange of information (via **interfaces** and **ports**) between computer equipment.

RAM—see **Random Access Memory**.

Random Access Memory—the portion of a computer's internal memory that may either be read or written to and is therefore changeable; it is usually **volatile**. Random access means that the time needed to read or write a piece of data is not dependent on its location within the memory. Abbreviated **RAM**.

Read Only Memory—the portion of a computer's internal memory that is permanently programmed and may be read but not changed; such programming is called **firmware**. Abbreviated **ROM**.

Record—in database management, a collection of related data items, or **fields**, which are treated as a single unit; comparable to a record in a manually kept file.

Register—a device within the **CPU** used for temporary storage of data during processing.

Resolution—the quality, in regard to clarity, sharpness, and density, of a video screen display.

ROM—see **Read Only Memory**.

Save—to store data in a secondary storage medium, such as a **floppy disk,** rather than in the computer's internal memory.

Scroll—the vertical or horizontal movement of a screen display, such as word processing text or a spreadsheet, in either direction.

Search—in database management, to examine a data file for those records meeting a specific set of criteria.

Search and replace—in word processing, the ability to locate a given **character string** anywhere it appears in a file and replace it with a different, operator-specified character string, e.g., replacing every use of "John Jones" with "Stan Smith."

Search key—data to be compared with specific items within records in order to locate desired records during a **search**.

Sector—on a **floppy disk**, a section of a **track**.

Serial input/output—transmission of data **bits** one at a time over a single wire.

Silicon chip—see **chip**.

Simulation—a type of program that simulates a physical or biological situation on a computer, e.g., an educational game that simulates the consequences of various decisions in the operation of a rocket.

Soft return—in word processing, a return (line ending) that is not kept when text is reformatted.

Soft-sector—a method for marking **floppy disk** sections using information written on the disk as opposed to **hard-sector** disks, which use physical holes.

Software—the sets of instructions, or **programs**, that cause **hardware** to perform specific functions; also includes related **documentation**.

Sort—to rearrange the **records** in a **file** according to a specific, logical order, e.g., alphabetically.

Spike—a brief but sharp surge in a power supply.

Spooling—the process of storing data temporarily in a **buffer** until an **input/output** device is ready to use it.

Standalone—a self-contained, single-purpose system, such as a dedicated word processor or circulation system.

Synchronous transmission—data transmission in which signals are sent at a fixed rate that is controlled by clock signals in the transmitter and receiver.

Systems software — programs that act as monitors to enable a computer's various components to function, or which cause the computer to run more efficiently; e.g., **operating systems**.

Terminal — a **peripheral device** that includes a keyboard, **video display monitor** and a **video generator**; alternatively, an **input/output** device that is **online** to a computer in another location.

Timeshare — a system that allows a number of users to share access to the same computer facility; although to the users it appears that they are all using the computer simultaneously, they are actually being serviced in sequence at very high speed.

Toggle — having two stable states, only one of which may be in effect at any given time, e.g., dynamic insert mode in word processing.

Track — a continuous path on a **floppy disk** or other medium such as magnetic tape, along which data is recorded. On a disk, the tracks are divided into sectors.

Tractor feed printer — a printer that has pins for feeding paper on adjustable tractors so that it is capable of handling paper of different widths.

Transistor — a semiconductor device for controlling the flow of electrical current.

Turnkey system — a packaged system, including both hardware and software, designed for a specific purpose; it is intended to be operated by persons with little or no knowledge of computer programming, systems, or operations.

User friendliness — description of a computer system in regard to ease of use and interactivity.

Video display unit — an **output** device that displays data on a **CRT** screen.

Video generator — a device contained in a computer or **terminal** that generates the signals that control the **CRT** screen display.

Volatile memory — memory that loses its contents if the system's power is turned off or lost.

Voltage regulator — a circuit that controls voltage output so that it remains consistent regardless of changes in the voltage passing through it.

Wild card — in searching or selecting, a character (usually an asterisk or question mark) that tells the computer to "accept anything in this position"; e.g., in conducting a search for a name when the operator is unsure of the spelling ("Smith" or "Smythe"), typing "Sm*th*."

Winchester drive — a **hard disk** unit in which the disk and the read/write assembly are encased in a hermetically sealed chamber to protect them against damage and/or data loss due to smoke or other types of particles.

Word wrap — in word processing, the ability to start a new line automatically whenever a word is typed that is too long to fit inside the margins.

Write-protect — a method for protecting a disk against inadvertent recording of data (and simultaneous erasing of data already present); on a **floppy disk** it is accomplished by a notch in the protective sleeve, which is either covered or uncovered depending on the individual computer system.

Appendix B: Resources

The following represents a selection of resources available concerning microcomputers, libraries, and education. As large as this selection is, it is not comprehensive; new resources are appearing almost literally every day. Still, the publications, organizations, individuals, and products listed here should provide any media specialist with a wide range of information and assistance in his or her microcomputer venture. Please note, however, that inclusion in this list does *not* constitute a recommendation unless specifically noted, as we were not able to personally examine each item.

The resources are organized by format (reference books, periodicals, newsletters, etc.) and further broken down by subject (library management, special education, etc.), with annotations and/or review sources, contact names, and price information (when available).

We want to thank the many people who took the time to answer our inquiries concerning their activities with microcomputers. The research for this section was most rewarding.

Please note when writing individuals and organizations, particularly nonprofit organizations such as libraries, it is a good idea to enclose a self-addressed, stamped envelope and/or postage with your request.

REFERENCE WORKS

Bibliographies

Children's Books for Computer Awareness and Literacy 1982. Compiled by Elizabeth S. Wall. Nokomis, FL: Bayshore Books, 1982.
   Bibliography of books for elementary school age children. Includes publishers, price, ISBN, and suggested grade levels.

"Classroom Test Your Courseware before You Buy It." By Ann Lathrop. *Educational Computer Magazine* (Jan./Feb. 1983): 34-37.
   Includes information about catalog mail-order distributors with liberal software on-approval policies, and sources of critical evaluations.

"Computer Literacy Bibliography." By Susan Friel and Nancy Roberts. *Creative Computing* (Sept. 1980): 92-97.
   Annotated and coded for age level. Includes sections on computer applications/societal issues; programming; computer science; what is a computer?; teaching resources; periodicals.

"Computer Literacy—Finding Effective Resources." By Barbara Kurshan. *Recreational Computing* (Jan./Feb. 1981): 45-47.

"Computer Literacy, Languages and Careers." By Phyllis Levy Mandell. *School Library Journal* (Apr. 1982): 19-22.
   Bibliography of available media—described, not evaluated.

"ComputerTown USA—Sources of Information ... Especially for Pet and TRS-80 Users." By Bob Albrecht and George Firedrake. *The Computing Teacher* 8 (Sept. 1980): 18-19.

Albrecht and Firedrake also publish a variety of materials particularly for users of PET, TRS-80s, and Ataris. Write Bob Albrecht for catalog at Dymax, P.O. Box 310, Menlo Park, CA 94025.

DP MagList. Larchmont, NY: Maglist Co., 1980. $4.00.

An annotated listing of some 46 data processing publications with the following information about each: publisher, frequency, target readership, editorial emphasis, cost. Some publications are free if certain requirements are met. Available from Maglist Co., P.O. Box 364, Larchmont, NY 10538.

"Dragonsmoke—Resources for the Radio Shack Color Computer." By Bob Albrecht and George Firedrake. *The Computing Teacher* 10 (Dec. 1982): 53-54.

Send Mr. Albrecht a SASE to receive an updated list when it is compiled.

Education Bibliography. San Diego: Department of Education, San Diego County, 1982. Free.

Categories include microcomputers, computer literacy, CAI drill and practice, tutorial, simulation, CMI, programming, and software. Available from Publication Sales, Department of Education, San Diego County, 6401 Linda Vista Road, San Diego, CA 92111-7399. Send stamped ($.54), 9½x12½ envelope.

ERIC Microcomputer Bibliographies. Syracuse, NY: ERIC, Syracuse University, 1981-1982. Free.

Six two-page annotated bibliographies: 1) Microcomputers: Issues and Trends; 2) Microcomputer Applications: General; 3) Microcomputer Applications: Elementary/Middle/Secondary Education; 4) Microcomputer Applications: Higher Education; 5) Microcomputer Hardware; 6) Microcomputer Software.

A four-page bibliography: Information Resources on Microcomputers: A Sampling of the ERIC Database.

A two-page information guide: Microcomputers: Some Basic Resources. Available from ERIC Clearinghouse on Information Resources, Syracuse University, Syracuse, NY 13210. SASE appreciated.

Guide to Resources in Instructional Computing. By Mary Kay Corbitt. Reston, VA: National Council of Teachers of Mathematics, 1982. $2.00 prepaid, 25-page guide.

Prepared for the Technology Advisory Committee. As the NCTM has a number of materials, you might want to write for a current listing of computer-related materials available when requesting this bibliography. Write to National Council of Teachers of Mathematics, 1906 Association Drive, Reston, VA 22091.

"How Can Educators Become Computer Literates?" By Darlene Myers. *The Computing Teacher* 8 (Nov. 1980): 34-42.

Contents include suggestions and concerns; organizations involved in educational computing; computing books for the beginner; texts for the educator.

Microcomputers and the Media Specialist: An Annotated Bibliography. Syracuse, NY: ERIC, Syracuse University, 1982. $4.25.

Compiled by Inabeth Miller with the assistance of Allan Sturrock; a 70-page ERIC publication which lists the latest papers and periodical and journal articles. Each entry is annotated and indicates the ERIC document number or the source. Available from ERIC, Information Resources Publications, 130 Huntington Hall, Syracuse University, Syracuse, NY 13210.

Microcomputing Periodicals, an Annotated Bibliography. By George Shirinian. Toronto: George Shirinian, Sept. 1982. $15.00, 65p.

Regularly updated bibliography; author requests input. It is divided into three sections: the first details publications that provide indexing to various periodicals; the second provides a list of all the periodicals on microcomputers that are currently in print; and the third gives information on those periodicals that have ceased publication or changed their name. Available from George Shirinian, 53 Fraserwood Avenue, #2, Toronto, Canada M6B 2NG.

" ... Where Are the Critical Reviews?" By Ann Lathrop. *The Computing Teacher* 9 (Feb. 1982): 22-26.

Directories

Classroom Computer News—1983 Directory of Educational Computing Resources. Watertown, MA: Classroom Computer News, annual. $14.95.

This directory contains a wealth of information. It has six parts: 1) Sources: People, Places, and Things; 2) Computer-Specific Resources; 3) Local and Regional Resources; 4) Continuing Education; 5) Calendar, Index of Advertisers, Index; 6) Yellow Pages. Sample inclusion: a list of user groups, periodical/newsletters and software directories for specific computers: Apple, Atari, Commodore, Radio Shack, Sinclair, Texas Instruments, and others. This is a recommended resource for every library. Available from Classroom Computer News, 341 Mt. Auburn Street, Watertown, MA 02172.

Micro Software Report. Library Edition. Edited by Jeanne M. Nolan. Torrance, CA: Nolan Information Management Services, 1982. $49.95.

Reviewed in *SCIL* (Oct. 1982): "first comprehensive listing of microcomputer software related to library applications." Available from Nolan Information Management Services, 21203-A Hawthorne Boulevard, Suite 5323, Torrance, CA 90509.

Microcomputer Directory: Applications in Educational Settings. Cambridge, MA: Harvard University, Monroe C. Gutman Library, annual. $15.00.

An excellent source of information about educational applications. The directory is indexed by subject area (libraries/media centers, administration, special education, etc.) and by state. Each entry includes a brief description of the application, the equipment used, funding, contact person, and address. Available from Harvard University Graduate School of Education, Appian Way, Cambridge, MA 01238. (Prepaid orders: add $1.00 for postage and handling, purchase orders add $2.50.)

On-Line Computer Telephone Directory. By Jim Cabron. Kansas City, MO. $5.95.

This directory was cited in an article on electronic bulletin boards in *Popular Computing* (Oct. 1982): 134-36. It provides the most up-to-date listings. Available from Jim Cabron, P.O. Box 10005, Kansas City, MO 64111. Back issues and summer issue still available for $2.85.

Indexes

Index to Volumes 8 and 9 of The Computing Teacher. From *The Computing Teacher* 10 (Sept. 1982): 30-48.

Reprints or back issues are available, ordering information is found on page 31 of the September 1982 issue.

Microcomputer Index. Santa Clara, CA: Microcomputer Information Services, quarterly. $30.00.

A subject index, including abstracts, for a cross-section of popular microcomputer magazines. (See Periodicals section.) Also now available on DIALOG. Available from Microcomputer Information Services, 2464 El Camino Real, #247, Santa Clara, CA 95051.

6-year Cumulative Index to Creative Computing and ROM. Volumes 1-6: 1974-1980. Morristown, NJ: Creative Computing. $2.00.

While individual issues in volumes 1 and 2 are no longer available, the *Best of Creative Computing*, volumes 1, 2, and 3 are available for purchase. The index also indicates which articles are included in these volumes. One of the index categories is book reviews, which might be helpful in selecting computer books. Available from Creative Computing, P.O. Box 789-M, Morristown, NJ 07960.

MONOGRAPHS AND SELECTED
JOURNAL ARTICLES
Computer History

From Dits to Bits: A Personal History of the Electronic Computer. By Herman Lukoff. Forest Grove, OR: Robotics Press, 1979. $12.95.
This autobiography of the director of technical operations at Sperry Univac, one of the first people to become involved with computers, recounts his experiences with five of the first computers, beginning with ENIAC. Reviewed in *Creative Computing* 6 (Nov. 1980): 188; *Interface Age* 5 (July 1980): 22. Available from Robotics Press, P.O. Box 555, Forest Grove, OR 97116.

From ENIAC to UNIVAC: An Appraisal of the Eckert-Mauchly Computers. By Nancy Stern. North Billerica, MA: Digital Press, 1981. $25.00.
Reviewed in *Kilobaud Microcomputing* (Dec. 1981): 233-34— " ... interesting, informative and well-written account.... "

Computer Literacy

Are You Computer Literate? By Karen Billing and David Moursund. Beaverton, OR: Dilithium Press, 1979. $9.95.
"Covers everyday use of computers, their parts, history, and programming; self quizzes in each chapter increase interest and allows reader to check his or her progress"— Ann Lathrop. Reviewed in *Personal Computing* 6 (Oct. 1980): 186.

Be a Computer Literate. By Marian J. Ball and Sylvia Charp. Morristown, NJ: Creative Computing, 1977. $3.95.
Reviewed in *The Computing Teacher* 8 (Dec. 1980): 51.

Computer Alphabet Book. By Elizabeth S. Wall. Nokomis, FL: Bayshore Books, 1979. $9.95.
Simple definitions of computer parts and terms. Useful at the beginning of any computer literacy program. Although this is an "alphabet book," it is useful for all ages. Available from Bayshore Books, P.O. Box 848, Nokomis, FL 33555.

Computer Consciousness: Surveying the Automated 80's. By H. Dominic Covvey and Neil H. McAlister. Reading, MA: Addison-Wesley, 1980. $6.95.
"Pulls together a wide range of 'buzz words,' describes them in context and explains much of the current technology. Excellent for one just starting to work in the area"— from *SCIL* (Oct. 1981): 7. Reviewed in *The Computing Teacher* 8 (Jan. 1981): 36-37; *Desktop Computing* 2 (Mar. 1982): 85; *Kilobaud Microcomputing* (Apr. 1981): 224.

Computer Dictionary and Handbook. By Charles J. Sippl and Roger J. Sippl. Indianapolis, IN: Howard W. Sams, 1980. $34.95.
Reviewed in *The Computing Teacher* 8 (Dec. 1980): 52-53.

Computer Fundamentals for Nonspecialists. By Joseph M. Vies. New York: AMACOM, 1981. $14.95.
Reviewed in *Popular Computing* (May 1982): 110.

Computer Literacy Curriculum Guide. St. Paul: Minnesota School Districts Data Processing Joint Board (TIES), 1982. $2.00 for TIES members; $10.00 for non-TIES members; $20.00 for nonresidents.

Described in *The Computing Teacher* 10 (Jan. 1983): 6. Available from TIES, Instructional Services, Attention: Distribution, 1925 W. Country Road B2, St. Paul, MN 55113.

Computer Literacy: Problem-Solving with Computers. By Carin E. Horn and James L. Poirot. Austin, TX: Sterling Swift Pub. Co., 1981. $13.95.

A textbook which also contains an extensive bibliography, glossary, and index. Reviewed in *Electronic Education* (Dec. 1981): 30; *The Computing Teacher* (Sept. 1981): 35-36; *The Computing Teacher* (Apr. 1982): 38-39; *Interface Age* (Feb. 1982): 134; *Electronic Learning* (Nov. 1981): 73. Available from Sterling Swift Publishing Co., 1600 Fortview Road, Austin, TX 78704.

Computer Programming for Kids and Other Beginners. Austin, TX: Sterling Swift Pub. Co., 1982. $9.95 for student books; $9.95 for teacher's guide.

Three different editions of a student book: Apple II, TRS-80 Model III, Radio Shack Color Computer, containing simple "hands-on" exercises, sample programs, and experimental-type questions. The teacher's edition may be used with any of the student versions.

Computers Are Fun. By Jean Rice and Sandy O'Connor. Minneapolis: T. S. Denison and Co., 1981. $3.95.

An introduction to computers for grades K-3. A teacher's resource and guide book is available to use with this book. Reviewed in *The Computing Teacher* (Mar. 1982): 38.

Computers for Kids. (Three versions: Apple, Atari, or TRS-80.) By Sally G. Larsen. Morristown, NJ: Creative Computing, 1981. $3.95.

A hands-on guide which includes section for parents and teachers. This book is also an excellent beginning book for teachers to use. Available from Creative Computing, P.O. Box 789-M, Morristown, NJ 07960. Specify version.

Course Goals in Computer Education, K-12. Tri-County Goal Development Project. Portland, OR: Northwest Regional Education Laboratory, 1979. $10.50.

This book is the result of a cooperative project of several Oregon school districts. It contains goals for use in planning and evaluating elementary and secondary school curricula in computer education. Should be helpful for any district developing a curriculum in this area. Available from Commercial-Educational Distributing Services, P.O. Box 8723, Portland, OR 97208.

Creative Kids Guide to Home Computers. By Fred D'Ignazio. Garden City, NY: Doubleday, 1981. $9.95.

Reviewed in *The Computing Teacher* (Mar. 1982): 38-39; *80 Microcomputing* (Apr. 1981): 31-32; *Recreational Computing* (July 1981): 40.

"Cupertino School District Develops Computer Literacy Curriculum." *The Computing Teacher* 9 (Sept. 1981): 27-34.

Contains a reprint of the Cupertino Computer Literacy Curriculum.

"Developing a District-Wide Computer-Use Plan." By Glenn Fisher. *The Computing Teacher* 10 (Jan. 1983): 52-59.

Copy of plan developed for Albany School District, which has three elementary schools, a middle school, a high school, and a continuation high school.

"Developing Computer Literacy in K-12 Education." Board of Cooperative Educational Services, Third Supervisory District, Suffolk County, NY. *The Computing Teacher* 9 (Nov. 1981): 43-48.

Complete reports can be purchased for $1.75 each from BOCES/LIRICS, 17 Westminster Avenue, Dix Hills, NY 11746.

Exploring with Computers. By Gary G. Bitter. New York: Messner, 1981. $7.95.
> Reviewed in *Popular Computing* (Mar. 1982): 127; *Educational Technology* (Feb. 1982): 54; *Kilobaud Microcomputing* (Dec. 1981): 232-33.

How You Can Learn to Live with Computers. By Harry Kleinberg. New York: J. B. Lippincott, 1977; Penguin, 1978.
> "Non-technical view of what goes on inside computers, of what they can, and cannot do, and of their potential impact"—from *SCIL* (Oct. 1981). Also reviewed in *The Computing Teacher* (Apr. 1982): 38-39.

The Illustrated Computer Dictionary. By Donald Spencer. Ormond Beach, FL: Camelot Publishing, 1980. $5.95.
> Camelot Publishing has a large number of computer books and teaching materials; write to P.O. Box 1357, Ormond Beach, FL 32074 for their latest catalog.

Introduction to Computers in Education/Elementary and Middle School Teachers. By David Moursund. Eugene: University of Oregon, 1981. $7.00.
> A manual on teaching about and teaching using computers, including over 75 activities to be used for self-instruction or for a formal inservice or preservice course for teachers at the elementary and middle school levels. Available from University of Oregon, International Council for Computers in Education, 135 Education, Eugene, OR 97403 (503/686-4414). Quantity discounts available.

Katie and the Computer. By Fred D'Ignazio. Morristown, NJ: Creative Computing, 1979.
> For story of this book read D'Ignazio's "The World Inside the Computer," *Creative Computing* (Sept. 1980): 40-44. Book reviewed in *The Computing Teacher* 9 (Mar. 1982): 38-39 and in *Recreational Computing* 9 (Sept. 1980): 51.

Larry Learns about Computers. By Michael Braude. T. S. Denison and Co., nd. $2.00.
> Grades three through six. Available from T. S. Denison and Co., Inc., 9601 Newton Avenue South, Suite 8223, Minneapolis, MN 55431.

The Micro Millennium. By Christopher Evans. New York: Viking Press, 1980. $10.95.
> Reviewed in *The Computing Teacher* (Sept. 1981): 36; *Creative Computing* (July 1981): 219; *Interface Age* (Aug. 1981): 142; *Popular Computing* (Feb. 1982): 103-104; *Kilobaud Microcomputing* (June 1981): 235-37.

Microcomputer Operation and Application Series. Syracuse University Center for Instructional Development. Syracuse, NY: Syracuse University, 1982. $2.00-$8.50; Slide/tape—$55.00.
> Series of programmed instructional units designed to cover specific microcomputers (Apple II Plus, Atari 410 and 800, TRS-80 I and III, Osborne 1—with Wordstar and SuperCalc). The sequences cover both operation and introductory application. Also have slide/tape introduction to computer literacy for computer novices, junior high to adult. Write for ordering information to Syracuse University Printing Services, 125 College Place, Syracuse, NY 13210.

My Computer Picture Dictionary. By Jean Rice and Marien Haley. Minneapolis: T. S. Denison and Co., 1981. $3.00.
> Reviewed in *The Computing Teacher* (Mar. 1982): 37-38. Available from T. S. Denison and Co., Inc., 9601 Newton Avenue South, Suite 8223, Minneapolis, MN 55431.

My Friend the Computer. By Jean Rice. Minneapolis: T. S. Denison and Co., 1981. $4.95.
> Grades four through seven. Reviewed in *The Computing Teacher* 8 (Dec. 1980): 51-52.

Running Wild, the Next Industrial Revolution. By Adam Osborne. New York: McGraw-Hill, 1979.
> This insider's look at computers in the 1980s provides insights into the future impact of computers on our lives.

The Story of Computers. By Charles T. Meadow. New York: Harvey House, 1970. $7.29.
Grades five through eight.

What Is a Computer? By Marion J. Ball. Boston: Houghton-Mifflin, 1972. $4.35.
Grades four through twelve.

A Young Person's Guide to Computers. By Paul M. Danzer. Milford, CT: Scelbi Publications. $7.95.
"A computer primer that will hold even the most active child's rapt attention"—from a review in *Popular Computing* (Mar. 1982): 125-26. Also reviewed in *Interface Age* (Mar. 1982): 134.

Computers

DON'T! or How to Care for Your Computer. By Rodnay Zaks. Berkeley, CA: Sybex, 1981. $11.95.
Reviewed in *Popular Computing* (Apr. 1982): 119-20—"DON'T is cheap insurance."

Guide to Microcomputers. By Franz J. Frederick. Washington, DC: Association for Educational Communications and Technology, 1980. $9.95.

Microcomputer Buyer's Guide. By Tony Webster. Rochelle Park, NJ: Hayden Book Co., 1981.
Computer reference guide. Reviewed in *Popular Computing* (Mar. 1982): 126-27.

Computers in Education

The Computer in the School: Tutor, Tool, Tutee. Edited by Robert Taylor. New York: Teacher's College Press, 1980. $14.95.
Reviewed in *The Computing Teacher* (Feb. 1981): 36; *The Computing Teacher* (Feb. 1982): 49-50; *Creative Computing* (Oct. 1981): 266-67.

Elementary ... My Dear Computer. By Marge Kosel. St. Paul: Minnesota Educational Computing Consortium, 1978.

Computers in the Classroom: A Guide for Secondary School Teachers. By Donald Spencer. Ormond Beach, FL: Camelot Publishing, 1982. $14.95.

Microcomputers and the 3R's: A Guide for Teachers. By Christine Doerr. Rochelle Park, NJ: Hayden Book Co., 1979. $7.95.
Reviewed in *Electronic Education* (Nov. 1981); 30; *The Computing Teacher* 8 (Nov. 1980): 59; *OnComputing* (Spring 1981): 40.

Microcomputers in Education, a Nontechnical Guide to Instructional School Management Applications. By Joiner, Vensel, Ross, and Silverstein. Holmes Beach, FL: Learning Publications, Inc., 1982. $24.95 (Cat #31-7 Hardcover) plus $1.50 shipping/handling.
A nontechnical language guidebook for educators describing recent accomplishments with microcomputers in schools, including both management and instructional applications. Available from Learning Publications, Inc., P.O. Box 1326, Holmes Beach, FL 33509.

Mindstorms. By Seymour Papert. New York: Basic Books, 1980. $14.95.
Reviewed in *The Computing Teacher* 8 (Mar. 1981): 52-53; *Classroom Computer News* (Mar. 1981): 26; *80 Microcomputing* (Feb. 1981): 14. Background for the use of LOGO.

Practical Guide to Computers in Education. By Coburn, Kelman, Roberts, Snyder, Watt, and Weiner. Reading, MA: Addison-Wesley, 1982. $10.95.
Reviewed in *Popular Computing* (Feb. 1983): 167-70. Recommended by Ann Lathrop in *Educational Computer* (July/Aug. 1982): 16.

Computers in Special Education

Computers and the Handicapped in Special Education and Rehabilitation. Eugene: University of Oregon, 1983. $7.00.
A resource guide with over 180 annotated citations, focusing on computer-assisted and computer-managed instruction in both educational and client settings. Available from ICCE, University of Oregon, 135 Education, Eugene, OR 97403, 505/686-4414. Quantity discounts available.

Computers, Education and Special Needs. Reading MA: Addison-Wesley, 1983.

Special Technology for Special Children. By E. Paul Goldberg. Baltimore: University Park Press, 1979.
Write to the publisher at 233 East Redwood Street, Baltimore, MD 21202.

Computers in Libraries

Automating Library Acquisitions, Issues and Outlook. By Richard W. Boss. White Plains, NY: Knowledge Industry Publications, 1982. $27.50.
Richard Boss is the coauthor of *Wilson Library Bulletin*'s monthly column, "Information Technology."

Basics of Online Searching. By Charles T. Meadow and Pauline Cochrane. New York: John Wiley and Sons, 1981. $15.95.
Examples based on BRS, DIALOG and ORBIT search services.

Computer-readable Data Bases: A Dictionary and Data Sourcebook. Edited by Martha E. Williams. White Plains, NY: Knowledge Industry Publications for the American Society for Information Science, 1979.

Computers for Libraries. By Jennifer Rowley. Hamden, CT: The Shoe String Press, Inc., 1980. $12.00.
An introduction to library automation with information on planning a computerized library system, including system components, information retrieval, technical processes, and circulation systems. Available from the publisher at 995 Sherman Avenue, Hamden, CT 06514.

Directory of Library Networks and Cooperative Library Organizations. Washington, DC: National Center for Education Statistics, 1980.
Available from the Superintendent of Documents, U.S. Government Printing Office, Washington, DC 20402.

The Library and Information Manager's Guide to Online Services. Edited by Ryan E. Hoover. White Plains, NY: Knowledge Industry Pub., 1980. $34.50, softcover $27.50.
Available from the publisher at 701 Westchester Avenue, White Plains, NY 10604, 800/431-1880.

"Library Applications of Microcomputers." By Theodore Hines. Greensboro: University of North Carolina.
This article lists numerous library applications for microcomputers, such as card catalog typing, ordering, bibliographic listings, newspaper indexing, and library statistics.

The article is kept in a word processing file and regularly updated. Available from Library Science/Educational Technology Division, School of Education, University of North Carolina, Greensboro, NC 27412. SASE.

Library Networks, 1981-82. By Susan K. Martin. White Plains, NY: Knowledge Industry Pub., 1981. $29.50, softcover $24.50.

Microcomputer Data Communication Systems. By Frank Derfler. Englewood Cliffs, NJ: Prentice-Hall, 1982. $12.95.
    Reviewed in *Popular Computing* (Oct. 1982): 51 – "If you are befuddled by computer jargon ... now there is help." Derfler is authoring a new column in *Microcomputing*: "Dial-Up Directory," which began in August 1982.

Microcomputers and Libraries, a Guide to Technology, Products and Applications. By Mark Rorvig. White Plains, NY: Knowledge Industry Publications, 1981. $27.50.
    Reviewed in *Small Computers in Libraries* (Feb. 1982) and *ACCESS: Microcomputers in Libraries* (Jan. 1982).

Microcomputers in Library Automation. By George A. Simpson. McLean, VA: The MITRE Corp., 1978. Approx. $3.00.
    Reviewed in *ACCESS: Microcomputers in Libraries* (July 1981): "A fine tutorial for those just entering library automation or the world of microcomputers; it should serve as a good introduction to other works written since 1978." Available from The MITRE Corporation, Metrek Division, 1820 Dolly Madison Boulevard, McLean, VA 22101.

Networks for Networkers: Critical Issues in Cooperative Library Development. Edited by Barbara Evans Markuson and Blanche Woolls. New York: Neal-Schuman Publishers, Inc., 1980. $21.95.
    Available from the publisher at 64 University Place, New York, NY 10003.

Online Public Access Catalogs: The User Interface. By Charles R. Hildreth. Dublin, OH: OCLC, 1982.

Online Search Strategies. Edited by Ryan E. Hoover. White Plains, NY: Knowledge Industry Publications, 1982. $37.50, softcover $29.50.
    Available from the publisher at 701 Westchester Avenue, White Plains, NY 10601, 800/431-1880.

Online Searching: A Primer. By Carol H. Fenichel. Marlton, NJ: Learned Information, 1981. $12.95.

The Professional Librarian's Reader in Library Automation and Technology. White Plains, NY: Knowledge Industry Publications, 1980. $24.50, softcover $17.50.

Public Access to Online Catalogs: A Planning Guide for Managers. By Joseph R. Matthews. Weston, CT: Online, Inc., 1982. $28.50.
    Designed for use at the beginning stages of an online catalog project. Available from Online, Inc., Book Dept., 11 Tannery Lane, Weston, CT 06883.

Programming

The BASIC Handbook. By David Lien. El Cajon, CA: Compusoft Publishing, 1981. $19.95.
    Good reference for those interested in typing in programs from books and magazines; contains a listing of almost 500 BASIC words used for over 250 types of computers. Reviewed in *Popular Computing* (Feb. 1982): 104; *Creative Computing* (Mar. 1982): 255; *80 Microcomputing* (Feb. 1982): 312. Available from the publisher at 1050 Pioneer Way, Suite E, El Cajon, CA 92020.

Creative Programming Manuals. Pasadena, CA: Creative Programming, Inc., 1980.
$10.00.

Series of seven workbooks for TRS-80, Apple, Pet, VIC, TI, or Atari computers. The workbooks, written at fourth grade reading level for use with students age eight through adult, cover commands in the BASIC language. There are also five "All Stars" manuals containing advanced projects intended to enhance logical thinking skills and encourage independent action in programming. The All Stars workbooks are designed to be used with any of the microcomputers and are sequenced with the seven basic programming manuals. Available from the publisher at 1020 South Arroyo Parkway, Pasadena, CA 91105, 213/682-3641. Quantity discounts available.

Flowcharting, a Tool for Understanding Computer Logic. By Nancy Stern. New York: John Wiley and Sons, 1975.

Introduction to Computers and Data Processing. By Gary Shelly and Thomas Cashman. Fullerton, CA: Anaheim Publishing Co., 1980.

Introduction to computers for high school students; teaching aids available include activity guides, tests, transparency masters.

Karel the Robot—A Gentle Introduction to the Art of Programming. By Richard Pattis. New York: John Wiley and Sons, 1981. $7.95.

Reviewed in *The Computing Teacher* (Nov. 1981): 42.

The Little Book of Basic Styles: How to Write a Program You Can Read. By John M. Nevison. Reading, MA: Addison-Wesley, 1978.

Guide to help you write clear, effective programs.

Programming for Poets: A Gentle Introduction to Programming Using BASIC. By Richard Conway and James Archer. Cambridge, MA: Winthrop Publishers, Inc., 1979.

The Secret Guide to Computers. 8 volumes. By Russ Walters. Boston, MA: Russ Walters, regular updates. $3.75/volume; set $29.70.

These books cover many aspects of computers and programming. The easy to follow information is written with humor (adult), and is periodically updated. The author is also available to answer questions by phone. Reviewed by Glenn Fisher, *The Computing Teacher* 9 (Sept. 1981): 36-37. Write to the author at 92 St. Botolph Street, Boston, MA 02116.

Sortmaster: Sorting Programs for Small Computers. A Book of Standard BASIC Programs. Norwalk, CT: Creative Computer Consultants, nd.

Reviewed in *The Computing Teacher* 8 (Feb. 1981): "excellent aids for users who need to sort data within a program, such as student names or grades." Available from the publisher at P.O. Box 23111, Norwalk, CT 06851.

Write, Edit, and Print: Word Processing with Personal Computers. By Donald H. McCunn. San Francisco: Design Enterprises of San Francisco, 1982. $34.95, $24.95 paperback.

Reviewed by Michael Schuyler, *ACCESS: Microcomputers in Libraries* 2 (Oct. 1982): "designed to allow the reader to create a complete word processing system.... There are better programs on the market.... However, if your intent is to learn BASIC programming, then this is a project which could very well take you from a beginner's level to be relatively conversant in the language. It provides the goal of a very useful program with immediate applications." Available from the publisher at P.O. Box 14695, San Francisco, CA 94114.

Software Sources and Evaluation Aids

Courseware in the Classroom: Selecting, Organizing and Using Software. By Ann Lathrop and Bobby Goodson. Menlo Park, CA: Innovative Division, Addison-Wesley, 1983. $9.95.

Ann Lathrop helped establish the Microcomputer Center—joint project of CUE (Computer-Using Educators) and the San Mateo County Office of Education and Softswap, a public domain software exchange. She has written a column "The Micro in the Media Center" for the past year in *Educational Computer* magazine. Bobby Goodson, as president of CUE, has also been involved with the Microcomputer Center and Softswap.

Educational Software Directory: A Subject Guide to Microcomputer Software. By Marilyn Chartrand and Constance D. Williams for Corporate Monitor, Inc. Littleton, CO: Libraries Unlimited, 1982. $22.50.

Comprehensive directory of educational software by subject for grades K-12. The first part is an informative annotated listing of programs arranged alphabetically by title within broad subject areas; the second lists publishers and distributors with the name, address, phone number, and a description of the company's products and previewing policies.

Special Computer Application Software

Introduction to Word Processing. By Zane K. Quible. Cambridge, MA: Winthrop Publishers, Inc., 1981.
Reviewed in *Electronic Education* (Dec. 1982): 38.

VisiCalc: Home and Office Companion. By David M. Castlewitz, Lawrence Chisauski, and Patricia Kronberg. Berkeley, CA: Osborne/McGraw-Hill, 1982. $15.99.
Spreadsheet applications; reviewed in *Popular Computing* (Dec. 1982): 163-64. This is just one of a variety of books with ideas for utilizing the spreadsheet programs. Watch for one coming that will emphasize library management.

Word Processing and Information Processing, a Basic Manual. By Dan Poynter. Santa Barbara, CA: Para Publishing, 1982. $11.95.

PERIODICALS

American Libraries. 50 East Huron Street, Chicago, IL 60611. Monthly; $25.00
Column, "The Source," contains a wealth of informational "briefs." Subheadings cover such topics as microcomputing, networks, resources, personal computing, etc.

Arithmetic Teacher. National Council of Teachers of Mathematics, 1906 Association Drive, Reston, VA 22091.
"Teaching with Microcomputers," 30 (Feb. 1983)—focus issue. Issue has a good variety of resource materials for teachers planning to use or already using microcomputers for instruction.

BYTE. Byte Publications, 70 Main Street, Peterborough, NH 03458. Monthly; $19.00.
A catalog of ads, good source for information concerning new products. The articles are generally aimed at those with some technical background, and are not for the novice. Each issue has a theme. You may want to purchase only those issues of particular interest. For example, in one issue recently the theme was LOGO, which would be of interest to educators. Look for back issues at computer stores. Indexed in *Microcomputer Index.*

Call A.P.P.L.E. 304 Main Street, Suite 300, Renton, WA 98055. Seven issues/yr.; $20.00 plus one time membership fee of $25.00 for Exchange Program.
Popular magazine with Apple owners; contains a great deal of programming information for all levels of programmers. Good source of reviews for Apple software and peripherals. Published by the Apple Puget Sound Program Library Exchange. Has periodic specials on Apple software and reference materials. Indexed in *Microcomputer Index.*

Classroom Computer News. Intentional Educations, Inc., 341 Mt. Auburn Street, Watertown, MA 02172. (617)923-8595. Bimonthly; $16.00.

Covers education applications of computers. Includes reviews of hardware, software, and books; announcements of new products; and practical articles by and for educators. Indexed in *Microcomputer Index.*

The Commodore Gazette. Compute! Publications, P.O. Box 5406, Greensboro, NC 27403. Monthly.

A new publication premiering in 1983, which will be written for beginning and intermediate level owners and users of the VIC-20, 64, and Ultimax computers.

CompuKids Computer Magazine for Beginners. CompuKids Magazine, P.O. Box 874, Sedalia, MO 65301. (816)826-5410. $16.00.

Compute! 625 Fulton Street, Greensboro, NC 26403. Monthly; $20.00.

Written for owners of computers using the 6502 chip, e.g., Apples, Commodores, and Ataris. Good resource for Commodore and Atari owners. Usually has several BASIC program listings. Indexed in *Microcomputer Index.*

The Computing Teacher. Dept. of Computer Science, University of Oregon, Eugene, OR 97403. Nine issues/yr.; $16.50.

One of the oldest educational computer magazines. Publication of International Council for Computers in Education (ICCE). Has articles for teachers using computers, and/or teaching about computers; articles addressing educational issues related to computers; book reviews, software reviews, film reviews, and articles concerning applications for computers in a wide range of curriculum areas. Good basic information source for teachers in elementary through high school.

Creative Computing. P.O. Box 789-M, Morristown, NJ 07960. Monthly; $25.00.

One of the oldest general computer magazines. Covers a wide variety of microcomputers and applications. Has good coverage of games and programs for the home user. Some issues have a theme such as education, and there are usually several articles related to education. This magazine is available at the general newstand, not just in computer stores. Indexed in *Microcomputer Index.*

Drexel Library Quarterly. School of Library and Information Science, Drexel University, Philadelphia, PA 19104. Quarterly; $6.00 per issue, or $20.00 per year.

"The Electronic Library," 17 (Fall 1981), includes: "You're in the Chips; or The Computer: What It Is and What It Can Do" by J. R. Matthews; "Library Information Delivery Systems: Past, Present, and Future" by B. L. Kenney; "The Human Element: Staff Development in the Electronic Library" by B. Conroy; "Financing the Electronic Library: Models and Options" by Waters and Kralisz; "Education for the Electronic Library" by C. E. Dowlin; "Remote Electronic Delivery of Information through Libraries" by R. T. Sweeney.

Educational Computer. P.O. Box 535, Cupertino, CA 95015. Bimonthly; $15.00.

Focuses on educational applications of computers K-12. Each issue has a library/media column and an administrative applications column. Articles address educational concerns and report on applications in the field. Reviews of software and products for education, Indexed in *Microcomputer Index.*

Educational Technology. 140 Sylvan Avenue, Englewood Cliffs, NJ 07632. Monthly; $49.00.

More scholarly, theoretical articles with research information on computers in education, written mainly by those in higher education. Also includes reviews of books and software. Indexed in *Microcomputer Index.*

80 Microcomputing. 80 Pine Street, Peterborough, NH 03458. Monthly; $25.00.

Specializes in covering the TRS-80 microcomputers. Good source for BASIC program listings, ads for TRS-80 products, reviews. Indexed in *Microcomputer Index.*

Electronic Education. Electronic Communications, Inc., Suite 220, 1311 Executive Center Drive, Tallahassee, FL 32301. (904)878-4178. Nine issues/yr.; $18.00.
First issue: Sept. 1981. Articles addressing issues in the educational use of computers; listing of educational computer conferences, workshops, etc.; new product descriptions; description of educational applications; reviews of books, software, and hardware.

Electronic Learning. Scholastic, 902 Sylvan Avenue, Englewood Cliffs, NJ 07632. 8 issues per year; $19.00.
Emphasis on educational applications for microcomputers. Provides a great deal of information on hardware for the novice, with explanatory articles and comparison charts. Reviews educational software. Articles by and about educators "in the field." First issue Sept./Oct. 1981. Indexed in *Microcomputer Index.*

The Electronic Library. Learned Information, Inc., 143 Old Marlton Pike, Medford, NJ 08055. (609)654-6266. Quarterly; $59.00.
A new journal (first issue Jan. 1983), " ... dedicated to the applications and impact of the new information technology in the library."

Information Technology and Libraries. Formerly called *Journal of Library Automation.* ALA, Library and Information Technology Division (LITA), 50 East Huron Street, Chicago, IL 60611. Quarterly; $15.00.

InfoWorld. 530 Lytton Avenue, Palo Alto, CA 94301. Weekly; $25.00.

Instructional Innovator. A.E.C.T. Publication, AECT (Association for Educational Communications and Technology), 1126 Sixteenth Street, N.W., Washington, DC 20036. Monthly; $18.00 or with AECT membership.

Interface Age. 16704 Marquardt Avenue, Cerritos, CA 90701. Monthly; $21.00.
Good general interest computer magazine. Regular reviews of hardware/software, with helpful charts. A middle-level publication focusing primarily on business applications. Includes a regular education column or article, as well as a regular column on data communications. Indexed in *Microcomputer Index.*

The Journal of Courseware Review. Vol. 1, No. 1. A Foundation Publication, Foundation for the Advancement of Computer-aided Education, 20863 Stevens Creek Boulevard, Bldg. B-2, Suite A-1, Cupertino, CA 95014. $5.95 plus $1.00 postage, or at computer stores or dealers.
The first volume reviews programs for the Apple II.

Learning. 19 Davis Drive, Belmont, CA 94002.
"Computers: The Key Word Is Learn; The Key Time Is Now" (Jan. 1982): 24-57, feature section. "Computers will become useful classroom additions for teachers who seize the initiative and learn what can—and should be done with them. On the other hand, teachers who wait passively for instructions may not like what they are told."

The Mathematics Teacher. National Council of Teachers of Mathematics, 1906 Association Drive, Reston, VA 22091.
"Microcomputers," 74 (Nov. 1981), a special issue; single copies $3.50 (Stock #203).

Microcomputing. Formerly *Kilobaud Microcomputing.* 80 Pine Street, Peterborough, NH 03458. Monthly; $25.00.
A general interest computer magazine with a variety of articles covering hardware, software, programming, etc. at different levels. In general this is a magazine for those with some computer knowledge. Regular columns include a data communication column, dial-up directory, and book reviews. Indexed in *Microcomputer Index.*

Peelings. P.O. Box 188, Las Cruces, NM 88001. Nine issues/yr.; $21.00.
Comprehensive reviews of software for the Apple. Usually reviews several similar programs in an issue to ease comparison. Indexed in *Microcomputer Index.*

Personal Computing. Hayden, 50 Essex Street, Rochelle Park, NY 07662. Monthly; $18.00.

A good general interest magazine for novice to middle level; not too technical. Mainly addresses issues and applications in business. Includes a regular "Answers" column, book reviews, software and hardware reviews and comparisons. Some articles concerning educational applications and issues. Indexed in *Microcomputer Index.*

Popular Computing. Formerly *OnComputing.* 70 Main Street, Peterborough, NH 03458. Monthly; $15.00.

Excellent general interest magazine for the novice. Articles are easy to read, well illustrated, and provide good variety of information for the beginner. Has software/hardware reviews. An easy magazine to read from cover to cover. Has a regular education column, a regular telecomputing column, book reviews, product announcements, "Ask Popular" column. Indexed in *Microcomputer Index.*

Purser's Magazine. For the TRS-80 Model I, Issue No. 15. P.O. Box 466, El Dorado, CA 95623. $5.00 plus $2.00 postage/handling.

Contains reviews and photographs for over 70 programs for the Model I.

School Courseware Journal. Formerly *CourseWare Magazine.* 1341 Bulldog Lane, Suite C, Fresno, CA 93710. (209)227-4341. Five issues/yr.

This is a magazine with programs on cassettes and diskettes for schools K-12. Address change announced in Oct. 1982 issue of *Computing Teacher.* Dr. Dan Isaacson, editor and publisher, said the new quarters provide space needed for installation of Atari and other equipment. This is in addition to Apple, PET, and TRS-80 microcomputers. The 1982/83 journal will be available for all four computers. *The Computing Teacher* 9 (Jan. 1982): 19-20 reviews an issue of the magazine. Each issue includes programs on tape of diskette, plus printed descriptions of the programs, listings in BASIC, lists of program variables, and an explanation in plain English of what each program line or group of lines does.

School Microware Reviews. Dresden Associates, P.O. Box 246, Dresden, ME 04342. Write for subscription information.

Softalk. Softalk Publishing, Inc., 11160 McCormick Street, North Hollywood, CA 91603. (213)980-5074. Monthly; $24.00 without sponsor, $18.00 with sponsor, free first year to Apple owner.

If you own an Apple, but you've never received *Softalk*, send your name, address, and Apple serial number with a request for a subscription to Softalk Circulation, P.O. Box 60, North Hollywood, CA 91603. *Softalk* is totally independent of Apple Computer, Inc.; sending your warranty card to Apple Computer will not inform *Softalk* of your existence.

Talmis Courseware Ratings. 115 North Oak Park Avenue, Oak Park, IL 60301.

Nielsen-like ratings from a representative sample of both elementary and secondary schools. Educators wishing to receive information on subscriptions to the rating newsletter should send their name and address to *Talmis.*

Today's Education. General edition (Apr./May 1982). National Education Association, 1201 Sixteenth Street, N.W., Washington, DC 20036. Published four times a year in Sept./Oct., Nov./Dec., Feb./Mar. and Apr./May; single copies $2.00.

NEWSLETTERS

Closing the Gap. Microcomputers for the Handicapped. Closing the Gap, Route 2, Box 39, Henderson, MN 56044. Six issues/yr.; $15.00 (prepaid—no purchase orders).

The purpose of *CTG* is to let people interested in computer applications for the handicapped know what is available and how to find it in this rapidly growing field. A sample copy may be obtained by sending $2.50 plus $.50 postage and handling.

CMC News (Computers and the Media Center). Jim Deacon, Editor. ES Task Group of ACM Computers, 515 Oak Street North, Canon Falls, MN 55009. Three issues (Fall, Winter, and Spring); $3.00 prepaid, back issues available.

Issue 1: Spring 1980. An excellent resource about happenings with micros in media centers. Includes user reports about commercial software used for library applications; news of library software sources; resource people with information and practical experiences to share; annotated lists of articles of special interest to library media personnel; and periodic annotated lists of subscribers. Every school library should find this newsletter a valuable resource.

C.U.E. Newsletter. P.O. Box 18457, San Jose, CA 95158. $6.00.

This newsletter comes with membership in the Computer-Using Educators Group, and is another good source of information. As the group's name implies, the newsletter concerns educational happenings with computers: reviews of products, software, hardware, books; reports about and from educational conferences; and update information about Softswap. It also serves as a vehicle for the exchange of ideas related to computer issues in education.

DLA Bulletin. University of California, Division of Library Automation, 186 University Hall, Berkeley, CA 94720. (415)642-9485. Irregular; free.

Variety of information about library automation, particularly at the University of California. Includes a glossary for each issue. Write to be added to mailing list.

EPIE Report on Microcomputer Courseware. EPIE (Educational Products Information Exchange) Institute, P.O. Box 620, Stony Brook, NY 11790. $25.00.

The first *EPIE Report on Microcomputer Courseware* will contain detailed analyses of all the major microcomputer mathematics packages currently on the market.

EPIE Special Report on Microcomputer Hardware. EPIE (Educational Products Information Exchange) Institute, P.O. Box 620, Stony Brook, NY 11790. $25.00.

The ETA Newsletter (Educational Technology for Alaska). Bee Tindell, Editor. Pouch F—State Office Bldg., Juneau, AK 99811. Free.

May/June 1982 issue included: descriptions of microcomputer applications, hardware reviews, a listing of microcomputer software for school administration, and a chart summarizing the features of nine microcomputer systems.

The Journal for VisiCalc Users. Software Arts, Inc., P.O. Box 815, Quincy, MA 02169.

One of a number of newsletters and magazines for users of spreadsheet programs.

Library Systems Newsletter. Library Technology Reports, American Library Association, 50 East Huron Street, Chicago, IL 60611. Monthly; $25.00.

MECC Data Line. MECC (Minnesota Educational Computing Consortium), 2520 Broadway Drive, St. Paul, MN 55112. Bimonthly; free.

Write to be added to mailing list.

MICROgram. Consortium for Quality in Educational Computing Products, EPIE and Consumers Union, P.O. Box 620, Stony Brook, NY 11790. (516)246-8664. Monthly; $48.00.

From *The Computing Teacher* (Jan. 1983): 35-46 — The consortium "has been created to serve as a consumer force working toward better quality educational computing products.... *MICROgram* is published to provide its readers with news about microcomputing products, and also, to function as an open forum for consortium members — a place where the consumer concerns of consortium members can be aired, discussed and organized into some much needed consumer clout in what, at present, is very much a 'sellers market.' "

MicroSIFT News. (Microcomputer Software and Information for Teachers). Northwest Regional Educational Laboratory, 300 Southwest Sixth Avenue, Portland, OR 97204.

This is a clearinghouse for evaluative information about educational software. The reviews are distributed through various state and local agencies as well as through some periodicals. The information is also retrievable through BRS (Bibliographic Retrieval Services — see Information Retrieval in this appendix). Write to NREL and have name added to mailing list to receive periodic newsletters.

The National LOGO Exchange. Elaine Larson, The National LOGO Exchange, P.O. Box 5341, Charlottesville, VA 22905. Monthly; $24.00.

A recently begun newsletter containing practical suggestions for implementing LOGO in the classroom.

NICE Newsletter. American Institutes for Research, P.O. Box 1113, Palo Alto, CA 94302. (415)493-3550. Quarterly; $15.00 individual.

NICE (Network for Industry, Computers, and Education) is concerned with helping both educators and those in industry who are concerned with providing today's young people with the necessary skills for functioning in our postindustrial era. NICE requests that you help the network work by sending information about collaborations between business and education to promote computer education in your school or community.

Small Computers in Libraries. Dr. Allan Pratt, Editor. Graduate Library School, College of Education, University of Arizona, 1515 East First Street, Tucson, AZ 85271. (602)626-3566. Monthly; $20.00.

Began in April 1981 stating as its principal objectives "1) to act as a clearinghouse for the sharing of information on micros in libraries and 2) to offer some guidance to those who are new to the field, in the form of glossaries, short tutorial articles, and reviews of both programs and books pertinent to this subject.... For *SCIL* purposes, we consider a micro to be a system costing under $10,000." This is an *excellent* source of information for libraries.

Technicalities. The Oryx Press, 2214 North Central, Suite 103, Phoenix, AZ 85004. Monthly; $24.00.

Newsletter concerned with "exploring the technical side of library and information systems and management.... Technicalities offers a spirit of dialog, a discussion of alternatives ranging from philosophical concerns to pragmatic how-to-do-it articles." — from first issue, December 1980.

Turtle News. Young People's Logo Association, 1208 Hillsdale Drive, Richardson, TX 75081. (214)783-7548.

YPLA publishes both *Turtle News* and *Logo Newsletter.* The association is open free of charge to anyone 18 or younger. Adults pay a fee.

Turtle Talk. Harvard Publishing, 118A Magazine Street, Cambridge, MA 02139. (617)547-3289. Bimonthly; $12.00; $3.00 for a sample copy.

This is another recently started newsletter to promote interest and provide a means of idea exchange among educators using LOGO. Planned regular features include a section on applications for special education.

BOOKLETS

Computer Literacy

An Introduction to Computing: Content for a High School Course. By Jean B. Rogers. Dept. of Computer and Information Science, University of Oregon, 135 Education, Eugene, OR 97403. (503)686-4414. $2.50, quantity discounts available.
An outline for a year-long computer science course at the secondary school level.

Kids Can Touch, a Child's Guide to the Apple II Plus Computer. By Patricia M. Shillingburg. 24 Beechwood Road, Summit, NJ 07901. (201)277-3837. $4.95 plus $1.00 postage, quantity discounts available.
A self-teaching guide which includes four chapters on programming and three chapters on the history of computers and their impact on society.

The Parent's Guide to Computers in Education. By David Moursund. ICCE, University of Oregon, 135 Education, Eugene, OR 97403. (503)686-4414. $3.50, quantity discounts available.
Describes in nontechnical language: why children should use and learn about computers; how computers work; ways students and teachers are using computers in schools and elsewhere; suggestions for parents; a plan for buying a home computer. Also includes a glossary and list of additional sources of information. New as of January 1983.

Precollege Computer Literacy: A Personal Computing Approach. By David Moursund. ICCE, University of Oregon, 135 Education, Eugene, OR 97403. (503)686-4414. $1.50, quantity discounts available.
This updated and expanded version of a paper, "Personal Computing for Elementary and Secondary School Students," which was presented by Mr. Moursund for a computer literacy conference held in December 1980 in Reston, Virginia, is a useful aid to developing school computer literacy programs.

School Administrator's Introduction to Instructional Use of Computers. By David Moursund. ICCE, University of Oregon, 135 Education, Eugene, OR 97403. (503)686-4414. $2.50, quantity discounts available.
An overview of instructional computer applications and their effects on curriculums.

Teacher's Guide to Computers in the Elementary School. By David Moursund. ICCE, University of Oregon, 135 Education, Eugene, OR 97403. (503)686-4414. $2.50, quantity discounts available.
A guide to instructional computer applications and computer education, including sample activities (many of which do not require a computer), a list of resources, and a glossary. Reviewed in *Computing Teacher* (Sept. 1981): 37.

Education

Illinois Series on Educational Applications of Computers. Computing-Teacher Education Papers, Urbana, IL. University of Illinois, Dept. of Secondary Education, 396 Education Building, Urbana, IL 61801. $.75 each, orders less than $6.00 must be prepaid.
Twenty-two booklets discussing all aspects of computers in education. Send for complete list.

Library Management

Guidelines for Cataloging Microcomputer Software. Wisconsin Educational Media Association. Don Jorgensen, McKinely Instructional Service Center, 1010 Huron Street, Manitowoc, WI 54220. Free to WEMA members, $1.50 plus $.50 mailing to nonmembers.

Software Evaluation

Evaluator's Guide for Microcomputer-Based Instructional Packages. MicroSIFT, project of Northwest Regional Educational Laboratory, ICCE Dept. 58, University of Oregon, 135 Education, Eugene, OR 97403. (503)686-4414. $2.50, quantity discounts available.

The Computer Technology Program of the Northwest Regional Laboratory developed this booklet, which includes a summary of MicroSIFT's evaluation process with detailed descriptions of all review components, review forms, sample reviews, and a glossary.

Guidelines for Evaluating Computerized Instructional Materials. National Council of Teachers of Mathematics. 1906 Association Drive, Reston, VA 22091. $3.75.

Ann Lathrop: "This is a very usable booklet, especially for the novice. The evaluation criteria are well developed, with clear explanations and examples, and the evaluation forms are both simple and easy to complete. Highly recommended."

Special Education

Learning Disabled Students and Computers: A Teacher's Guide Book. By Merrianne Coon, David Ouellette, and Joan Thormann. ICCE University of Oregon, 135 Education, Eugene, OR 97403. (503)686-4414. $2.50, quantity discounts available.

Published in January, 1983, for those concerned with meeting the needs of learning disabled children; includes a resource section with a glossary and references to publishers, books and organizations involved with computers and special education.

LIBRARY APPLICATIONS SOFTWARE

NOTE: When considering any software, it is strongly recommended that you contact a user if possible. Often you may do this through the many computer user groups and/or organizations, if not through the original distributor.

Abacus Computing, 75 Hewett Street, Rochester, NY.

A file management system being used by some libraries for inventory, indexing, film books, purchase orders, etc.

American Micro Media, P.O. Box 396, Red Hood, NY 12571. (914)756-2557.

Carries the programs from Library Software Company and Right On for library management. This is one of the companies described by Ann Lathrop in her article "Mail-Order Distributors with Liberal Software On-Approval Policies" in the Jan./Feb. 1983 issue of *Educational Computer.*

Apple Presents Apple: An Introduction to the Keyboard. Apple Computer, Inc. Available at Apple dealers.

This program on disk was originally a part of the Apple Family System and is now available from Apple dealers. An easy "introduction to the keyboard," via the keyboard, for students and staff. Reviewed in *Classroom Computer News* (Jan./Feb. 1983): 58-59.

Audio-Visual Equipment Program. Avant-Garde Creations, P.O. Box 30160, Eugene, OR 97403.

BIBLIOMOD. Blue Lakes Software, 3240 University Avenue, Madison, WI.

BIBLIOTEK. Scientific Software Products, 3171 Donald Avenue, Indianapolis, IN 46224. (317)299-0467.

Program not written to handle complete bibliographic data, but intended for the cataloging of private collections of scientific reprints. It could, however, be useful in small technical libraries which have similar needs to individual scientists and researchers. Contact Scientific Software for user names.

CALICO. Computer Assisted Library Instruction Co., Inc., P.O. Box 15916, St. Louis, MO 63114.

A series of self-instructional programs prepared as guides for using periodical indexes, almanacs, *Bartlett's Familiar Quotations, Current Biography*, and poetry indexes. More programs are being developed. Demo disk available. Write for more information. In the Jan./Feb. 1982 issue of *Educational Computer* Ann Lathrop uses the Periodical Indexes program to illustrate the use of a critical evaluation guide for software. Three of the programs are reviewed in the November 1, 1982 issue of *Booklist*. Programs were developed and tested by a group of librarians. An article about the program development was published in *Show-Me Libraries* (Mar. 1982).

Capital Systems Groups, Inc., 11301 Rockville Pike, Kensington, MD 20895. (301)881-9400.

Six programs: CHECKMATE™ (serials control); GOLDEN RETRIEVER™ (acquisitions, inventory, and other database storage and retrieval functions); BOOKDEX (for monographic and report indexing); NEWSDEX (for serials indexing); CARD for AACR2 (catalog card production) and THESAURUS BUILDER (for thesaurus construction). Minimum hardware requirements include a full 24x80 screen and an ASCII keyboard, a printer and disk drives (varies for each). Some demo disks available and separate manuals may be purchased.

CARDPREP. Pierre P. and Linda J. Barrette, Route #1, 48 Highlander, Carbondale, IL 62901.

This is a program to generate complete sets of catalog cards as well as complete sets of labels. The program was designed and programmed by two librarians. It requires an Apple II computer with 64K memory, an upper/lowercase adapter chip, and a printer capable of handling card stock.

Catalog Card and Label Printer. William F. Wehner, K-12 MicroMedia, P.O. Box 17, Valley Cottage, NY 10989. (201)391-7555.

Compared with Telemarc III in *Small Computers in Libraries* (July 1982). Requires an Apple II Plus, lower case adapter, and printer. The cataloging style is based on the book *Commonsense Cataloging* by Esther J. Piercy.

Catalog Card and Label Printing Program. Clinton-Essex-Franklin Library System, 17 Oak Street, Plattsburgh, NY. 563-5190.

This is an in-house program developed to print out complete sets of catalog cards and pocket, card, and spine labels. Equipment needed: 64K Apple Plus, a disk drive, a Videx Videoterm 80 column board and Videx keyboard enhancer, a Microsoft Softcard and an Epson dot matrix printer.

CHECKMATE™. CLASS (California Library Authority for Systems and Services), 1415 Koll Circle, Suite 101, San Jose, CA 95112.

A standalone, turnkey system. Software is fully supported and maintained by CLASS. Demonstration diskette available ($21.50). Distributed east of the Mississippi through CSG Capital Systems Group, Inc., 11301 Rockville Pike, Kensington, MD 20895. Hardware requirements: Micro with at least 64K (e.g., HP 125 or TRS-80 Mod. III), CP/M or TRSDOS, eight-inch floppy disk drives or hard disk. Application language: Microsoft BASIC, printer.

Circulation Management System. Orchard Systems, 207 East Third Street, Waunakee, WI 53597. (608)849-5727.

System designed to operate on the Apple II, 48K, DOS 3.3, one disk drive and 132 column printer. Tracks up to 600 items from time of check-out to time of return. Libraries with more than 600 items checked out at one time could use the system by dividing circulation into categories, or using the program only for overdues.

Charles W. Clark Co., 168 Express Drive South, Brentwood, NY 11717. (516)231-1220.
One of the catalog mail-order distributors with liberal software on-approval policies described by Ann Lathrop in *Educational Computer* (Jan./Feb. 1983). Has library skill instruction software.

Computer Cat™. Colorado Computer Systems, Inc., 3005 West Seventy-fourth Avenue, Westminster, CO 80030. (303)426-5880.
Online "card" catalog. Operates on an Apple II Plus (or Bell and Howell equivalent), 48K plus a language card, one floppy disk drive, Corvus hard disk, monitor, and printer. For a multi-station system Omninet can be added. For details see chapter 7.
A leaflet about special applications for Computer Cat can be obtained from Think Small Computers, Inc., 8600 Concord Lane, Westminster, CO 80030. (303)428-2929. It includes directions for adapting Computer Cat to handle equipment inventory, reservations, equipment check-in/check-out and service location. Also included are directions for using a small data field to hold codes for indicating which items in a set are active or inactive. For example, the system could be used with a catalog holding multiple collections to identify all the locations for a specific title. These applications may be used with other programs also.

CTI Circulation Systems. Computer Translation, Inc. (CTI), 1455 South State Street, Orem, UT 84057. (801)224-1169.
This system handles basic circulation functions, including check-out, check-in, patron file, overdue notices, and statistics. It is being used at Goddart High School, 300 North Kentucky, Roswell, NM 88201. The program requires an Apple II Plus 48K, one floppy disk drive, one hard disk, monitor, 16K language card, lightpen, printer, and software. CTI has several systems. Write for complete information.

Data Sheet: Photophile™, Image Storage and Retrieval System. Peripheral Visions, Inc., 5285 Northeast Elam Young Parkway, Suite B500, Hillsboro, OR 97123. (503)640-1317.
A filing and cross-referencing system for slides and negatives. The company has other record-keeping, bibliographic type programs. Contact for further information.

DB Master™. Stoneware, 50 Belvedere Street, San Rafael, CA 94901. (415)454-6500.
A popular database management program for the Apple which is being used by many libraries. Both floppy disk and hard disk drive versions available.

dBaseII™. Ashton-Tate, 9929 West Jefferson Boulevard, Culver City, CA 90230.
A popular database management system being used by many libraries. This program requires some programming knowledge; it is not "turnkey" software.

DTI Data Trek, 121 West E Street, Second Floor, Encinitas, CA 92024. (714)436-5055.
Library automation software packages: five integrated modules which may be purchased separately—catalog, circulation, acquisitions, serials, and lab notebook systems. The programs run under the CP/M or MP/M operating systems and so will run on a variety of microcomputers. They were originally developed for special libraries but are now also installed in at least one school district. Contact DTI for user names.

Educational Activities, Inc., P.O. Box 392, Freeport, NY 11520.
Media and equipment management software.

Electronic Library Systems. InfoSoft, 12219 Wildpine Drive, Houston, TX 77039. (713)442-4040.
An online card catalog program that runs under CP/M. It is being tested at Furneaux Elementary School, Carrollton, TX 75007.

Elementary Library Media Skills. Combase, Inc., Suite 890, 333 Sibley Street, St. Paul, MN 55101.
Ruth Sather developed and tested an elementary computer literacy program and is now designing and developing an elementary library media skills computer-based program.

The program will run on an Apple II and is scheduled for release in 1983. For more information contact Combase.

EyeGate Media, Inc., 146-01 Archer Avenue, Jamaica, NY 11435.
Has several library instruction programs for the Apple, TRS-80, and Pet.

Follett Library Book Company—"Quality Courseware" Catalog, Follett Library Book company, 4506 Northwest Highway, Crystal Lake, IL 60014. (800)435-6170.
Follett carries library management and library skills instruction software for a variety of microcomputers. It is one of the companies described in "Mail-Order Distributors with Librarl Software On-Approval Policies," by Ann Lathrop in *Educational Computer Magazine* (Jan./Feb. 1983). The library software packages developed by Robert Stevens of Richmond Software in Canada are being distributed in the United States by Follett. Contact them for more information.

Gaylord Library Systems—Library Products/Supplies Company, P.O. Box 4901, Syracuse, NY 13221. (315)457-5070.
Write for Gaylord Microcomputer Products and Services Catalog. They carry several library management programs such as The Overdue Writer and Telemarc III.

GOLDEN RETRIEVER™. CLASS (California Library Authority for Systems and Services), 1415 Koll Circle, Suite 101, San Jose, CA 95112.
A general purpose file maintenance and information retrieval program; indexes, stores, searches, and retrieves information in a variety of formats. Demo disk available ($21.50). Hardware requirements: Micro with 64K (e.g., HP125, TRS-80 III), CP/M or TRSDOS, eight-inch floppy disk drives or hard disk, printer. Distributed east of the Mississippi through CSG Capital Systems Group, Inc., 11301 Rockville Pike, Kensington, MD 20895.

The Highsmith Co., Inc., P.O. Box 800, Fort Atkinson, WI 53538. (414)563-9571.
Highsmith, a leading supplier of library products, carries many computer products: software, popular reference books, paper, diskettes, storage and maintenance items. Write for their microcomputer catalog.

Information Master. High Technology Software Products, P.O. Box 14665, 8001 North Classen Boulevard, Oklahoma City, OK 73113.
A data management system—see article about library application in *ACCESS: Microcomputers in Libraries* (Oct. 1981).

J. L. Hammett Co., P.O. Box 545, Braintree, MA 02184. (800)225-5467.
Has library circulation program The Bookworm, described in "Some Sure-Fire Microcomputer Programs" by Blanche E. Woolls and David V. Loertscher, *School Library Journal* 28 (Aug. 1982). Hammett is one of those described in the article "Mail-Order Distributors with Liberal Software On-Approval Policies" by Ann Lathrop in *Educational Computer Magazine* (Jan./Feb. 1983).

Jinsam. Jini Micro-Systems, Inc., P.O. Box 274 Kingsbridge Station, Riverdale, NY 10463. (212)796-6200.
A flexible, menu-driven database management system for all versions of 32K Commodore computers and disk drives. Reviewed in *Educational Computer Magazine* (May/June 1982). Has a users' newsletter.

K-12 MicroMedia, P.O. Box 17, Valley Cottage, NY 10989. (201)391-7555.
Distributes library management and library skills instruction software. One of the distributors described in article "Mail-Order Distributors with Liberal Software On-Approval Policies" by Ann Lathrop in *Educational Computer Magazine* (Jan./Feb. 1983).

Librarian. Geosystems, Inc., 802 East Grand River, Williamston, MI 48895.
A filing and key word retrieval program.

Library Circulation Management. K-12 MicroMedia, P.O. Box 17, Valley Cottage, NY
    10989. (201)391-7555.
    Developed for small school libraries, this program records information for 300
students borrowing up to six books each. Two disk drives can accommodate up to 800
students. TRS-80 and Apple versions are available. This program is being used at the Baker
City High School (1015 South Third West, P.O. Box 659, Baker, Montana 59313) on a
TRS-80 III with an 80 character printer.

Library Circulation System. Winnebago Software Co., 109 West Main Street, Caledonia,
    MN 55921.
    A circulation program for an Apple II Plus, 48K that uses a bar code reader.

Library Monitor. Colorado Computer West, P.O. Box 206, Kremmling, CO 80459.
    (303)724-9364.
    A library management program.

Library Processes System. EDUCOMP, 919 West Canadian Street, Vinita, OK 74301.
    Card printing program designed for TRS-80 two-disk systems, with a minimum of
48K, and a heavy-duty tractor feed printer. Available for Models I, II, and III. Write for
descriptive flyer.

Library Skills, Intel-Tutor Software. K-12 MicroMedia, P.O. Box 17, Valley Cottage,
    NY 10989.
    Reviewed in *The Computing Teacher* 10 (Dec. 1982): 40.

Library Skills: What's There and How to Find It. Micro Power and Light Company,
    1108 Keystone Park, 13774 North Central Expressway, Dallas, TX 75243.
    Reviewed by MicroSIFT, Northwest Regional Educational Laboratory, 300
Southwest Sixth Avenue, Portland, OR 97204, (503)248-6800. Write for copy of review.
Program also available through several mail-order distributors. Read review in *The
Computing Teacher* 8 (Mar. 1981): 39-40.

Library Software Co., P.O. Box 23897, Pleasant Hill, CA 94523.
    A variety of library programs developed by Robert Skapura, a high school librarian:
The Overdue Writer; The Elementary Overdue Writer; The Overdue Collector; The
Overnight Writer; AV Catalog Printer; Bibliography Writer; Card Catalog Generator.
These programs are available through several mail-order catalogs: Highsmith, Follett, etc.
The Overdue Writer has been on the market for some time and is in widespread use. See
article by Robert Skapura in *School Library Media Quarterly* (Summer 1982) about its
development. Many libraries have found this a good package for introducing the library
staff to computers. For example, Eric Anderson tells how they have used it in *The
Computing Teacher* 9 (May 1982): 13-14. The manual is very well done.

Library Usage Skills. Title IV-C, Jim Deacon, Project Director, Computers and the Media
    Center, Cannon Falls Public Schools, 820 East Minnesota Street, Cannon Falls, MN
    55009.
    Deacon received a two-part grant. The first part was to develop library usage skills for
fourth, seventh, and tenth graders. The skills package was scheduled for completion in
January of 1983. The second part of the project is to develop a circulation system using a
bar code reader. Contact him for current information.

Massachusetts Vocational Curriculum Resource Center (MVCR), Minuteman Tech,
    758 Marrett Road, Lexington, MA 02173-7398. (617)863-1863.
    MVCR has developed a variety of library applications using commercial software such
as DB Master™ and PFS Filing System™. Some of these have been described in *Small
Computers in Libraries* and/or you may write the center for descriptions of their activities.

Maxwell Library Systems, Suite 26, 186 Alewife Brook Parkway, Cambridge, MA
    02138. (617)497-7432.

Carries TRS-80 library programs based on the database manager system MAXIMANAGER, which is required in order to use them: Newspaper Index, Catalog Card Production, Periodicals Control, Information and Referral Files, Community Calendar. The programs are described in *Small Computers in Libraries* (Nov. 1982).

Mile High Media—Electronic Message System for Interlibrary Loan. Mile High Media, 1435 Race Street, Denver, CO 80206. (303)388-8318.

Mile High Media is a small consulting firm specializing in library, computer, and audiovisual services. It operates or maintains the system for members of the Colorado Council of Medical Librarians on a Northstar Horizon with 64K, two quad density 5¼-inch disk drives, two terminals, and a modem. Software required includes RCONS (Remote Console Operated Northstar) from Microstuff Company of Atlanta, Georgia. Other software in the system was developed by Mile High Media.

Nonesuch Circulation System. Ringgold Management Systems, Inc., P.O. Box 368, Beaverton, OR 97075. (503)645-3502.

This circulation system is configured to use one or more microcomputer-based circulation stations linked to a large disk storage unit. It is capable of handling multiple circulation stations, each consisting of a microcomputer video/keyboard, bar code reader, and floppy disk drive. The smallest system can handle a library with any combination of circulating items and patrons up to 50,000 records.

Ol'Sam. Franklin Institute Research Laboratory, Inc., Twentieth and Race Streets, Philadelphia, PA 19103. (215)448-1167.

A microcomputer system on a North Star that assists in searching major online bibliographic databases. Read detailed description in *Small Computers in Libraries* (Aug. 1981).

Overdue Program. Maine Township High School West, 1755 Wolf Road, Des Plaines, IL 60018.

Developed in-house, this program allows for printed passes, lists by homeroom teacher, and list of overdues according to class level. Runs on an Apple II or Franklin ACE 100 and is available for purchase.

Overdue Program. Geoffrey Tomlin, J. N. Burnett Junior Secondary School, Richmond, BC, Canada V6G 1L2.

"Organizing Library Overdues," *The Computing Teacher* 8 (Sept. 1980): 48-49, describes this program and gives ordering information.

Overdue program for large high schools. Cooper City High School, 9401 Stirling Road, Cooper City, FL 33328. (305)434-8000.

This program for managing overdues was developed by a second year mathematics student on independent study, in cooperation with the library media staff. Process described in *Florida Media Quarterly* 6 (Spring 1981): 19-21.

PFS™ Programs. Software Publishing Corp., 1901 Landings Drive, Mountain View, CA 94043.

File management and report writing programs being used for a number of library applications.

Pinellas County Schools—Library/Media Computer Pilot Project. Carlton E. Hoffman, Director of Media Services, and Hope Botterbusch, Pinellas County Schools, 1960 East Druid Road, Clearwater, FL 33502.

The Pinellas School District has implemented an in-house project that utilizes microcomputers for library/media management tasks. Several programs have been developed and are available for purchase. The pilot libraries began using the programs in the first semester of 1982-1983 school year and more will be added in the second semester. Programs are for TRS-80.

Profile. Radio Shack.

A file management program being used for library applications on the TRS-80s.

Project Mini-Cap (Mini-Computer Assisted Program). Point Pleasant High School, 2312 Jackson Avenue, Point Pleasant, WV 25550-2096. (304)675-1350.

A Title IV-C project that developed a program for the TRS-80 III to completely computerize the library management tasks—circulation, inventory, statistical analysis, cataloging, etc.

Readability Index.

See review of program for Pet or TRS-80 in *The Computing Teacher* 8 (Jan. 1981): 42. Program available from Educational Activities, Inc.

Readability Programs.

A number of articles have been written about readability programs, some of which contain program listings: *Educational Computer Magazine* (Sept./Oct. 1982): 26; *ACCESS: Microcomputers in Libraries* (Apr. 1982): 12; *Creative Computing* (Apr. 1980); *Creative Computing* (Mar. 1981): 166-78; *Creative Computing* (Apr. 1981): 152-54; *Interface Age* (May 1981): 27; *Desktop Computing* (Jan. 1982): 46-47.

Richmond Micro Software—Library Management Software for the Apple. Follett Library Book Co.: Quality Courseware, 4506 Northwest Highway, Crystal Lake, IL 60014. (800)435-8170.

Five programs developed by Robert Stevens and tested in Canadian schools: On-Line Circulation System, Ordering System, Catalog Card and Label Printer System, Cataloging System, Magazine Control System. Contact Follet for more information and dates for demonstration workshops in your area.

Right On Programs. Division of COMPUTEAM, Inc., P.O. Box 977, Huntington, NY 11743. (516)271-3177.

Has an Elementary School Overdue Program, Accession Number program and a variety of library skills instructional programs. Programs are also distributed through Academic Software, K-12 MicroMedia, and Queue, Inc. The Overdue and Accession Number programs are available on disk or cassette for Apple and Commodore PET. They were developed and used by an elementary library media specialist. Write for their latest catalog.

School Management Systems, 5973 Nandina Street, Sweet Home, OR 97386. (503)367-4747.

Has several library and school management programs developed and tested by a library media director in an Oregon school district: CARDPRIN/II; LIBSTARS; Fund Accounting; and others. Most operate under CP/M 2.2x and are written in CBASIC2. Write for full information.

SIAS (Student Information Accessing System). Delta Software Company, 14110 Washington Drive, Plymouth, MI 48170. (313)455-2388.

A circulation program that runs on an Apple II.

Sunburst. Sunburst Communications, Inc., 39 Washington Avenue, Pleasantville, NY 10570. (800)541-1934.

Has library management and library skills instruction software. One of the distributors described in "Mail-Order Distributors with Liberal Software On-Approval Policies" by Ann Lathrop in *Educational Computer Magazine* (Jan./Feb. 1983).

Telemarc III. Catalog Card Corporation, Gaylord Library Systems—distributor, P.O. Box 4901, Syracuse, NY 13221.

Cedar Rapids (Iowa) Community Schools has been using this program since the spring of 1982 and would be glad to answer questions. They have been very satisfied and mentioned as one of its strengths the ease of use and the small amount of staff training needed to implement it. Telemarc III is compared with another card printing program in *Small Computers in Libraries* (July 1982).

TIES (Total Information Education Systems) of Minnesota, 1925 West Country Road B2, St. Paul, MN 55113.
Has two library/reading programs: Media Skills, Readability Analysis. Their catalog is being revised; write for latest information.

25:02. Softrend, Inc., P.O. Box 1462, Charlotteville, VA 22902.
A program specifically designed for maintaining bibliographic information.

Visidex™. Visicorp, 2895 Zanke Road, San Jose, CA 95134.
One of the file management programs being used for library applications.

MEDIA AND MEDIA SOURCES

Computer Literacy

This list contains a number of sources for good films to use in computer literacy classes. *The Computing Teacher* periodically has a "Computer Literacy Film Reviews" column and solicits contributions. As these resources are constantly changing, you will want to write and have your library added to the mailing lists, in order to receive information about the current film holdings and their costs.

Alameda County Superintendent of Schools, Learning Resource Services — Publication Sales, 685 A Street, Hayward, CA 94541.
Classroom Applications of Microcomputers, a series of four videocassettes, provides an introduction to computer use in the classroom. These are tapes of inservice sessions given by Glenn Fisher, School Computer Specialist in Alameda County. Available in either ¾- or ½-inch format for $50.00 each or $160.00 for the set of four. Good material and examples presented. 1) Classroom Applications of Microcomputers; 2) Using a Computer in the Classroom; 3) Educational Software; 4) Teaching Computer Literacy and Programming. Could be viewed individually or in groups.

Allis Chalmers Film Library, 4431 West North Avenue, Milwaukee, WI 53208.

AVC Media Library, Audio-Visual Center, University of Iowa, Iowa City, IA 52240.

BFA Educational Media (Film Associates of California), 2211 Michigan Avenue, Santa Monica, CA 90404.

Brigham Young University, Educational Media Services, 290 Herald R. Clark Building, Provo, UT 84602.

British Broadcasting Corporation, 55 Bloor Street West, No. 1220, Toronto, ON, Canada M4W 1A5.
A number of the BBC films have been reviewed in *The Computing Teacher*. See the index for Vols. 8 and 9 (Film Reviews, p. 45) in Vol. 10 (Sept. 1982).

Business Education Films, 7820 Twentieth Avenue, Brooklyn, NY 11214.

Changing Times Education Service. EMC Corporation, 180 East Sixth Street, St. Paul, MN 55101.

Children's TV International, Suite 1207, Skyline Place, 5265 Leesburg Pike, Falls Church, VA 22041.
Adventures of the Mind — six 15-minute videocassettes, available for preview. This series has been shown on some PBS television stations.

Contemporary/McGraw-Hill Films, Film Rental Library. McGraw-Hill Book Company, P.O. Box 590, Highstoron, NJ 08520.

Control Data Corporation, Photo Library, HQN11U, P.O. Box O, Minneapolis, MN 55401.

Coronet Films, 65 E. South Water Street, Chicago, IL 60601.
Write for list of computer-related films. Some, such as *Data Processing: An Introduction* (reviewed in *Computing Teacher* 8 [Feb. 1981]) are available from film libraries.

CRM McGraw-Hill Films, 110 Fifteenth Street, Del Mar, CA 92104.
The documentary special on computers in education, *Don't Bother Me, I'm Learning*, which was produced by One Pass Video and sponsored by ComputerLand, is available through your local ComputerLand stores.

Digital Equipment Corp. Film Library—Public Relations Dept., 146 Main Street, Maynard, MA 01754.

Educator's Guide to Free 16mm Films. Educators Progress Service, Inc., Randolph, WI 53956. Annual publication.

Encyclopaedia Britannica Educational Corp., 425 North Michigan Avenue, Dept. 10A, Chicago, IL 60611.

Film Fair Communications, 10900 Ventura Boulevard, Studio City, CA 91604.
Source for computer-related films such as *The Computer*.

Films, Inc., 8124 North Central Park Avenue, Skokie, IL 60076.
Source for computer-related films such as *The Silicon Factor: So What's It All About*, reviewed in *The Computing Teacher* 10 (Dec. 1982): 20.

Films Incorporated, Wilmette, IL 60091. (800)323-4222.
Source for computer-related films such as *Painting by Numbers*, reviewed in *The Computing Teacher* 10 (Dec. 1982): 21.

General Electric Corp., Educational Films, Corporation Park, Scotia, NY 12302.

Guidance Associates, Communications Park, P.O. Box 300, White Plains, NY 10602.
Source for computer-related media such as *Computers: From Pebbles to Program*.

IBM Corporation, Old Orchard Road, Armonk, NY 10504.

Indiana University, Audiovisual Center, Bloomington, IN 47401.

Journal Films, 909 West Diversey Parkway, Chicago, IL 60614.

Kent State University, AV Services, Kent, OH 44242.

MacMillan Films, Inc., 34 MacQuesten Parkway, South, Mt. Vernon, NY 10550.

MECC (Minnesota Educational Computer Consortium), 2520 Broadway Drive, St. Paul, MN 55113-5199. (612)638-0627.
Using the Computer in the Classroom: Training Materials.... Materials developed by MECC for teaching an introductory course to instructional computing for educators using the Apple are available from MECC. An Atari version will be released soon. For more information see description in *The Computing Teacher* 10 (Dec. 1982): 6, or contact MECC.

Modern Talking Pictures, Film Scheduling Center, 2323 New Hyde Park Road, New Hyde Park, NY 11040.

National Audio-Visual Center, General Services Administration Order Section/BB, Washington, DC 20409.

Northwestern Bell Telephone Co. (or local Bell office), Program Service, 224 South Fifth Street, Room 1335, Minneapolis, MN 55402.

Pacific Telephone Film Libraries, 1145 North McCadden Place, Los Angeles, CA 90038.
Or contact your local phone company for a list of computer-related films such as *The Thinking??? Machines*, reviewed in *The Computing Teacher* 8 (Nov. 1980): 43.

"Preparing Slide Presentations on Computers." By John K. Elberfeld.
Article in Oct. 1982 issue of *The Computing Teacher* (pp. 34-35): "Fewer than ten people can comfortably watch a video monitor, but several hundred can watch a slide show at the same time."

Remington Rand, Div. of Sperry Rand Corp., 1290 Avenue of the Americas, New York, NY 10011.

Sandia Laboratories, Division 3153, Alburquerque, NM 87185.

SFFL (Santa Fe Film Library), 80 East Jackson Boulevard, Chicago, IL 60604.

Sperry-Univac, P.O. Box 500, Blue Bell, PA 19422.

Syracuse University, Film Rental Library, 1455 East Colvin Street, Syracuse, NY 13210.

Time-Life Films, 16mm Dept., 43 West Sixteenth Street, New York, NY 10011.

TRW Systems Group, One Spack Park, Redondo Beach, CA 90278.

University of Arizona Film Library, Tucson, AZ 85721.
Distributes computer-related films such as *Automation: The Next Revolution*, reviewed in *The Computing Teacher* 8 (Dec. 1981): 32.

University of California, Extension Media Center, Berkeley, CA 94720.

University of Illinois Film Library, 1325 South Oak Street, Champaign, IL 61820.
IU has a number of computer literacy films that have been reviewed in *The Computing Teacher*. See *The Computing Teacher* index for Vols. 8 and 9 (Film Reviews, p. 45) in Vol. 10 (Sept. 1982).

University of Iowa, Audiovisual Center Media Library, C-5 East Hall, Iowa City, IA 52242.

University of Minnesota, Audio-Visual Library Services, 3300 University Avenue S.E., Minneapolis, MN.

University of Southern California, Division of Cinema, Film Distribution, University Park, Los Angeles, CA 90007.

University of Wisconsin Film Library, La Crosse, WI.
Has computer-related films, such as *Theta* reviewed in *The Computing Teacher* 8 (Dec. 1981): 31.

Westinghouse Broadcasting Co., 90 Park Avenue, New York, NY 10017.

General Information

Alaska State Film Library, ETA Program, Department of Education, Pouch F - State Office Building, Juneau, AK 99811.
Troubleshooting Your Apple Computer consists of three programs: *It's Probably the Diskette, But If It's the Equipment*, and *An Ounce of Prevention Keeps the Apple Doctor Away*. The programs are accompanied by worksheets and may be adapted for teacher inservice programs. To order, send a blank ¾ videocassette and $15.00; ask for catalog order No. 85469.

Information Retrieval

ERIC, MICROsearch Demonstration. ERIC Clearinghouse on Information Resources
Publications, 130 Huntington Hall, Syracuse University, Syracuse, NY 13210. $10.00,
plus $1.00 postage and handling.
A demonstration diskette set with a manual is available, with a choice of Educational
Technology or Library/Media items on the sample database diskette. A new quarterly
subscription to database diskettes is now available to run on the Apple II Plus. Two to
three diskettes, at $6.00 each, will be needed each quarter. A good demo to illustrate
database searching.

ORGANIZATIONS

ACU (Association of Computer Users). ACU Research and Education Division, Inc.,
4800 Riverbend Road/P.O. Box 9003, Boulder, CO 80301. (303)443-3600. $65.00.
An independent nonprofit association offering comparisons of the most popular small
computers, a software locator service, a monthly journal, and consumer guides. Some of
the benchmark reports are available individually. Write for more information.

ADCIS (Association for Development of Computer-Based Instructional Systems).
ADCIS International Headquarters, Computer Center, Western Washington University, Bellingham, WA 98225. (206)676-2860. $75.00, institutional; $100.00, sus-
taining; $30.00, individual; chapter membership only—varies.
Publications: *ADCIS News*, newsletter—six times per year; *Journal of Computer-
Based Instruction*—quarterly. Regional chapters: Northeastern U.S.; MidEastern U.S.;
Front Range of Colorado/Wyoming. A number of special interest groups have been
formed. ADCIS has an annual conference, plus workshops and chapter and/or SIG
meetings.

AEDS (Association for Educational Data Systems), 1201 Sixteenth Street, N.W.,
Washington, DC 20036.
For educators and data processing professionals at all levels of education. Primarily
concerned with administrative information systems, it has branched out to include
microcomputers and instructional applications. Publications: *AEDS Bulletin, AEDS
Monitor, AEDS Journal.*

ASIS (American Society for Information Science), 1010 Sixteenth Street, N.W.,
Washington, DC 20036. (202)659-3644.
Write for more information.

BEST NET. Project Best/AECT, Suite 214, 1126 Sixteenth Street, N.W., Washington,
DC 20036. (202)466-4780.
This electronic mail system links 43 state sites, ten U.S. Department of Education
regional offices and the Project BEST (Basic Education Skills through Technology) office
in an information exchange. Write for more information.

Bibliographic Retrieval Services, Inc., BRS/Education Service Group, 1200 Route 7,
Latham, NY 12110. (518)783-1161.
Operates national network which includes access to SPIN, The School Practices
Information Network. Includes a database of commercial curriculum materials including
the entire Curriculum Development Library produced by Fearon-Pitman publishers.

CompuServe Information Service, 5000 Arlington Centre Boulevard, Columbus, OH
43220. (614)457-8650.
CompuServe offers online access to a variety of information of interest to the home
computer owner, electronic mail, and news. Schools are using this service also, particularly
for the current access to news. (See article in *The Computing Teacher* [Feb. 1982]. Also see

"CompuServe: A Potpourri of Information Services," *Popular Computing* [Mar. 1982]: 74-78.)

ComputerTown™ — "Bringing Computer Literacy to Entire Communities.... " Computer-Town, 1263 El Camino Real, P.O. Box E, Menlo Park, CA 94025. Personal, leader, group, and commercial memberships available.

The model from which the present organization grew began in 1979 as a research project, receiving some National Science Foundation funding. The goal of the project was to bring computer literacy to local communities, and to form a working model for similar projects around the world. There are now some 80 ComputerTown sites. Membership includes a News Bulletin (a good source of information), support services, discounts, publications, etc. Write for more information. Copies of back bulletins available.

DIALOG™ Information Retrieval Services, Inc., 3460 Hillview Avenue, Palo Alto, CA 94304.

Offers 40 million abstracts and records in over 150 databases, including technical reports, conference papers, patents, newspaper, journal, and magazine articles in science, technology, social science, humanities, business, and economics. Of special interest to libraries: Books in Print and The Microcomputer Index. Now available to home users is a portion of DIALOG's database called "Knowledge Index."

MACUL (Michigan Association for Computer Users in Learning). MACUL, Larry Smith, Wayne County Intermediate School District, P.O. Box 807, Wayne, MI 48184. $5.00.

Organized in 1975. Group publishes a yearly journal and a newsletter (five per year), holds conferences, and has a software exchange program.

Micro Timesharing Co., 20 Carmel Avenue, Salinas, CA 93101. (408)424-0596.

One of several sources for coin operated computers for installation in public libraries at no cost to the library. The company provides programs, service and maintenance. The library will receive a royalty.

New York Times. New York Times Information Service, Mt. Pleasant Office Park, 1719-A Route 10, Parsippany, NJ 07054. (201)539-5850.

OCLC (Online Computer Library Center). OCLC, Inc. 6565 Frantz Road, Dublin, OH 43017.

Operates international network used by libraries to acquire and catalog library materials, arrange interlibrary loans, and maintain location information. At present, OCLC has over 7.4 million bibliographic records.

RICE (Resources in Computer Education). Northwest Regional Laboratory, 300 Southwest Sixth Avenue, Portland, OR 97204. (800)547-6339.

Currently there are more than 1,500 descriptions of microcomputer courseware for use in elementary and secondary education, and a file of more than 150 producers or developers of such software.

RLIN. Research Libraries Information Network, Encina Commons, Stanford University, Stanford, CA 94305.

Offers search-only bibliographic data to nonmembers of RLG. Contains over 4 million bibliographic records.

SDC. System Development Corporation, 2500 Colorado Avenue, Santa Monica, CA 90406.

Eighty databases online are available through the ORBIT™ Information Retrieval System covering petroleum/energy, business, labor and labor-related areas, textile industry information, sports coverage and others.

SOFTSWAP Microcomputer Center. San Mateo County Office of Education, 333
   Main Street, Redwood City, CA 94063.
   SOFTSWAP was organized through the cooperation of CUE (Computer-Using
Educators) and the San Mateo County Office of Education. A variety of microcomputers
is housed here and a number of commercial software programs are available for preview.
The center has a large amount of public domain software, which volunteers have previewed
and enhanced. These programs are available free to those bringing their own disks to the
center or by mail for a nominal fee. For a complete catalog and ordering information send
$1.00 to Ann Lathrop, SOFTSWAP.

The Source. Source Telecomputing Corporation, 1616 Anderson Road, McLean, VA
   22102. (703)821-6660.
   Includes New York Times Summary, UPI, financial data, access to staff of reference
researchers, over 100 education programs.

Special Education CUE (subgroup of Computer-Using Educators in California), Joanne
   Doell, P.O. Box 18547, San Jose, CA 95158.
   Those involved in special education have had interest group meetings at the CUE
conferences. Send a SASE for more information on the group's activities.

Special Education Service Delivery—Project EduTech. EduTech, Log AB, JWK International, 7617 Little River Turnpike, Annandale, VA 22003.
   Project EduTech provides information on technological solutions to problems of the
handicapped and disseminates the data in print form to state education agencies. The
group responds to individual requests for information and is seeking more information for
its files as well.

PEOPLE

Anderson, Eric S. Director, Library/Media Services, Dakota Community Unit 201,
   Dakota, IL 61018.
   "Putting Micros to Work in the Media Center" in *The Computing Teacher* 9 (May
1982), describes some of Mr. Anderson's experiences with micros for library applications.

Bruestle, Greg. South Jr. High, 233 Twelfth Avenue South, St. Cloud, MN 56301.
   Mr. Bruestle has developed a film rental program, which is described in *CMC News*
(Spring 1980).

Brune, Charlotte. Durango High School, P.O. Box 2467, Durango, CO 81301.
   For information on using The Source as a "news" database. Durango High School
selected The Source as an alternative to Times microfilm.

Chase, Richard. Red Wing High School, Red Wing, MN 55066.
   Mr. Chase has developed several library management programs, which are available
for purchase at very reasonable prices (overdue, inventory, etc., for floppy disk drives). He
has an Apple II Plus system with a Corvus™ hard disk and the Omninet system.

Christian, Deborah. DAC Consulting Services, P.O. Box 784, Oakridge, OR 97463.
   (503)782-2111.
   Deborah Christian is the editor/publisher of *ACCESS: Microcomputers in Libraries.*

Costa, Betty. Think Small Computers, Inc., 8600 Concord Lane, Westminster, CO
   80030. (303)428-2929.
   Library media consultant, with emphasis on library applications using
microcomputers.

Dewey, Patrick R. North-Pulaski Library, 4041 W. North Avenue, Chicago, IL 60639.
   (312)269-2900.

Mr. Dewey and his staff have developed a Personal Computer Center for their patrons. This involved developing a number of materials, including a users guide. Dewey describes some of their experiences in *Small Computers in Libraries* (Apr. 1982). If you are considering this type of activity, it would be worthwhile to contact him. For the Users Guide and/or Public Computing Newsletters, send a 9x5 SASE to Patrick R. Dewey.

Fiebert, Elyse E. Radnor High School, 130 King of Prussia Road, Radnor, PA 19087.
    Ms. Fiebert is in her fourth year (1982-1983) of using DIALOG to teach students online searching skills. She teaches these skills as a regular part of the library program.

Freund, Alfred L. Data Management Associates, 24 Pond Hill Avenue, Warwick, NY
    10990. (914)986-1094.
    Mr. Freund, as director of the Ramapo Catskill Library System, 619 North Street, Middletown, NY 10940, has developed a book order system capable of handling 15,000 online, 130 byte records, using the Commodore CBM 8032 computer and a software package called OZZ. Freund is also the director of the microcomputer consulting firm, Data Management Associates.

Hawley, Steven C. Greenhills-Forest Park City School District, Project Office,
    1501 Kingsbury Drive, Cincinnati, OH 45240. (513)851-8781.
    This library has developed a microcomputer application called ACCS (Annehurst Curriculum Classification System), in which they have identified more than 800 numerical codes to describe the content of educational materials. They found the program especially helpful in matching curriculum objectives with specific activities, inventorying resources, and making purchasing decisions.

Konopatzkie, Pat. Elmira High School, Elmira, OR 97437.
    Ms. Konopatzkie's work is described in "Computers and the Media Center: A Principal's Perception" by Gary Zosel, Elmira High School, in *The Computing Teacher* (Mar. 1982): 34-37.

Lathrop, Ann. Library Coordinator, San Mateo County Office of Education,
    Redwood City, CA.
    Ms. Lathrop's background includes work as a teacher and a librarian in both elementary and secondary schools. She is coordinator of the SOFTSWAP, an exchange of public domain microcomputer software. She authored a regular column in *Educational Computer* (The Micro in the Media Center) and is the coauthor of *Courseware in the Classroom: Selecting, Organizing, and Using Educational Software* (Reading, MA: Addison-Wesley, 1983).

Marland, Ed. Benjamin Franklin Junior High School, 33555 Annapolis, Wayne, MI
    48184. (313)595-2420.
    Mr. Marland is using microcomputers for AV equipment inventory, maintenance records, indexing, film bookings, purchase orders, etc. He is also using the Apple as a terminal for database searching with students, using DIALOG and The Source.

Minemier, Betty M. Junior High School, Dansville, NY 14437.
    Ms. Minemier is willing to share locally produced library programs for TRS-80: overdue list, shelf list, bibliographies, etc.

Nolan, Jeanne M. Information Management Services, 21203-A Hawthorne Boulevard,
    Suite 5323, Torrance, CA 90509. (213)259-3329.
    Dr. Nolan is a consultant, speaker, workshop presentor/trainer, and author. She also develops and brokers library/information management software, and is publisher of the *Micro Software Report*, library edition.

Ruby, Carl E. Witt Elementary School, 10255 West 104th Drive, Broomfield, CO 80020.
    Mr. Ruby is using microcomputers for a variety of library management tasks with database management and sorting programs.

Sather, Ruth. Eau Claire Public Schools, Longfellow School, 512 Balcom Street, Eau Claire, WI 54701.

Ms. Sather has written an article, "Microcomputer, Media Center and Kids!" (in *The Computing Teacher* 9 [Dec. 1981]: 23-26), which describes her experiences developing an Elementary School Computer Literacy Program which is now being marketed. A media specialist, she is developing a Library Skills Program to be released in the Spring of 1983.

Smith, Janice. Supervisor of Media Services, Adams County School District No. 12, District Media Center, 10291 North Huron, Denver, CO 80221. (303)451-8889.

Ms. Smith's media center is using a film management system developed by Research Technology, Inc. using an ADS Multivision II microcomputer with a Centronics printer. The system correlates teaching objectives with the film management. In addition, the district media staff is using a wide variety of commercial software for management and processing.

Appendix C:
Caring for Your Computer

Computers have acquired an unfortunate reputation for being unreliable, and the earlier computers actually did spend as much or more time "down" as up and running. Microcomputers, along with advances in speed and capacity, also offer,considerably more reliability and durability. They are, however, vulnerable to carelessness, mishandling, power quirks, and ignorance. Properly treated, your computer should give years of faithful and reliable service. Following are a few basic rules for keeping your computer system "up." We also highly recommend adding to your library a comprehensive guide to computer care such as *DON'T! or How to Care for Your Computer* by Rodnay Zaks, published by Sybex, Inc.

1) *Read the manual*—at the very least read the section on Care and Cautions. Many components or systems have individual quirks which dictate certain procedures. Certain types of hard disks, for example, must be powered up only *after* the computer itself is turned on. Reversing the order could mean losing a whole disk's worth of data. Some systems may be powered up with disks in the disk drives; to do so with other systems can mean lost data. Know your system's special needs before you start to use it.

   Your dealer should show you how to set up your system, such as what plugs in where and how (remember, it is possible to plug things in the wrong way!). He may also show you some basic care procedures, such as cleaning a disk drive. You should also be familiar with the utilities on your operating system disk that are used for testing various parts of the system.

2) Keep it clean. Computer components themselves and especially storage media such as disks and tapes are very vulnerable to dirt and dust, fingerprints, and even hair. And NEVER, NEVER eat, drink, or smoke while using (or in the vicinity of) the computer.

3) Use anti-static mats or sprays if you have a lot of static electricity in the library. A shock can be as "painful" to a computer and its memory as to a person! If your school power supply is erratic or you live in an area that is subject to thunderstorms or power failures, invest in a voltage regulator, powerline filter or backup power supply.

4) We've said it before, we'll say it again. **BACK UP**—every time you add or change data. Also, keep backup copies of all programs. Backup copies should be kept in a safe place separate from working copies. DO NOT SKIP THIS STEP—EVER. The exact method used for backup will depend on the type of storage medium and the operating system you are using. Consult your manual, and/or have your vendor show you the technique(s) for backing up data with your system.

   When you are doing frequent data entry, such as for an online catalog or a circulation system, use a rotating backup system. NEVER backup on your most recent backup. A good method is to use a different disk for each day of the week, and backup on the next-to-last day's disk. For example, Wednesday's data would be backed up on Monday's disk, Thursday's data on Tuesday's disk, and so on. That way any major or minor catastrophe would result in only one day's work being lost. It is also a good idea to make daily printed reports, just in case.

5) Caring for floppy disks: Floppies are a wonderfully convenient way to store data. They are also terribly vulnerable to:

Dirt — including dust, fingerprints, smoke, soft drinks, hair, eraser or pencil lead particles, and food. When not in use, even for a few minutes, disks should be kept in their protective sleeves. Never touch the exposed portions of a disk.

Magnets — including those found in telephone receivers and color television tubes. Also suspect metal objects such as screwdrivers, keys, and paper clips.

Extreme temperatures — window sills, cars, and radiators are not safe storage areas.

Pressure — especially direct pressure such as that caused by writing on the disk with a pencil or ball point pen. Labels should be written before you attach them to the disk. If you must write on an already labeled disk, use a felt tip pen. Also, disks should never be laid down where other objects might be placed on top of them. Store disks vertically in a safe place when not in use, and don't try to cram too many into one box.

Bending, creasing, and folding — will keep your disk from making proper contact with the read/write head in the drive.

Forcing or jamming into a drive — always make sure that the disk is facing the right way (know your system!) and be GENTLE.

Gobbling — various minor or major events that cause a computer to "eat" the disk and destroy the data on it. The only protection against this is frequent BACKUP.

6) Caring for a hard disk: Like floppies, hard disks are vulnerable to dirt, smoke, and liquids. In fact, since the distance between the read/write head and the disk is so small, a particle of cigarette smoke is enough to cause a head crash, i.e., allow the read/write assembly to come into contact with the disk itself. At the least a head crash will destroy your data, and at the most it will destroy your disk. Winchester drives, because the disk and read/write assemblies are in a hermetically sealed chamber, are fairly well protected. They can, however, be "wiped" by a ringing telephone, by improper use (such as powering up or down in the wrong order), by physical damage, such as dropping, and by power irregularities. Among other things, hard disks should not share outlets with other appliances such as coffee makers or vacuum cleaners — in fact, you should avoid using any other powerful device while the hard disk is running. And always BACK UP to tape or floppies.

7) Plan your computer area. Make sure that all the components are placed where they are both stable and easy to reach. Printers, especially, can vibrate a good deal. Also make sure that cables are tucked out of the way where they can't be tripped over or accidentally unplugged. The computer system should, if at all possible, use a dedicated circuit to avoid power interference.

8) Educate the users. A list of disk do's and don'ts plus reminders prohibiting food or drinks and encouraging gentleness could be posted at each computer station. Also, each user should be required to go through an orientation session before being allowed to use the computer.

9) Keep a journal. Make this a habit from the first day you acquire your system. Keep track of all procedures, including backups, with dates and descriptions. It is especially important to note any unusual events or problems with either hardware or software. Describe what the operator did and what happened. This can be enormously useful when you or by-the-hour service personnel are hunting down hardware or software bugs.

10)   What to check before calling the service department: First, try the operation again. If it doesn't work the second time, turn everything off, then turn it all back on and try once more. If the problem persists, suspect the software first. Try a backup copy of the software (you do have a backup copy, don't you?). If you still can't get it to work, then you can begin to suspect a hardware malfunction. Check all the cables and circuit boards to be sure they are plugged in properly. If you have duplicate components, you can try substitutions — such as a different CRT.

When you must have a service person call, try to be present while the problem is being corrected. If it is something simple, such as a blown fuse, you may be able to fix it yourself next time. However, unless you feel very confident that you know what you are doing, DON'T open the equipment and start trying do-it-yourself diagnosis and repair. At the least, you may invalidate the warranty.

Appendix D: No Computer in the Budget? Alternative Funding Possibilities

There are a number of sources outside regular budget allotments that might be used to introduce or supplement computer applications in school and public libraries. These sources include federal and state block grants, district funds, a wide list of foundations, local community groups (including parent organizations, student groups, Friends of the Library, etc.), and computer companies themselves. Locating these sources and then persuading them to fund projects involving computers will take research, creativity, and persistence, but even in these days of higher costs and lower budgets, money is available to those who know whom and how to ask for it.

With the possible exception of student groups (such as school computer clubs), any potential funding source will require some form of written and/or oral proposal that explains clearly and specifically the goals, objectives, and methods of the proposed project(s). Although the art of grant writing is outside the scope of this book, there are numerous resources available to anyone seeking to learn it, including books, magazine articles, and even courses at adult education and university extension centers. The main points to remember are these:

1) You must be able to state exactly why you are seeking the funds and what you intend to do with them. The proposal must document clearly the need for and benefits of the proposed project, along with its goals, objectives, and expected outcomes.

Most of the special funding for libraries has had an instructional slant, primarily toward the teaching of library skills, although some grants have been made for the purpose of making library management more time and cost effective. The objective in the latter cases has been to free the library staff to provide more and better patron services. However, it is also important to note that the media center is a logical place to base computer activities for an entire school (see chapter 5, "The Library as a Computer Resource Center"). Therefore, the media specialist will probably be deeply involved in selecting, funding, and implementing computer-oriented projects that go beyond the library.

2) Know your potential sources. Both government and foundation funds tend to have very specific requirements for recipients. These requirements range from geographic and demographic restrictions to the specific types of projects that are eligible. Most agencies will provide guidelines upon request, listing restrictions and requirements for submitting proposals, so there is no need to waste time and effort preparing a proposal for a program for which you may not be qualified. Once you have decided where to submit your proposal, research the organization to determine the best approach, including the way to format the proposal. This will depend on such factors as the organization's main interests and areas of priority, its familiarity with your specialty, and the attitudes of the selection committee. Some organizations demand a formal, by-the-rules grant proposal; others prefer a straightforward, "plain talk" statement. Find out what your target organization wants.

3) Include specific methodology, time frame, and budgetary requirements in the proposal, as well as the credentials of the person or persons who will actually be carrying out the project. You will also need to include the method(s) to be used for evaluating the success of the project and determining whether and how well your objectives have been met. Your project, after all, represents an investment by the funding organization, and they will want to know if the investment was worthwhile.

4) Timing is important. It can be anywhere from six weeks to six months or even longer between the submission of a proposal and notification of action upon it. Also, many organizations will only accept proposals at specific times of the year. Preparing a proposal is a long-term project in itself.

The following are some potential sources for funds for educational and/or library projects involving computers:

Block Grants. The Reconciliation Act of 1981 consolidated over 33 formerly discretionary programs for elementary and secondary education. Under Chapter II of the revised block grants program, local education agencies ("LEA's," i.e., school districts) will now be receiving about $5 to $10 per student to be distributed by the districts themselves. Chapter II is divided into four subchapters, three of which might include monies for library media programs: subchapter A, Basic Skills Development; subchapter B, Educational Improvement and Support Services; and subchapter C, Special Projects. Funds are distributed by state education agencies to the districts according to a formula similar to the one used for the old ESEA-Title B program (from which the majority of the block grant funds come). In order for an LEA to receive funds, it must submit to the state an application that includes a description of the planned allocation of funds. Therefore any library media projects to be funded out of block grants must be included in the LEA's original application.

In most cases, district level funding recommendations will be made by the superintendent of schools in conjunction with a committee of teachers, administrators, and parents. You should make sure that the committee includes at least one library media specialist — you? Library programs are more likely to receive funds if their proponents can show how the programs will benefit programs in other areas as well. Criteria will vary from district to district, but a well-thought-out and well-presented proposal could result in the purchase of computers for individual schools, or possibly a district level cooperative project.

For further information on the block grant program, particularly in regard to educational technology, contact: AMP Block Grant Center for Media and Technology, Attn: Anne Cullather, 1101 Connecticut NW, Washington, DC 20036, (202)857-1195. Though intended primarily for companies marketing products to grant recipients, the services of the center are available to educators as well.

District Funds. Each district has its own methods for determining budget allotments. Often budget decisions are made almost out of habit, or based on "tradition." Administrators at district level might be interested to learn that a library can be equipped with a good quality microcomputer system, serving the entire student body, at a cost less than that of a wrestling mat, which serves only a small proportion of students.

Foundations and Government Grants. There are a number of foundations, both public and private, that delight in funding worthy educational projects. Although only a minority of the grants are specifically earmarked for technology-related programs (see below), a proposal for a creative project that *includes* one or more microcomputers could very well qualify for funding. One foundation that has shown a particularly strong interest in innovative projects for education is the General Mills Foundation. (Contact: W. R. Humphries, Jr., Executive Director, General Mills Foundation, P.O.

Box 1113, Minneapolis, MN 55440.) To find out about other possibilities, check a nearby large library or one of 60 regional collections affiliated with the Foundation Center in New York. Contact the center at 888 Seventh Avenue, New York, NY 10106, (212)975-1120 or toll-free (800)424-9836, for the location of the collection nearest you. The center has also published a directory, which is available in most public libraries. The following is a list of other publications that can be helpful to grant seekers. Many of them are available at public libraries and/or from district professional collections:

Apple Computer Educator's Information Booklet, a free guide to classroom computer use, with a section on government funding. It is available from the Education Marketing Division, Apple Computer, Inc., 10260 Bandley Drive, Cupertino, CA 95014, (408)996-1010.

The AV Connection: The Guide to Federal Funds for Audio-Visual Programs, an annually updated guide published by the National Audio-Visual Association (NAVA), which includes information on federal programs that make funds available for audio-visual equipment, materials, and services (including computers). It is available from NAVA, 3150 Spring Street, Fairfax, VA 22031 (703)273-7200, for $29.95.

The Catalog of Federal Domestic Assistance, a comprehensive listing of funds available through federal agencies, and two daily publications, *The Federal Register* and *The Commerce Business Daily*, all published by the U.S. Superintendent of Documents, U.S. Government Printing Office, Publications Dept., Washington, DC 20402.

Foundation Center Source Book Profiles and *About Foundations: How to Find the Facts You Need to Get a Grant*, both from the Foundation Center, 888 Seventh Avenue, New York, NY 10106.

Foundations Reports, a bimonthly magazine that provides listings of foundation grants, cross-referenced by state, subject area, and receiving institution.

Funding Report for Microcomputers, a 44-page booklet published by Bell & Howell with abstracts of 19 federal programs, along with advice on writing proposals and obtaining funds through state education departments. Though it was published in 1979 and is therefore partially out of date, it is still useful. The handbook is available free from Bell & Howell dealers or from Bell & Howell Audio-Visual Products Division, 7100 North McCormick Road, Chicago, IL 60645.

Grants—How to Find Out about Them and What to Do Next, Plenum Press, 227 West Seventeenth Street, New York, NY 10011.

The Grants Register, St. Martins Press, 175 Fifth Avenue, New York, NY 10010. An annually updated directory of funding organizations, with grants indexed by subject.

In addition, a number of the periodicals mentioned in appendix B, particularly those aimed at educators, such as *Educational Computer* and *Electronic Learning*, publish frequent articles on obtaining funds for microcomputer-related projects.

Computer Companies. Three of the largest microcomputer manufacturers have established formal grant programs for distributing hardware, software, and money for worthwhile and *innovative* educational projects. Several other companies, though they do not have grant programs as such, are not adverse to hearing from individuals and institutions with good ideas for using their equipment. Whether seen as a philanthropic commitment to education or as industry competition for the very large educational market, these programs represent tremendous benefits for educators and students. Although each company has its own criteria for choosing recipients, there are some common factors to keep in mind. First, you must know something about computers, or team up with someone who does. The grants are not being made for the purpose of teaching basics, or for repeating work that has already been done. Rather, they are aimed at funding creative, original projects on any scale, including anything from development of a marketable software package to special school or community computer programs. Whatever the type of project, your chances are better with a single, carefully-thought-out idea than with a shotgun approach.

Information on each of the formal programs is available from:

Apple Education Foundation. At the time of this writing, the Apple Education Foundation's emphasis is on providing hardware in exchange for software development, specifically nationally marketable packages that take advantage of the special properties of microcomputers to expand teachers' ability to teach. Therefore, project proposals must include the skills of an actual programmer or programmers. For specific guidelines, contact Apple Education Foundation, 20525 Mariani Avenue, Cupertino, CA 95014.

Atari Institute for Educational Action Research. Atari is especially interested in "humanistic" uses for computers, such as in the areas of art and music. The institute provides seed grants of hardware, software, or money for imaginative projects that can serve as model programs for organizations and communities all over the country, in both formal and informal educational settings. Application information is available from The Atari Institute for Educational Action Research, 1196 Borregas Avenue, Sunnyvale, CA 94086.

Tandy TRS-80 Educational Grants Program. Tandy's program is the newest of the three; its aim is to provide equipment, including hardware, software, and accessories, to educators with ideas that promote microcomputer technology and education. Within that broad spectrum, Tandy will divide the year into four grant periods, with each period focusing on a different topic. Sample topics for 1983 include the use of microcomputers in educating the handicapped and disadvantaged, and unique and innovative microcomputer applications in education. For a current information packet, write Tandy TRS-80 Educational Grants Program, Radio Shack Education Division, 400 Tandy Atrium, Fort Worth, TX 76102.

The following companies do not have formal grant programs, but are nonetheless interested in innovative proposals for projects using their equipment:

Commodore Business Machines, Inc., Computer Systems Division, 681 Moore Road, King of Prussia, PA 19406. Attn: Bruce Downing.

Osborne Computing Corporation, Public Relations Department, 26538 Danti Court, Hayward, CA 94545. Attn: Sandy Taylor.

Texas Instruments, Educational Marketing Division, P.O. Box 10508, Mail Station 5816, Lubbock, TX 79408. Attn: John W. Alden.

School and/or Community Fund-Raising. Local fund-raising ideas range from bake sales to full-scale community fund drives. In order to launch a successful fund-raising project, you will need to have specific goals, first in terms of what you want to obtain — five new computers for classroom use, special software, a new printer? — and then in terms of monetary requirements. Then you will need a dedicated and energetic committee, preferably including students, teachers, parents, and community business leaders, to carry out the campaign. Get as much publicity as possible, through open houses and PTA presentations — particularly effective if you already have micros that can be used for hands-on demonstrations — local newspaper coverage, handouts and newsletters, and so on. Local business leaders are often willing to support educational projects, perhaps in the form of matching donations, and local service organizations may be willing to help as well. Set a time frame for achieving your goals and be persistent.

Another way to raise money for computer projects is to earn it, using computers! This is particularly true in schools and communities with active computer clubs. One high school club in California, for example, raised money by working with the school athletic department during a "Lift-a-thon" fund drive. The club computerized the pledge list, printing and mailing statements to people who had pledged money for the Lift-a-thon, in return for 10% of the proceeds. Besides making money, club members got to carry out a challenging project. Such ideas are limited only by club and committee members' imaginations and energy.

Coin-operated computers are also becoming popular for public library use. They are available through several vendors (see appendix B), or you may wish to devise your own system, perhaps charging a fee for software use as well.

Public interest in and support for computer-related education is growing at a tremendous rate. Parents want their children to be exposed to computers, and in fact, often would not mind a little exposure themselves. Take advantage of this interest to enlist their support, as well as the support of the students themselves. If your library is a public one, you are in a position to offer computer services to the community as a whole. Ask the community to help make those services available. Everyone will benefit.

Appendix E:
Sample Comparison
and Evaluation Charts

Included in this section are several sample forms which might be used to evaluate potential computer purchases. The exact nature of your charts will, of course, depend on the specific needs of your particular library, but these examples should give you a good starting point for developing your own evaluation methods.

Chart 1 is a comparative analysis of the different methods of acquiring software, as discussed in chapter 2; charts 2-5 represent some different methods of software evaluation; and chart 6 is a sample comparison chart for evaluating hardware systems.

We are grateful to those who have allowed us to reprint their work here.

Chart 1 — Comparative Analysis of Software Systems*

FEATURE	IN-HOUSE DEVELOPMENT	CUSTOM DEVELOPMENT	PURCHASED SOFTWARE	PURCHASED SERVICES
Development Cost	Very high development cost.	Design and programming costs higher than in-house; but total cost could be less.	Package cost estimated at 20 to 50% or less of in-house development. Implementation costs may exceed in-house.	No development cost unless tailoring modifications are required. Implementation cost will vary with amount of internal system modification required.
Development Lead Time	Long lead time due to system design, programming and testing.	Lead time shorter than in-house, but still lengthy.	Shorter lead time than in-house. Will require time for system familiarization and installation.	Minimum lead time. Support usually provided by service bureau to speed implementation.
Development Risk	Risk high due to the many variables involved.	Lower risk than in-house, but is relative to the capabilities of the vendor and system complexities.	Low risk is relative to the level of package use and complexity of requirements.	Low risk relative to experience and quality of the service bureau.

*Reprinted by permission of McDonnell Douglas Automation Company.

Chart 1 (cont'd)

FEATURE	IN-HOUSE DEVELOPMENT	CUSTOM DEVELOPMENT	PURCHASED SOFTWARE	PURCHASED SERVICES
Company Acceptance	Should receive wide and easy acceptance if user heavily involved in requirements definition and development.	Should be accepted if user has been involved in selection, requirements definition and development.	Some resistance; can be overcome by planning and user commitment, beginning with involvement in selection.	Some resistance; user may accept external processed system if involved in selection and is convinced of strong, continuing vendor support.
System Quality	Some errors will be latent in most development efforts; general quality will be as good as staff capabilities.	Quality will be as good as vendor ability; level of errors is reduced by vendor specialized skills.	Quality of base packages should be superior to in-house software; modification to method of operation and enhancements may have an effect on quality.	Because the system is in use, the quality should be superior to in-house; no operation quality factors should impact user since service bureau operates the system.
System Flexibility	Will be as good as that which was planned for; high initial cost will reduce the chance of enhancements soon.	Level of flexibility should exceed in-house.	System flexibility will be higher than in-house; designed for broad market and usually has numerous features included. Enhancements will be somewhat tied to the vendor ability to change and update the package.	System flexibility will be high; systems should have dynamic characteristics as service bureau should continually enhance the system to meet new requirements and improved hardware.

(Chart 1 continues on page 190)

Chart 1 (cont'd)

FEATURE	IN-HOUSE DEVELOPMENT	CUSTOM DEVELOPMENT	PURCHASED SOFTWARE	PURCHASED SERVICES
Implementation Support	Level of support controlled by staff availability and skill.	Level of support will be consistent with contract terms; in-house support will have to be developed to augment vendor support.	Support is usually limited to software installation and initial user training. Prime effort of vendor is directed toward package sale.	Support is directed toward rapid, successful implementation since revenue is primarily related to the amount of processing after implementation.
Documentation	Generally lower quality than other sources; usually the last area of system development to be completed.	Documentation should be better than in-house if the vendor has people skilled in preparing it.	Documentation level and quality vary; quality can be quite good but initial appearance may not properly reflect the true quality.	Documentation quality tends to be highest among all sources since attention is directed towards helping the user process with minimal problems; quality varies among vendors.
System Operation	Generally will run efficiently on current equipment; changes in equipment may cause operating inefficiencies.	Should operate more efficiently than in-house because of broader knowledge gained in designing for a variety of hardware shops; care must be taken to assure that operation and user ease of operation has been fully considered.	Generally designed to operate efficiently only on the machine for which it was initially designed; user operations characteristics may not be consistent with your standards, and may require noticeable effort to "fine tune".	Usually designed to meet user needs in an efficient manner and well tuned to run efficiently in the service bureau's environment.

Chart 1 (cont'd)

FEATURE	IN-HOUSE DEVELOPMENT	CUSTOM DEVELOPMENT	PURCHASED SOFTWARE	PURCHASED SERVICES
Maintenance	Total maintenance must be performed by user.	Maintenance may be performed by user after acceptance; time must be allocated to learn system.	Maintenance costs may be reduced substantially if maintenance contracts are available.	Maintenance is included in the service; no effort is required by user.
Enhancements	Growth to meet future needs dependent on the skill with which the initial design was developed and on staff availability.	Enhancements done by the vendor can be expensive if his original staff is not available. The alternative will require learning time by in-house programmers to become familiar with design techniques.	Vendor personnel may be available to make modifications; otherwise, your programming staff will have to become familiar with programs and make changes, possibly voiding warranties and maintenance contracts.	Systems tend to be most flexible with periodic system enhancements; service bureau will usually make changes for clients since programming support staff is available.
User Support	Require continued training and allocation of personnel familiar with manufacturing systems.	Must be provided in-house following the acceptance of the working system.	Initial user training may be provided by the vendor; subsequent support will be the users' responsibility.	On-going support with manufacturing and DP background will usually be available to assist users.

Chart 2—Software Evaluation*

RATING: Circle the letter abbreviation which best reflects your judgment.

IMPORTANCE: Circle the letter which reflects your judgment of the relative importance of the item in this evaluation.

	RATING	IMPORTANCE	
	SA–Strongly Agree A–Agree D–Disagree SD-Strongly Disagree NA–Not Applicable	H–HIGH L–LOW	
CONTENT	SA A D SD NA	H L	Content is accurate
	SA A D SD NA	H L	Content is organized in a clear, concise way
	SA A D SD NA	H L	Content is free of race, ethnic, sex or other stereotypes.
	SA A D SD NA	H L	Student is allowed to build on skills
	SA A D SD NA	H L	Graphics/color/sound are used for appropriate instructional purposes
	SA A D SD NA	H L	Learner controls the rate and sequence of presentation and review
	SA A D SD NA	H L	Program is relevant to the curriculum
INSTRUCTIONAL QUALITY	SA A D SD NA	H L	Flexibility in skill leveling is allowed
			Principles of learning are employed:
	SA A D SD NA	H L	Retention
	SA A D SD NA	H L	Motivation
	SA A D SD NA	H L	Transfer
	SA A D SD NA	H L	Reinforcement
	SA A D SD NA	H L	Teaches to one objective
	SA A D SD NA	H L	Bloom's Taxonomy is employed beyond the knowledge level
	SA A D SD NA	H L	Students are allowed to exit from program
	SA A D SD NA	H L	Directions are easy to use
	SA A D SD NA	H L	Program is well documented
TECHNICAL QUALITY	SA A D SD NA	H L	Intended users can easily and independently operate the program
	SA A D SD NA	H L	Program is free from errors
	SA A D SD NA	H L	Visual display is readable
	SA A D SD NA	H L	User support materials are comprehensive

*Reprinted by permission of School District No. 12, Adams County, Colorado.

Chart 2 (cont'd)

SOFTWARE EVALUATION

Courseware Description	*Technical Information*

Program Title _____

Call Number _____

Developer/Publisher Names_____

_____

Release Date _____ Cost _____

Vendor _____

Subject Area _____

With which instructional objectives does this software correlate?

_____

Copyright Privileges   No _____   Yes _____

   If allowed, restrictions? _____

Estimated time for student interaction with the program to achieve the objectives. (Can be stated as total time or time per day)

_____

Type of Program:

   Computer-Assisted Instruction (Please check all applicable descriptions)

   Drill and Practice _____   Problem Solving _____

   Tutorial _____   Informational Retrieval _____

   Game _____   Other _____

   Simulation _____

   User Grade Level:

   1   2   3   4   5   6   7   8   9   10   11   12

   Reading Level _____

Computer Managed Instruction

   Learning Management _____

   Diagnosis _____

   Prescription _____

Administrative

   Data Base Management _____

   Text Editing _____

   Turnkey System   Yes _____   No _____

   Best used by _____

Computer Company _____

Computer Model_____

Memory Capacity _____

DOS: 3.2 _____   3.3 _____   Other, specify_____

_____

Number of Disk Drives _____

Required Hardware:

   Color Monitor _____   Paddles _____

   B/W Monitor _____   Wand _____

   Printer _____   Graphics Table _____

Special Requirements (hardware, application, software)

_____

_____

Language _____

Storage Media:

   Cassette _____   Cartridge _____

   Disk _____   Other, specify _____

   _____

   Floppy Disk _____   Sectors

                              13 _____   16 _____

   Hard Disk _____   Type _____

(PLEASE COMPLETE EVALUATION ON REVERSE)

Reviewer's Name _____

Date of Review _____

Authorized as available for sharing   Yes _____   No _____

School _____

(If owned by school):   Program location in school _____

Comments _____

_____

School District No. 12, Adams County
11285 Highline Drive
Northglenn, Colorado 80233

Chart 3—Classroom Evaluation of Microcomputer Courseware*

NOTE: Please copy this form and use it to contribute reviews to the SOFTSWAP file. Send your reviews to: Ann Lathrop, San Mateo County Office of Education, 333 Main Street, Redwood City, CA 94063.

CALIFORNIA LIBRARY MEDIA CONSORTIUM FOR

CLASSROOM EVALUATION OF MICROCOMPUTER COURSEWARE

FOLD HERE AND STAPLE TO RETURN (ADDRESS ON REVERSE)

- -

Program title_____

Disk/tape/package title (if different)_____

Microcomputer brand, model_____ ___K memory needed

Language __BASIC (or_____) Publisher_____ Cost_____

Peripherals needed_____ __Disk __Tape __Cartridge __Other(_____)

Supplemental materials/equipment needed_____ Backup possible?_____

    *   *   *   *   *   *   *   *   *   *   *   *   *   *   *

Reviewed by_____ grade level/subject_____

School/District_____ Phone (   )_____

Address_____

May we use your name in the published review?_____

THANK YOU FOR YOUR HELP. PLEASE RETURN IMMEDIATELY TO THE ADDRESS ON THE BACK.

*Reprinted by permission of California Library Media Consortium, San Mateo County Office of Education.

Chart 3 (cont'd)

CHECKLIST OF EVALUATION CRITERIA

YES NO N/A

GENERAL:

__ __ __ 1. Is this an effective/appropriate use of the computer?

__ __ __ 2. Are the objectives/purpose of the program well defined?

__ __ __ 3. Does the program achieve its objectives/purpose?

__ __ __ 4. Is the program technically sound, free of programming errors, easy to operate?

__ __ __ 5. Does it provide a useful summary or report of student performance?

__ __ __ 6. Is the program free of excessive competition and violence?

__ __ __ 7. Is it free of racial, sex, and ethnic stereotypes?

__ __ __ 8. Is the documentation sufficient?

CONTENT:

__ __ __ 1. Is the content factually correct?

__ __ __ 2. Is the presentation logical, well organized, with internal consistency?

__ __ __ 3. Can the instructor modify the program (word lists, data, speed, etc.)?

__ __ __ 4. Are the interest level, difficulty level and vocabulary level compatible?

INSTRUCTIONS (available within the program)

__ __ __ 1. Are they clear, complete and concise?

__ __ __ 2. Can user skip them and return to them as needed (HELP)?

__ __ __ 3. Is user told how to end program? start over? reenter where user left?

__ __ __ 4. Can user control speed and sequence of paging?

__ __ __ 5. Is there a menu to allow user to access specific parts of the program?

INPUT:

__ __ __ 1. Is input consistent, using common conventions and symbols?

__ __ __ 2. Can user correct input if necessary before continuing program?

__ __ __ 3. Is there a cursor or other indicator to show where input is to go?

__ __ __ 4. Does the computer give a helpful response to input errors?

__ __ __ 5. Is the amount of typing required appropriate to the grade level?

SCREEN OUTPUT:

__ __ __ 1. Is the screen format neat and uncluttered?

__ __ __ 2. Are punctuation and grammar correct?

__ __ __ 3. Is the correct answer, or appropriate help, given after a reasonable time or after a given number of errors?

__ __ __ 4. Does the program branch to easier or harder material in response to user input?

__ __ __ 5. Are responses to errors non-judgmental, free of harsh or demeaning comment?

__ __ __ 6. Is the positive feedback for correct response more interesting/enjoyable/exciting than is the response to errors/failure?

__ __ __ 7. Does the program use motivational devices effectively?
CIRCLE those used. STAR (*) ones used effectively to enhance the program.

__timing __scoring __game format __personalization __color __sound

1/82 __graphics for instruction __graphics for reward __random order

(Chart 3 continues on page 196)

Chart 3 (cont'd)

GRADE LEVEL(S) (circle) k 1 2 3 4 5 6 7 8 9 10 11 12 college teacher use

SUBJECT AREA(S)_____

SCOPE

__single concept program
__program is one part of a
    larger instructional series
__complete instructional unit

GROUP SIZE

__individual use
__small group (2 to 5)
__large group/class

DOCUMENTATION

__in program
__guide/manual
__student materials
__none

TYPE OF PROGRAM

__simulation (a model of a portion of the real world)
__educational game
__game
__drill and practice
__tutorial (presents new material for student to learn)
__problem solving
__testing
__authoring system (allows teacher to develop a program)
__classroom management
__other _____

BRIEF DESCRIPTION OF THE PROGRAM

Objectives_____

_____

Content_____

_____

Classroom uses_____

_____

Strengths/weaknesses_____

_____

STUDENT RESPONSE

Did your students like the program?_____

Did they want to use the program repeatedly, or share it with friends?_____

Did they learn from it?_____

_____

PLEASE USE ANOTHER SHEET IF YOU HAVE ADDITIONAL COMMENTS

OVERALL OPINION ***** OVERALL OPINION ***** OVERALL OPINION ***** OVERALL OPINION

__Great program! I recommend it highly!
__Pretty good/useful -- consider purchase.
__OK, but you might wait for something better.
__Not useful. I don't recommend purchase.

Chart 4 – Software Evaluation Form and Checklist*

The Computing Teacher

FIGURE 1
SOFTWARE EVALUATION FORM & CHECKLIST
(Permission to reprint is granted)

DATE:_____   EVALUATOR: _____

PROGRAM NAME _____   WRITTEN FOR _____ COMPUTER

VENDOR-AUTHOR_____   IN _____ LANGUAGE

ADDRESS _____

CITY, ST., ZIP _____

PHONE _____

COST $_____

PROGRAM CLASS (Check one or more boxes)   **SYSTEM REQUIRED** (Check one or more boxes)

☐ Computer assisted instruction   ☐ 16K   ☐ 32K   ☐ 48K COMPUTER

☐ Computer managed instruction   ☐ DISK DRIVE

☐ Administrative   ☐ TAPE

☐ (Other) _____   ☐ PRINTER   ☐ W/GRAPHICS

_____   ☐ PLOTTER

INTENDED USER (Check one or more boxes)

☐ Teachers

☐ Students _____ Grade Level

☐ Other _____

_____

**PROGRAM MODE ** ** (Check one or more boxes)

☐ Drill & Practice*   ☐ Test Construction or Analysis*

☐ Instructional Game*   ☐ Tutorial Instruction*

☐ Instructional Management*   ☐ Programming Utility

☐ Instructional Support*   ☐ Information

☐ Problem Solving or Research*   ☐ Other (please specify) _____

☐ Simulation*   _____

GENERAL DESCRIPTION OR PURPOSE OF PROGRAM

**The definitions of the eight starred modes of educational applications of computers have been the focus of five years of work by Dr. J. Richard Dennis of the University of Illinois at Urbana/Champaign, and are available through Dr. Bob Kansky, Science/Math Teaching Center, Box 3992- University Station, Laramie, Wyoming 82071.

(Chart 4 continues on page 198)

*Reprinted by permission of *The Computing Teacher.*

Chart 4 (cont'd)

The Computing Teacher

FIGURE 1a

OVERVIEW OF PROGRAM CHARACTERISTICS

	LITTLE	SOME	MUCH
A. DOCUMENTATION AVAILABLE	☐	☐	☐
B. INSTRUCTOR ORIENTATION NEEDED	☐	☐	☐
C. USER ORIENTATION NEEDED	☐	☐	☐
1. Directions (Verbal)	☐	☐	☐
2. Directions (Written)	☐	☐	☐
3. Systems Errors Handled?	☐	☐	☐
4. Keyboard Input by User	☐	☐	☐
5. Dependence on Background or Prior Knowledge	☐	☐	☐

D. USER TARGET(S)
- ☐ Individual
- ☐ Group

E. INTERACTION
- ☐ Cooperation
- ☐ Competition

CHARACTERISTICS OF TEACHING STRATEGY/MOTIVATION
- ☐ Games
- ☐ Color
- ☐ Audio
- ☐ Graphics
- ☐ Student Control
- ☐ Ancillary Materials & Worksheets

SOUNDNESS OF CONTENT IS —
- ☐ Mathematically and Computationally Correct
- ☐ Conceptually Correct and Contemporary
- ☐ Compatible with Other Instructional Material in Use
- ☐ Instructionally Significant

ALL OVER GENERAL RATING
- ☐ Poor
- ☐ Fair
- ☐ Good
- ☐ Excellent
- ☐ Superior

OTHER COMMENTS

_____
_____
_____
_____
_____

FORM DESIGN: BOB HILGENFELD, SCHOOL DISTRICT #1, ROCK SPRINGS, WYOMING

Chart 5—Software Review and Rating Form

Reviewer's Name _____Date _____

Subject/Grade Level Taught _____

Name of Program _____Source_____

Author's Name_____ Machine Used_____

1. What were the Objectives for this program?

2. Subject Area(s)_____

3. Instructional level(s)_____

4. Pre-requisite skills:_____

5. Type of Activity: Drill & Practice_____Tutorial_____
   Remediation_____Enrichment_____Problem Solving_____
   Simulation_____Strategy Game_____Video Game_____

6. Is this activity a good application for computers?_____

7. Is there documentation? (Instructions, Teacher's Guide, Methods
   of implementing changes, references to other resources.)_____

8. Does this program contain a "Title Page" with author & Source?___

9. Does the program allow the following functions?
   Possibility of student quitting?_____
   Teacher lock up so student must complete program?_____
   Clear instructions with ability to return to them at will?_____
   Student control of screen page changes?_____
   Personalized interaction?_____
   Encouraging positive reinforcement?_____ Varied?_____
   Gentle means of negative reinforcement? _____Varied?_____
   Does the program give answers?_____After how many tries?____
   Can the answers be locked?_____Retrieved?_____
   Does the student know how many problems he is to do?_____
   Does the program tell the student how many have been done?_____
   Is the program randomized or is it the same each time it is run?___
   How many choices of format?_____
   Can the program be easily changed to accept teacher data?_____
   Is this by file or by data changes?_____

(Chart 5 continues on page 200)

Chart 5 (cont'd)

Does the program require students to record data or plan action on paper?_____

Is the program timed?_____In what way?_____

Does the program reward the child by providing a game or graphics display for problems correct?_____

Is a score board given?_____Does it include:
Time to complete program?_____Number of correct responses?_____
% correct?_____Listing of problems that gave the student trouble?_____
Does the program give the option of reviewing the problems missed with a tutorial presentation?_____

At the end, does the student get to try the program again or is the program terminated automatically?_____

Was the program easy to follow and to understand what the student was to do?_____

Did the program use interesting graphics?_____Was there variety?_____

Did the program have animation?_____

Did the program follow a sequence or did it allow branching if a student responded correctly?_____

10. If a simulation, or problem solution does the event follow actual dates, events, places, etc. accurately?_____Is the simulation as close to reality as possible?_____ Does it use the computer's ability for animation?_____ Does it require the student to record data, plan action and pose solutions on paper?_____ Does it give the student clues as to wrong choices or is the student "bombed"?_____Does it require good interaction?_____

SUMMARY EVALUATION: Rate each category. A=Excellent B, C, D, F=Terrible

Level of interest._____   Educational Value._____ Program polish

(amateurish, incomplete, bugs, ease of use, etc.)_____ Quality of

documentation._____ Use of graphics and/or animation?_____

Response to knowledgeable student?_____Use of computer as a unique

instructional tool?_____ Positive, personalized interaction?_____

Summary of student performance?_____Ease of adaptation by teacher?___

OVERALL VALUE: A   B   C   D   F   (A=Every school should have one.)
                             (F=Not worth the effort to load & view.)
Please write a short summary of the program including strengths and weaknesses, functions listed in item 9 and a personal reaction to the value of the program for your classroom.

Chart 6—Hardware Comparison Chart

DESIRED SOFTWARE APPLICATIONS IN ORDER OF IMPORTANCE:

1. Word processing

2. Accounting, fund

3. Database management/file
   management

4. Spreadsheet/statistical
   analysis

5. Special Applications

	Computer A	Computer B	Computer C
1.Established stand alone single application package	1,4	2,3	1,2,3,4
(one package that meets needs of first application priority)			
2. Compatible software pkgs available:	1,4	2,3	1,4
(packages from one developer which will interface and meet the needs of more than one application on your priority list)			
3.Operating Systems:			
Standard	CP/M	CP/M86	(?)DOS
Others		UNIX	CP/M
4.Memory:			
RAM	48K	128K	64K
ROM	NA	20K	12K
Expandable to	64K	512K	NA
5. Programming Languages available:			
Standard	MBASIC	MBASIC	(?)BASIC

(Chart 6 continues on page 202)

Chart 6 (cont'd)

Others	FORTRAN Pascal	"C" Pascal	Pascal
6. Keyboard:			
Attached	yes		
Detached		yes	yes
Numeric pad			yes
Cursor keys		yes	
Function keys		yes	yes
7. Video display:			
Color(b/w,amber...)	green b/w	amber green b/w	green b/w
Attached	yes		
Detached		yes	yes
Adjustable		yes	
Graphics	yes	yes	yes
Pixels Horizontal, Vertical (number of "dots" in pattern)	180,90	400,360	240,160
8. Character display (40,54,72,80)	54	80	40
Expandable		120	80
9. Lower Case	no	yes	
Expandable			yes
10. Graphics	no	yes	yes
11. Color possible			yes
12. Sound possible			yes

Chart 6 (cont'd)

13. Interfaces:

# of serial(RS-232C)		3	2
# of parallel	1	1	1
Expandable			

14. Printer

Dot Matrix	x		x
Daisywheel		x	x
Graphics	x		
# of columns	80	132	80

15. Vendor:

Reliable/Established	
Will train/hand-hold	
Service/warranty	

16. COST

CPU/Keyboard	
Video display Unit	
Drive(s)	
Floppy	
Hard	
Printer	
Cables & interfaces	
Other	

BE SURE HARDWARE MATCHES SOFTWARE REQUIREMENTS!

Bibliography

ACCESS: Microcomputers in Libraries 1-2 (July 1981-Oct. 1982 inclusive).

Ansfield, Paul J. "Humanizing the Installation of Microcomputers." *Catholic Library World* 54 (Nov. 1982): 151-54.

Arnold, Anne Jurmu. "Getting That Computer into Your School." *Learning* (Oct. 1982): 46-50.

Asher, Richard. "Retrospective Conversion of Bibliographic Records." *Catholic Library World* 54 (Nov. 1982): 155-61.

Author unknown. "An Adventure into Data Base Management Concepts." Hewlett Packard Publication No. 5953-4511 (Jan. 1980): 1-10.

Author unknown. "The Cutting Edge: Creating Online Systems in the Classroom." *American Libraries* 13 (Nov. 1982): 622.

Author unknown. *DataPhase Systems: Glossary of Computer Terms*. Kansas City: DataPhase Systems, Jan. 1981, booklet.

Author unknown. "Dual-processor Micros Ease Market Transition." *Computer + Software News* (Jan. 3, 1983): 10.

Author unknown. "Guide to Software: What You Should Know before You Buy." *Computer Readout 1981*:57-59, 101-102.

Author unknown. "Interview with Seymour Papert, Author of Mindstorms ... Computers Are Objects to Think With." *The Instructor* (Mar. 1982): 86-89.

Author unknown. "Results of Teacher Attitude Survey on Computers." *The Instructor* (May 1982): 76-77.

Barden, William, Jr. "What Do You Do after You Plug It In?" *Popular Computing* 1-2, 3 (Nov. 1981-Jan. 1983 inclusive), regular column.

Barrette, Pierre P. "Selecting Digital Electronic Knowledge: A Process Model." *School Library Media Quarterly* 10 (Summer 1982): 320-36.

Beiser, Karl. "Microcomputer Periodicals for Libraries." *American Libraries* 14 (Jan. 1983): 43-48.

Berger, Ivan. "How to Buy a Disk System." *Popular Computing* 1 (Apr. 1982): 92-96.

Berst, Jesse. "Ten Pitfalls to Avoid in Acquiring a Word Processor." *Interactive Computing* (Journal of the Association of Computer Users) 8 (Apr. 1982): 98-104.

Berst, Jesse. "Ten Pitfalls to Avoid in Buying a Small Computer System." *Interactive Computing* (Journal of the Association of Computer Users) 7 (May/June 1982): 4-9.

Bierman, Kenneth J. *Automation and the Small Library*. Small Libraries Publication No. 7, American Library Association, 1982.

Boehmer, Sister M. Clare. "ASC Computerizing on a Shoestring." *Catholic Library World* 54 (Nov. 1982): 162-65.

Bourque, Joseph. "An Apple for the Teacher: Classroom Computers." *Popular Computing* 1 (Mar. 1982): 47-50.

Brown, Carol W. *The Minicomputer Simplified.* New York: The Free Press, Div. of Macmillan Publishing Co., Inc., 1980.

Burns, Bill. "dBase II: System of Assembly-Language Programs." *InfoWorld* (Aug. 17, 1982); *InfoWorld's Critics' Guide to Microcomputer Software.* Palo Alto, CA: Popular Computing, Inc., 1982. pp. 21-23.

Byrne, Richard B. "As through a Glass Darkly: For the Unknowable Media Future." *School Library Media Quarterly* 10 (Fall 1981): 22-28.

Carl, David L. "Library Media Specialists and Instructional Development: A Probe of the Literature via Microcomputer." *School Library Media Quarterly* 10 (Winter 1982): 158-63.

Charp, Sylvia. "Trends — Time-Sharing, Microcomputers — Networking." *T.H.E. Journal* 10 (Nov. 1982): 82-83, 99.

Chenoweth, Russ. "A Word Processor in the Library." *Library and Information Technology* 1 (June 1982): 160-63.

Classroom Computer News 1-3 (Mar./Apr. 1982-Jan./Feb. 1983 inclusive).

The Computing Teacher 8-10 (Sept. 1980-Jan. 1983 inclusive).

Corbin, John. *Developing Computer-Based Library Systems.* Phoenix, AZ: Oryx Press, 1981.

Cound, William T. *COLONET: Microcomputers in Libraries.* Denver: Colorado State Library Network, 1982.

Creative Computing 7-9 (Jan. 1981-Jan. 1983 inclusive).

Dahmke, Mark. "Telecomputing: Local Networks Save Money, Increase Reliability." *Popular Computing* 1 (6): 138-40.

DeChenne, James A., and Bob Evans. "Let MICROCOMPUTERS Cure Your Scheduling Headaches." *Instructional Innovator* 27 (Oct. 1982): 26.

Dewey, Patrick R. "Computers, Fun and Literacy." *School Library Journal* 29 (Oct. 1982): 118.

Ditlea, Steve. *A Simple Guide to Home Computers.* New York: A and W Visual Library, 1979.

Dyer, Susan R., and Richard Forcier. "How to Pick Computer Software." *Instructional Innovator* 27 (Sept. 1982): 38-40.

Educational Computer 1-3 (Sept./Oct. 1981-Jan./Feb. 1983 inclusive).

Electronic Education 1-2 (Nov. 1981-Jan. 1983 inclusive).

Electronic Learning 1-2 (Sept./Oct. 1981-Oct. 1982 inclusvie).

Emmens, Carol E. "About Maggie's Place: Library Computer System in Colorado Springs, Colorado." *School Library Journal* 29 (Sept. 1982): 53.

Gilmer, Anne. "The Compleat Grantsman," *Classroom Computer News* 1 (Jan.-Feb. 1981): 1, 6-7.

Givens, Beth. "Montana's Use of Microcomputers for Interlibrary Loan Communications." *Information Technology and Libraries* 1 (Sept. 1982): 260-64.

Glotfelty, Ruth. "Stalking Microcomputer Software." *School Library Journal* (Mar. 1982): 91-94.

Golden, Susan. "Online Serials Circulation in a Library Network." *Wilson Library Bulletin* 56 (Mar. 1982): 511-15.

Good, Phillip. "Choosing the Right Business Software." *Popular Computing* 1 (Apr. 1982): 33-38.

Gordon, Anitra, and Karl Zinn. "Microcomputer Software Considerations." *School Library Journal* 28 (Aug. 1982): 25-27.

Grady, David. "A Hard Look at the World of Educational Computing." *Personal Computing* 6 (8): 40-44.

Heck, William P., Jerry Johnson, and Robert Kansky. *Guidelines for Evaluating Computerized Instructional Materials.* Reston, VA: National Council of Teachers of Mathematics, 1981.

Horn, Carin E., and James L. Poirot. *Computer Literacy Problem-Solving with Computers.* Austin, TX: Sterling Swift, 1981.

Howe, Samuel F. "On-Line Data Bases." *Media and Methods* 19 (Sept. 1982): 21.

Hunter, David. "Hard Times Are Coming." *Softalk* (Sept. 1981): 88-89.

Jones, Mildred, and Beatrice Simmons. "Utilizing the New Technologies in School Library Media Centers: A Report to the Association." *School Library Media Quarterly* 9 (Summer 1981): 231-34.

Kelly, Jane Y. "Changing Jobs—The Automated Undercurrent." *Technicalities* 1 (Apr. 1981): 8-9.

Kelly, Mahlon G. "Buying Software." *Popular Computing* 1 (Apr. 1982): 27-30.

Kesselman, Martin. "Special Report: National Online Meeting Held in New York." *Wilson Library Bulletin* 56 (June 1982): 754-56.

Kinzler, Milt. "The Microcomputer and the Building Media Specialist." *School Learning Resources* 1 (Spring 1982): 24.

Leimbach, Judy. "Spotlight on Computers: Students in Control." *School Library Journal* 28 (Aug. 1982): 37.

Lord, Hal. "MICROCOMPUTERS The State of the Art." *The Medium* (Sept. 1982): 1-2.

Lundeen, Gerald. "The Role of Microcomputers in Libraries." *Wilson Library Bulletin* (Nov. 1980): 178-85.

Magrath, Lynn L. "Computers in the Library: The Human Element." *Information Technology and Libraries* 1 (Sept. 1982): 266-70.

Malinconico, S. Michael. "Technology, Change and People: Hearing the Resistance." *Library Journal* 108 (Jan. 15, 1983): 111-13.

Marcum, Deanna, and Richard Boss. "Information Technology." *Wilson Library Bulletin* (Jan. 1981): 362-63, 398.

Marcum, Deanna, and Richard Boss. "Information Technology (Automated Serials Control)." *Wilson Library Bulletin* 57 (Oct. 1982): 154-55.

Marcum, Deanna, and Richard Boss. "Information Technology (MARC Format)." *Wilson Library Bulletin* 56 (June 1982): 764-65.

Marcum, Deanna, and Richard Boss. "Information Technology (Non-bibliographic Databases ... Source Files)." *Wilson Library Bulletin* 57 (Sept. 1982): 54-55.

Markuson, Barbara E., and Blanche Woolls, editors. *Networks for Networkers: Critical Issues in Cooperative Library Development.* New York: Neal Schuman Publishers, Inc., 1980.

Mason, Robert M. "Mason on Micros: What Good Are Microcomputers, Anyway?" *Library Journal* 108 (Jan. 15, 1983): 108-10.

Matthews, Joseph R. "Online Public Access Catalogs: Assessing the Potential." *Library Journal* (June 1, 1982): 1067-71.

Mcglynn, Daniel R. *Personal Computing: Home, Professional and Small Business Applications.* New York: John Wiley and Sons, 1979.

Moskowitz, Mickey. "Developing a Microcomputer Program to Evaluate Library Instruction." *School Library Media Quarterly* 10 (Summer 1982): 351-56.

Murtha, Stephen M., and Mitchell Waite. *CP/M Primer.* Indianapolis: Howard W. Sams and Co., Inc., 1982.

Nyren, Karl. "News in Review 1982." *Library Journal* 108 (Jan. 15, 1983): 93-104.

Olivieri, Peter. "Mind Your Own Business." *Softalk* (Aug. 1981-Feb. 1982 inclusive), regular column.

OnComputing 1-3 (Summer 1979-Fall 1981 inclusive).

Personal Computing 5-6 (Jan. 1981-Jan. 1983 inclusive).

Pool, Gail. "Magazines: Personal Computer.... " *Wilson Library Bulletin* (Jan. 1982): 376-78.

Popular Computing 1-2 (Nov. 1981-Jan. 1983 inclusive).

Rice, Jean. *Teacher's Guide and Activity Book to Accompany My Friend the Computer.* Minneapolis: T. S. Denison and Co., Inc., 1981.

Rice, Jean, and Marien Haley. *My Computer Picture Dictionary.* Minneapolis: T. S. Denison and Co., Inc., 1981.

Shillingburg, Patricia M. *A Child's Guide to the Apple II Plus Computer.* Summit, NJ: Patricia M. Shillingburg, 1982.

Simpson, George A. *Microcomputers in Library Automation.* McLean, VA: The MITRE Corporation, 1978.

Skapura, Robert. "The Overdue Writer: A Program Long Overdue." *School Library Media Quarterly* 10 (Summer 1982): 347-50.

Skvaria, Donna. "Computertown, OK!" *Catholic Library World* 54 (Nov. 1982): 170-74.

Small Computers in Libraries 1-2 (Apr. 1981-Dec. 1982 inclusive).

Snow, Carl E. "Word Processing: A First Step to On Line Scheduling." *T.H.E. Journal* 9 (Mar. 1982): 74-75.

Spencer, Donald D. *The Illustrated Computer Dictionary.* Columbus, OH: Charles E. Merrill Publishing Co., 1980.

Steffin, Sherwin. "Software to Learn From: How to Choose It." *Softline* (Nov. 1981): 18-19.

Stone, Barney. "Letter to the Editor." *Softalk* (Dec. 1981): 15.

Swanson, Don R. "Miracles, Microcomputers, and Librarians." *Library Journal* (June 1, 1982): 1055-59.

Thomason, Nevada. "Microcomputers and Automation in the School Library Media Center." *School Library Media Quarterly* 10 (Summer 1982): 312-19.

Townsend, Carl. *How to Get Started with CP/M.* Beaverton, OR: Dilithium Press, 1981.

Twaddle, Dan R. "School Media Services and Automation ... Survey and Annotated Bibliography...." *School Library Media Quarterly* 7 (Summer 1979): 257-68, 273-76.

Watt, Daniel. "The Brouhaha over Computers in the Classroom ... Are We Providing the Education Children Need to Function in a Computer-based Society?" *Popular Computing* 1 (May 1982): 36-45.

Watt, Daniel. "Should Children Be Computer Programmers?" *Popular Computing* 1 (Sept. 1982): 130-33.

Winfield, Gary R. "Are Computers Teachers?" *Hi-Ties News* (HI-TIE, Colorado State University): 9-10, 12.

Wollman, Jane. "Coin-Operated Computers." *Popular Computing* 1 (Apr. 1982): 141-43.

Wollman, Jane. "Software Piracy and Protection: Are You Breaking the Law?" *Popular Computing* 1 (Apr. 1982): 99-106.

Woolls, Blanche, and David Loertscher. "Some Sure-Fire Microcomputer Programs." *School Library Journal* 28 (Aug. 1982): 22-24.

Wozny, Lucy Anne. "Online Bibliographic Searching and Student Use of Information." *School Library Media Quarterly* 11 (Feb. 1982): 34-42.

Zaks, Rodnay. *DON'T! or How to Care for Your Computer.* Berkeley, CA: Sybex, 1981.

Zamora, Ramon, "Courseware Magazine: Educational Computing." *InfoWorld* (Aug. 31, 1981); *InfoWorld's Critics' Guide to Microcomputer Software.* Palo Alto, CA: Popular Computing, Inc., 1982. pp. 25-27.

Zsiray, Stephen W., Jr. "Microcomputers in the School Library Media Center: Building the Media Collection." *School Learning Resources* 1 (Summer 1982): 15-17.

Zussman, John Unger. "DB Master and PFS: Data-base Programs Compared." *InfoWorld* (Apr. 13, 1981); *InfoWorld's Critics' Guide to Microcomputer Software.* Palo Alto, CA: Popular Computing, Inc., 1982. pp. 12-14.

Index